English-Thai
Thai-English

Compiled by Scot Barmé and Pensi Najaithong

TUTTLE Publishing

Tokyo | Rutland, Vermont | Singapore

Published by Tuttle Publishing, an imprint of Periplus Editions (HK) Ltd.

www.tuttlepublishing.com

© 2014 by Periplus Editions (HK) Ltd

ISBN 978-0-8048-4289-1

Distributed by:

North America, Latin America and Europe
Tuttle Publishing
364 Innovation Drive, North Clarendon, VT 05759-9436 USA.
Tel: 1(802) 773-8930 Fax: 1(802) 773-6993
info@tuttlepublishing.com; www.tuttlepublishing.com

Asia Pacific
Berkeley Books Pte. Ltd.
61 Tai Seng Avenue #02-12, Singapore 534167
Tel: (65) 6280-1330 Fax: (65) 6280-6290
inquiries@periplus.com.sg; www.periplus.com

17 16 15 14   5 4 3 2 1   1402CP

Printed in Singapore

CONTENTS

INTRODUCTION

This Mini Thai Dictionary gives entries that are based on everyday colloquial Thai although more 'polite' or 'formal' ones are also included, where appropriate. To ensure that you are aware of these distinctions both 'colloquial' and 'formal' entries are clearly indicated, as is the case with various idioms and slang terms listed.

In compiling this work we have done our best to include the most commonly used Thai words. It should be emphasized, however, that in a book of such limited scope, it has been impossible to provide a totally comprehensive listing of vocabulary items. Even so we believe that this dictionary will meet the needs of all those users who would like to develop a proficiency in the language and a better understanding of a distinctively different socio-cultural world.

To help you get a better sense of how different Thai words function there are also a number of specific examples of usage provided. Merely providing lists of words and their Thai or English equivalents does not really give the user enough to work with if they are interested in moving beyond a rudimentary, and often unsatisfactory, level of communication.

Numerous examples of how the particular meanings of Thai words/expressions are formed are also provided. These examples are given in parentheses and appear as follows: (literally, 'word A'-'word B' and so on). A case in point is the way the Thai word for 'river' is formed. In English 'river' is a single word. In Thai, however, 'river' – **mâeh-náam** แม่น้ำ – is a combination of two distinct and completely different words. The first of these is '**mâeh**', or 'mother', and the second is '**náam**', or 'water'. In other words 'river' in Thai is literally 'mother'-'water' (or 'mother of water(s)'). Similarly, the English word 'tear(s)' (i.e. the tears of someone crying) in Thai is **náam-taa** (literally, 'water'-'eye[s]') น้ำตา, the word '**taa**' here meaning 'eye(s)'.

From examining the examples provided in the English-Thai section of the dictionary you should be able to not only extend your vocabulary and improve your facility with the language, but also develop a better understanding of the type of English typically spoken by many Thai people. Regardless of your language background it is natural to use your mother tongue as a type of template when speaking another language. That is until you begin to make a serious effort to understand the underlying nature of the language you are trying to learn and develop a fuller sense of it in its own terms. In Thai, for example, there is no definite article (i.e. 'the') or indefinite article (i.e. 'a'), and the verb form, unlike English, does not change with variations in person and tense (the past, present, and future are indicated in Thai by other words in conjunction with the verb). And nouns in Thai do not change their form to signify singular or plural. Again this is indicated

Introduction

by other words used in conjunction with the noun. As a consequence many Thai speakers of English speak in what is usually referred to as 'broken English' (or 'Tinglish' as some would have it) – this being strongly influenced by their native Thai language template. And, obviously, non-Thais do much the same thing when speaking Thai.

Here it should be mentioned that there is a significant, and ever increasing, number of English words in Thai, many concerned with technological advances and innovation. At the same time there is also a growing body of 'non' technical words and expressions that have been incorporated into Thai. Such instances are clearly indicated by the inclusion of the marker (from English) next to such entries. Inevitably, English borrowings into Thai have been 'Thai-ified' and, at times, are not immediately clear or comprehensible to the native English speaker. In all cases an attempt has been made to provide a usable form of pronunciation for these various English 'loan' words.

A final note: In addition to 'polite', 'formal', 'colloquial' terms and a smattering of widely used 'idioms', a number of common crude, vulgar words are included and clearly marked. These particular entries are for the benefit of the curious reader – a form of FYI, as it were. However, it is strongly advised that you avoid using any such words until you have gained a good level of familiarity with Thai society and the way Thai people interact. Under no circumstances experiment using such language with strangers as the consequences of doing so could, potentially, be very unpleasant.

General overview of some key aspects of Thai

In one very basic sense Thai is like English – it has an alphabet. Thai words, like those in English, are composed of particular combinations of letters – both consonants and vowels. In the Thai case, however, different vowels are written before, above, below or after consonants, or a combination of these positions. And in a very small number of cases, the vowel sound, while the same as other written forms, is not written at all; rather it is 'inherent' and has to be learned.

Thai has its own distinctive script which is similar to the closely related language of neighboring Laos. Thai, like Lao, is written without spaces between the words. In written Thai, however, spaces do occur between what we might loosely call 'grouped associated ideas'.

It should be emphasized that there is no ideal way of writing – that is romanizing or transliterating – Thai words in English. There are a number of 'systems' for romanizing Thai and, regrettably, none of them (including that used in this dictionary) is ideal. In fact, at times, some of the systems used to romanize Thai words are rather unhelpful when it comes to getting the pronunciation correct. For example, you may have seen the common, polite everyday greeting for 'hello' 'sàwàt dii' written as 'sawasdii/dee' or 'sawas dii/dee'. There is no issue with the

Introduction

'**dii/dee**' which simply sounds like the English letter 'd'. As for the '**sawas**' what has occurred is that the writer has employed one of the romanization systems which adhere strictly to the actual Thai spelling. In written Thai, the final 's' in '**sawas**' is indeed spelled with an 's' letter, but what needs to be understood is that when 's' (and in Thai there are a number of different letters representing 's') appears at the end of a syllable or word it is pronounced as a 't' sound (although some consider this to be closer to a 'd' – hence you will sometimes see 'sawad dii/dee', or, for the popular noodle dish, '**pad/phad thai**' rather than the more accurate '**phàt thai**' – the word '**phàt**' actually sounding closer to the English golfing term 'putt'). In a following section all of the syllable final consonant sounds in Thai are provided.

In summary, while Thai and English share many of the same sounds there are a number of instances where there are no comparable sounds between the two languages. Hence it is a good idea, whenever possible, to ask a Thai friend or acquaintance to look at a particular word or phrase in the Thai script provided and help you with your pronunciation.

Tones

Thai is a 'tonal' language, which means variations in tone or pitch determine the meaning of a word. Thus the assistance of a native Thai speaker to help you approximate the correct tones would be invaluable.

Some people find the idea of 'tones' particularly daunting but, in fact, tones in Central Thai (the name of the official language in Thailand) are not as impenetrable as these individuals imagine. Indeed, there are a relatively small number of words where it is vital to get the tone absolutely correct to be understood (for example, see the entries for 'near' and 'far'). These days with a large and growing number of foreigners visiting Thailand, not to mention a significant and ever expanding expatriate 'community', more and more Thais are becoming accustomed to non-native speakers 'mangling' their language to one degree or another when trying to speak it. So often meaning can be conveyed, partially through context, even if one's tones are slightly off kilter. To say this is not to reduce the significance of tones, for ultimately they are crucial; rather it is to encourage you, the learner, to use the language as much as you can and develop your confidence, and hopefully your interest, so as to help you move on to another level.

In Central Thai there are five tones: mid, low, falling, high and rising. In the system of romanization used in this dictionary the mid-tone is unmarked. The other tones are represented by the following symbols written above the relevant syllable (in the case of words with a number of syllables) or the word if it is monosyllabic: low tone `; falling tone ˆ; high tone ´; and rising tone ˇ.

Here are some examples of the tones with words given in romanized form – their English meaning in

Introduction

parentheses – and in Thai script. Try having a Thai friend or acquaintance pronounce the words written in Thai to get some idea of the differences in tone, then practise saying them yourself.

1. Mid tone (unmarked)	mai (a mile – from English)	ไมล์
2. Low tone (ˋ)	mài (to be new)	ใหม่
3. Falling tone (ˆ)	mâi (a Thai word for 'no')	ไม่
4. High tone (ˊ)	mái (wood)	ไม้
5. Rising tone (ˇ)	mǎi (silk)	ไหม

Note: What English speakers perceive as the same word pronounced with different tones are, in fact, regarded as completely different words by Thai people. Thus Thais do not consider the examples given above as one word with five different tones, but rather as five distinct and completely unrelated words. To Thai ears these various words are as different as the words 'seed' and 'seat' are to a native English speaker, the two words whose final sounds many Thais find hard to distinguish.

Romanized Thai

English pronunciation is often very confusing to non-native speakers as individual letters do not correspond to a single unchanging sound. Take the vowel sound 'e', for example, which is pronounced in a number of ways. Consider the 'e' sounds in the following: 'mother,' 'women,' 'they,' 'he,' and so on. Thai pronunciation, by contrast, is much more 'phonetic', that is vowels and consonants have but one sound which does not change in different words as is the case in English.

Vowels

In Thai there are both 'long' and 'short' vowels. This distinction between long and short vowels is very important. The 'basic' or 'standard' vowels in English – a, e, i, o, u – all are found in Thai but with both a 'long' and 'short' form. In the short form used in this dictionary the following are written the same as in English, but the sound is very short:

a   sounds like ah! as in 'Ah! haa (there you are)' (not aah)

e   sounds like eh! (not ee)

i   sounds like when you begin pronounce the letter 'e' and then stop very abruptly

o   sounds like oh! in the exclamation 'Oh! Ooh (here's trouble)'

u   sounds similar to the 'ou' sound in 'you', but, as with all these sounds, very, very short

As for the 'long' sounds of the same five vowels they are written as follows:

aa   which sounds like 'ar' in 'far'

eh   which sounds like 'ey' in 'hey' (i.e. Hey, you!)

ii   which sounds like 'ee' in 'free'

Introduction

oh which sounds like the 'o' in 'go'
uu which sounds like the 'ue' in 'true'

In addition to vowel sounds listed above there are a number of other vowels which do not occur in English although some of them have a sound easily recognizable to the English ear. For example:

am pronounced like the 'um' in 'rum'
uai pronounced u as in the English 'u' + 'ay' as in 'way' i.e. u-ay, but written 'uai'

The following vowel sounds have both a 'long' and a 'short' form. However, in the instances below the 'short' form is not as abrupt as in the selection of vowels listed above, yet there is a clear distinction between 'long' and 'short' which is best demonstrated by a native speaker with good, clear enunciation.

ae is pronounced like the word 'air'
ai pronounced like the English word 'I', or 'eye' – as in the word 'Thai'
ao is pronounced like 'ow' in the word 'cow'
eo is pronounced 'ey-o' the 'ey' as in 'hey'
ia is pronounced like the 'ia' in the name 'Maria'
iao is pronounced like the sound 'e-oh'
iu is pronounced like the 'ew' in 'new'
oi is pronounced like 'oy' in the word 'boy'

ueh (อือ) no equivalent in English. However, you can try pronouncing it by doing this – clench your teeth together while imagining you're sitting on the toilet trying to squeeze something out. While this may seem a somewhat unusual form of instruction it should help you approximate the correct sound.

uea (เอือ) is pronounced much the same as 'ueh' but with an 'a' or 'ah' sound added at the end. So begin by clenching your teeth together for the 'ue/ueh' sound and then open your mouth as you voice the 'a/ah'

The description of the following vowel sounds is for the 'long' form:

aw is pronounced like 'aw' in the word 'lawn', or similar to the English word 'or'

oeh is pronounced like 'ir' in the word 'skirt', or the 'ur' in 'hurt'

The short form of these vowels is very short – for the 'aw' sound consider the following entry from the dictionary:

island **ka-w** ('aw' pronounced very short like 'oh!' in 'Oh! Ooh' with a 'g' sound in front – the whole word sounds something like 'goh!') เกาะ

As for the short form of **oeh** it is similar in duration to the **aw** although it is found in far fewer words.

Introduction

Consonants

The majority of Thai consonants are similar to those in English, although there are a number of important differences. The consonants listed below are in the 'initial' position, that is, at the beginning of a word.

ROMANIZED LETTER(S)	APPROXIMATE ENGLISH SOUND
*k	similar to 'g', sounds like 'k' in 'skin'
kh	'king'
*ng	'singer'
j	similar to 'j', sounds like 'j' in 'jet' but a little softer
ch	'charge'
d	'do'
*t	'star'
th	'tie'
n	'narcotic'
b	'bar'
*p	'spa'
ph	'poor'
f	'far'
m	'me'
y	'you'
r	'rat'
l	'sling'
w	'wing'
s	'see'
o	'on'

*Note: The English sound 'ng' only occurs (with a slight exception – see below) in the syllable-final position of a word, as in 'sing', 'bring', etc. However, 'ng' occurs both at the beginning and end of Thai words and syllables. The closest comparable English sound to the syllable initial 'ng' in Thai is the sound that occurs at the beginning of the second syllable of words such as 'singer' (i.e. sing-nger), or 'wringer' (i.e. wring-nger). You may find it useful to practise pronouncing the 'ng' sound at the beginning of various Thai words by trying the following: say 'sing', 'sing','singer, singer', then 'nger, nger'.

*The Thai sounds represented by the letters 'k', 't' and 'p' should not be confused with the English 'k', 't' and 'p' sounds. When these occur at the beginning of English words, as in 'king', 'top' and 'pit', they are aspirated sounds. That is, they are pronounced with an associated 'puff' of air. Try placing your hand in front of your mouth and say 'k', 't', 'p'. In the system of romanization used in this dictionary the aspirated k, t and p sounds are written 'kh', 'th' and 'ph', the puff of air being represented by the letter 'h'. By contrast, the k, t and p sounds are unaspirated. That is, they are pronounced without an associated puff of air. These three unaspirated sounds do not occur by themselves in English, but similar sounds do occur in some English consonant clusters such as 'sk', 'sp' and 'st'. The 'k', 't' and 'p' sounds in 'sk', 'st' and 'sp' are pronounced without a puff of air.

Syllable-final Consonant Sounds

In Thai only eight consonant sounds occur in the syllable-final position. These eight sounds can be divided into two groups – stops and sonorants. Stops are sounds whose pronunciation ends abruptly, while sonorants are sounds whose pronunciation can be sustained for some time. For example, the 't' in 'hot' is a stop while the 'n' in 'bin' is a sonorant. It is possible to sustain the 'n' in 'bin' for a long time – 'binnnnn....', but the 't' in 'hot' has a short, sharp sound which brings the pronunciation of that word to a sudden stop once it has been spoken.

The seven final consonant sounds in Thai are:

STOPS	COMPARABLE ENGLISH SOUND
k	sick
t	flat
p	sip

The final stop is not indicated by a symbol in this dictionary. However it is the sound that was mentioned above when discussing the word 'island' – it is the short 'oh!' sound as in 'Oh!Ooh'.

SONORANTS

ng	wing
n	bin
m	jam
y	joy
w	now

Syllable-initial Consonant Clusters

Only a relatively small number of consonant clusters (i.e. two or more consonants together) occur in Thai, compared to English. All Thai consonant clusters occur in syllable-initial position. No consonant clusters occur at the end of Thai words. The consonant clusters are as follows:

kr, kl, kw, khr, khl, khw, tr, pr, pl, phr, phl.

Also fr and fl which only occur in English loan words.

'R' and 'L' sounds in Thai

The pronunciation of 'r' and 'l' sounds in Thai varies according to the speech style or register. In the formal style of educated Thais 'r' and 'l' are usually pronounced quite clearly and distinctly. However, in casual and informal conversation, and among less educated people 'r' and 'l' both tend to be pronounced as 'l' in the syllable-initial position. In consonant clusters in informal Thai 'r' is often replaced by 'l' and sometimes both 'r' and 'l' sound are omitted altogether from consonant clusters. Note that the change of 'r' sound to 'l' in casual spoken Thai does not alter the tones of words, which remain unchanged. Compare the following examples:

FORMAL STYLE PRONUNCIATION
khráp (Male polite particle)

INFORMAL STYLE PRONUNCIATION
kháp (similar to 'cup' with a high tone)

Introduction

plaa (a fish)	**paa**
ruai (to be rich)	**luai** (luu-ay)
àrai (What?)	**àlai**
kràthá (a pan)	**kàthá**

In closing it should be pointed out that many of the words in this dictionary with two or more syllables have hyphens included to help you with your pronunciation. Here, for example, is the word for the month of August: **sǐng-hǎa-khom**.

We wish you 'Good luck' on your journey into the Thai language or, as the Thais would say, **'Choke dee'**.* โชคดี

---

* While this particular rendering of Thai might cause some to laugh, make jokes or bad puns it's very close to what the Thai for 'Good luck' actually sounds like.

English–Thai

A

abandon (leave – a car, a girlfriend, etc.) láthîng, ละทิ้ง, or simply thîng ทิ้ง

abdomen châwng tháwng ช่องท้อง

able to să-mâat สามารถ; **ability** khwaam să-mâat ความสามารถ

aboard *See* 'on board'

abort, an abortion tháeng แท้ง, tham tháeng ทำแท้ง

about (approximately) pràmaan ประมาณ, or raaw raaw ราวๆ

about (regarding, concerning) kìao-kàp เกี่ยวกับ, or rûeang เรื่อง (used in a meaning of 'subject/topic' for informal expression)

above, on top (of) khâang bon ข้างบน

abroad, overseas tàang prà-thêet ต่างประเทศ, or mueang nâwk เมืองนอก;

to be abroad/overseas—to be living abroad/overseas—either of these equally common expressions: yùu tàang prà-thêet อยู่ต่างประเทศ, or yùu mueang nâwk อยู่เมืองนอก

absent (not be here/there) mâi yùu ไม่อยู่, e.g. he/she is not here khăo mâi yùu เขาไม่อยู่

abstain (to give up something) lôek เลิก

abuse (mistreat/hurt) tham rái ทำร้าย; to abuse (verbally, to scold/berate) dàa (somebody) ด่า – most common – wâa (somebody) ว่า

academic (an academic – a university lecturer) aajaan (pronounced like 'ah-jarn') อาจารย์; (the general term for) things 'academic' wíchaa-kaan วิชาการ

accent, an (when speaking) săm-niang สำเนียง

accept, to yawm ráp ยอมรับ

accident, an ù-bàttì-hèht อุบัติเหตุ

accidentally, by chance dohy bang-oehn โดยบังเอิญ, or (COLLOQUIALLY) bang-oehn บังเอิญ

accommodation thîi phák ที่พัก

accompany, to pai pen phûean ไปเป็นเพื่อน (literally, 'go'-'be'-'friend')

according to (what he/she said) taam thîi... ตามที่...

account (e.g. bank account) ban-chii บัญชี; an accountant nák ban-chii นักบัญชี

accuse, to klàaw hǎa กล่าว หา

ache (as in 'headache/ toothache, etc.) pùat ปวด

acid kròt กรด

acne (pimple/s) sĭw สิว

acquaintance, an (not a friend as such) khon rúu jàk คนรู้จัก

acquainted/familiar (e.g. to be acquainted with some-thing) khún khoei kàp คุ้น เคยกับ

across from... trong khâam kàp... ตรงข้ามกับ...

act, to (do) (COLLOQUIAL) tham ทำ, or (in more formal, bureaucratic language) pàtibàt ปฏิบัติ

action kaan kràtham การ กระทำ

activity kìt-jà-kam กิจกรรม; **activist** (i.e. a social activist) nák kìt-jà-kam นักกิจกรรม

actor/actress (general term for 'performer') nák sà-daehng นักแสดง

actual (real) pen jing เป็นจริง

actually (as in 'actually he doesn't have a car') thîi jing ที่จริง

add (plus, i.e. +) bùak บวก

add, to phôehm เพิ่ม

addict, a (drug) khon tìt yaa คนติดยา

addicted, to be (to drugs, sex, types of food, soap operas, etc) (COLLOQUIAL) tìt ติด

address thîi yùu ที่อยู่

adjust pràp ปรับ

admire/praise, to chom ชม

admit/confess yawm ráp ยอมรับ

adopt, to v ráp líang รับเลี้ยง;
  N an adopted child bùt bun
  tham บุตรบุญธรรม

adorable (lovable) nâa rák
  น่ารัก

adore, to rák mâak รักมาก

adult phûu yài ผู้ใหญ่

adultery (for someone to
  engage in adultery – an affair
  with a 'married' man/woman)
  pen chúu เป็นชู้ (NOTE: for an
  adulterer often just the single
  word chúu ชู้ is used. *Also
  see* entry under 'womanizer')

advance, go/move forward
  kâaw nâa ก้าวหน้า

advance money, a deposit
  ngoen mát jam เงินมัดจำ

advantage (benefit) phŏn
  prà-yòht ผลประโยชน์; to
  take advantage (of someone)
  ao prìap เอาเปรียบ

advertise/advertisement
  khôht-sà-naa โฆษณา
  (NOTE: this word also means
  'propaganda')

advice N kham náe nam คำ
  แนะนำ

advise/suggest, to v náe
  nam แนะนำ

aerobics (from English)
  ae-robìk แอโรบิกส์; to do
  aerobics lên ae-robìk
  (literally, 'play'-'aerobics') เล่น
  แอโรบิกส์

aeroplane/airplane, an
  khrûeang bin เครื่องบิน

affair (as in that's 'my affair/
  my business' — the word
  for 'story' is used) rûeang
  เรื่อง, (for a married person
  to have a lover, i.e. an affair)
  (COLLOQUIAL) mii chúu มีชู้

affect, to mii phŏn tàw มี
  ผลต่อ

affection khwaam rák khrâi
  ความรักใคร่

affirm/confirm, to yuehn
  yan ยืนยัน

afford, to săa-mâat mii dâi
  (literally, 'able'-'have'-'can')
  สามารถมีได้

afraid/scared, to be klua
  กลัว

Africa (from English) áep-frí-
  ka แอฟริกา

after lăng jàak หลังจาก; later
  thii lăng ทีหลัง

afternoon (after midday till 4
  p.m.) tawn bàai ตอนบ่าย

3

afternoon/late afternoon (4 pm to dusk) tawn yen ตอนเย็น

afterwards, then lăng jàak nán หลังจากนั้น

again (another – person, bottle of beer, etc.) ...ìik ...อีก: e.g. 'play (name of game) again' lên ìik เล่นอีก; 'can I have another bottle of beer?' khǎw bia ìik khùat (literally, 'request/ask for'-'beer'-'another'-'bottle') ขอเบียร์ อีกขวด

age aa-yú อายุ; to ask someone's age, i.e. 'How old are you?' khun aa-yú thâo-rài (literally, 'you'-'age'-'how much?') คุณอายุเท่าไหร่

agency (company) bawrísàt tua thaen บริษัทตัวแทน

agent/representative n tua thaen ตัวแทน (NOTE: often the English word 'agent' is used with Thai pronunciation 'a yên' เอเย่นต์)

aggressive, to be kâaw ráaw ก้าวร้าว; (COLLOQUIAL) someone looking for trouble khon hǎa rûeang (literally,

'person'-'looking for'-'a story/ an issue') คนหาเรื่อง; to look for trouble hǎa rûeang หาเรื่อง

ago thî láew ที่แล้ว; two years ago sǎwng pii thî láew (literally, 'two'-'year'-'ago') สองปีที่แล้ว

agree, to (with someone) hěn dûai เห็นด้วย

agree to do something, to tòklong tham ตกลงทำ

agreed! tòklong ตกลง

agreement khâw tòklong ข้อตกลง

agriculture kà-sèht-trà-kam เกษตรกรรม

aid See 'help'

AIDS rôhk èhds โรคเอดส์

air aa-kàat อากาศ

air conditioned ...pràp aa-kàat (literally, 'adjust'-'air') ...ปรับอากาศ, or (more colloquially) ae แอร์

air force, the kawng tháp aa-kàat กองทัพอากาศ

air hostess (colloquial, from English) ae แอร์; the term naang fáa (literally, 'woman'-'sky') นางฟ้า is also used colloquially

airmail mehl aa-kàat เมล
อากาศ

airport (COLLOQUIAL) sà-nǎam
bin สนามบิน

alarm tuean phai (literally,
'warn'-'danger') เตือนภัย;
alarm clock naàlí-kaa plùk
(literally, 'clock'-'wake')
นาฬิกาปลุก

alcohol, liquor (spirits) lâo
เหล้า

alien (as in strange, different,
unusual) plàehk แปลก;
alien (from outer space)
má-nút tàang daaw (literally,
'human'-'different'-'planet')
มนุษย์ต่างดาว

alike, the same mǔean
เหมือน

alive, to be yang mii chii-
wít ยังมีชีวิตอยู่

all (the whole lot)/altogether
tháng mòt ทั้งหมด

allergic (to something)/an
allergy pháeh แพ้

alley, lane, side street (in
Bangkok, in particular, can
also refer to a substantial
road) soi ซอย

alligator See 'crocodile'

allow/give permission, to
à-nú-yâat hâi อนุญาตให้

allow (let someone) yawm
ยอม

allowed/permitted to dâi
ráp à-nú-yâat ได้รับอนุญาต

all right See 'okay'

almost kùeap เกือบ

alone (be by oneself) khon
diao คนเดียว

already láew แล้ว (a term
that indicates completion);
'gone' pai láew (literally, 'go'-
'already') ไปแล้ว

although/even though
thǔeng máeh wâa ถึงแม้ว่า

also (as well) dûai ด้วย: e.g.
he/she will go also/as well
khǎo pai dûai (literally, 'he/
she'-'go'-'also/as well') เขา
ไปด้วย

alternative/choice mii
thîi lûeak มีที่เลือก, or mii
thaang lûeak มีทางเลือก

altogether See 'all'

always sà-mǒeh เสมอ

amateur sà-màk-lên
สมัครเล่น

amazing (as in 'that's
unbelievable!' 'incredible')

mâi nâa chûea ไม่น่าเชื่อ, also
má-hàt sà-jan มหัศจรรย์

ambassador, diplomat
(general term) thûut ทูต

ambulance rót phá-yaa-baan
รถพยาบาล

America à-meh-rí-kaa
อเมริกา

American khon à-meh-rí-
kan คนอเมริกัน

among, between rá-wàang
ระหว่าง

amount jam-nuan จำนวน

amphetamine (COLLOQUIAL) yaa
bâa (literally, 'drug/medicine'-
'crazy/mad') ยาบ้า; ice yaa
ái ยาไอซ์

amulet (i.e. the ubiquitous
Buddha image amulets
worn by many Thai people,
both male and female) phrá
khrûeang พระเครื่อง

amusing/funny, to be tà-lòk
ตลก, or tà-lòk khòpkhăn
ตลกขบขัน

ancestor banphá-bu-rùt
บรรพบุรุษ

ancient bohraan โบราณ; very
old kào kàe เก่าแก่

and láe (pronounced with a

very short 'eh' sound with 'l'
in front) และ, or kàp กับ

anger khwaam kròht ความ
โกรธ

Angkor/Angkor Wat
ná-khawn wát (literally,
'city'-[of] 'temple(s)') นครวัด

angry, to be kròht โกรธ, also
moh-hŏh โมโห

animal, an sàt สัตว์

ankle khâw tháo ข้อเท้า

anklet kamlai khâw tháo
กำไลข้อเท้า

anniversary, an khróp râwp
ครบรอบ

announce, to prà-kàat
ประกาศ

annoy/bother, to róp kuan
รบกวน

annoyed, to be ramkhaan
รำคาญ

annual prà-jam pii ประจำปี

another (more) ìik ... อีก...:
e.g. 'another one' (as in
'another plate of food' etc.
ìik jaan nùeng อีกจานหนึ่ง);
a second word for 'another'
is ùehn อื่น (which is used in
this sense: 'another person'
khon ùehn คนอื่น)

6

answer (response) ɴ kham
tàwp คำตอบ

answer, to (respond) v tàwp
ตอบ

answer the phone ràp thoh
rá sàp รับโทรศัพท์

answering machine
khrûeang ràp thoh-rá-sàp
เครื่องรับโทรศัพท์

ant(s) mót มด

antenna (TV, radio) săo
aa-kàat เสาอากาศ

antique(s) khăwng kào ของเก่า

anus (polite/medical term)
thawaan nàk ทวารหนัก;
(vulgar, common term) ruu
tùut (literally, 'hole'-'arse')
รูตูด

any (the equivalent of the
English word 'any' is generally
implied in Thai questions
and responses without any
specific word as such. For
example, to say 'do you have
any money?' is khun mii
ngoen măi [literally, 'you'-
'have'-'money'-'question
marker']คุณมีเงินไหม;
here there is no word that
specifically means 'any', it

is understood. To respond
'yes, I do' is simply mii มี
which means 'have'. To
answer 'no, I don't have any'
you can say either mâi mii
[literally, 'no'-'have'] ไม่มี or,
mâi mii loei [literally, 'no'-
'have'-'at all'] ไม่มีเลย. The
idea of 'any' is understood,
but not expressed as a word.
In certain limited cases,
however, there is a Thai
word that means 'any/some'.
This is used in the following
example, the same English
question asked above but
in another form in Thai: 'do
you have any/some money?'
khun mii ngoen bâang măi
[literally, 'you'-'have'-'money'-
'any/some'-'question marker']
คุณมีเงินบ้างไหม. Here the
word bâang บ้าง may be
translated as 'any/some')

anybody, anyone (at all) (the
word kâw ก็ is pronounced
very similar to the English
word 'gore', but short and
with a falling tone) khrai kâw
dâi ใครก็ได้

7

anything (at all) àrai kâw dâi
อะไรก็ได้

anywhere (at all) thîi năi kâw
dâi ที่ไหนก็ได้

**apart (from….), in addition
to…** nâwk jàak…. นอกจาก….

apartment (from English)
à-páatméhn อะพาร์ตเมนต์

ape/monkey ling ลิง

apologize to (e.g. for
stepping on someone's foot)
khăw thôht ขอโทษ

apology (e.g. 'my apologies'
– on hearing of someone's
serious illness/death)
sà-daehng khawm sĭajai
แสดงความเสียใจ

apparently yàang hěn
dâi chát อย่างเห็นได้ชัด;
apparently (it seems as if…)
praa-kòt wâa ปรากฏว่า

appear/become visible, to
praa-kòt ปรากฏ

appearance/attitude, looks
thâa thaang ท่าทาง

appetizer/entrée/starter
khăwng wâang ของว่าง

apple (from English) áep-pôen
แอปเปิล

appliance, an (electrical)

khrûeang fai fáa เครื่องไฟฟ้า

apply, to (for permission)
khăw à-nú-yâat ขออนุญาต

apply, to (for work/a job)
sà-màk สมัคร

appointment nát-mǎai นัด
หมาย, or simply nát นัด; to
have an appointment mii
nát มีนัด

approach, to (in space) khâo
hǎa เข้าหา

approach, to (in time) klâi
wehlaa ใกล้เวลา

appropriate/suitable, to be
mà-w sǒm เหมาะสม

approve (of something) hěn
sǒmkhuan เห็นสมควร; to
approve (something) à-númát อนุมัติ

approximately prà-maan
ประมาณ

April meh-sǎa-yon เมษายน

architect sà-tǎa-pà-ník
สถาปนิก

architecture sà-tǎa pàt-tà-
yá-kam สถาปัตยกรรม

area phúehn thîi พื้นที่, or
bawrí-wehn บริเวณ

area code/post code rá-hàt
รหัส

argue, to thá lá-w ทะเลาะ
(NOTE: a very common Thai term meaning 'to argue/dispute an issue/contradict/talk back' is thǐang เถียง)

argument, an kaan thòk thǐang การถกเถียง

arm khǎen แขน

army, the kong thá-hǎan กองทหาร, or commonly kong tháp กองทัพ

aroma (pleasant smell) klìn hǎwm กลิ่นหอม

around (approximately) raaw raaw ราวๆ

around (here, nearby) thǎew níi แถวนี้

around (surrounding) râwp râwp รอบๆ

arrange, to jàt kaan จัดการ

arrangements kaan jàt kaan, การจัดการ; to make plans waang phǎehn วางแผน

arrest, to jàp จับ, or jàp kum จับกุม; to be arrested dohn jàp โดนจับ

arrive/reach, to maa thǔeng มาถึง, or simply thǔeng ถึง

arrogant yìng หยิ่ง, or jawng hǎwng จองหอง

art sǐnlápà ศิลปะ, or simply sǐn ศิลป์; artist sǐnlápin ศิลปิน

arthritis rôhk káo โรคเกาต์

article (in newspaper) bòt khwaam บทความ

artificial (as in an artificial limb, or copy of a brand name product) thiam เทียม

ashamed, embarrassed nâa lá-aai น่าละอาย

ashtray thîi khìa bùrìi ที่เขี่ยบุหรี่

Asia eh-sia เอเชีย

ask (a question) thǎam ถาม

ask about, to thǎam kìao kàp ถามเกี่ยวกับ, or simply thǎam rûeang ถามเรื่อง

ask for, request khǎw ขอ

asleep/slept nawn làp นอนหลับ, or nawn นอน

ass/arse (bottom) (COLLOQUIAL) tùut ตูด

assemble/gather together, to rûap ruam รวบรวม

assemble, put together (e.g. a bicycle) prà-kàwp ประกอบ

assist, to chûai ช่วย

assistance khwaam chûai lǔea ความช่วยเหลือ

association N sà-maa-khom สมาคม

as soon as (COLLOQUIAL) phaw พอ

assume (suppose, imagine) sŏmmút สมมุติ/สมมติ

asthma (medical condition) rôhk hàwp hùeht โรคหอบ หืด, or colloquially hùeht หืด

astonished, to be prà-làat jai ประหลาดใจ

as well dûai ด้วย

at thîi ที่; **at home** thîi bâan ที่บ้าน

athlete (sports person, male/female) nák kii-laa นักกีฬา

ATM (from English) eh-thii-em เอทีเอ็ม

atmosphere/ambience ban-yaa-kàat บรรยากาศ

at night, nighttime tawn klaang khuehn ตอนกลาง คืน, or simply klaang khuehn กลางคืน

atom (from English) à-tawm อะตอม

at once, immediately than thii ทันที

attached file/attachment fai thîi nâep maa ไฟล์ที่แนบ

มา (NOTE: the most commonly used English terms related to computers, the Internet, etc. are generally also used in Thai – the word 'file', for example, is fai ไฟล์)

attack (in war) johm tii โจมตี

attack (with words) dàa wâa ด่าว่า

attain, reach, arrive thǔeng ถึง

attempt, an khwaam phá-yaa-yaam ความพยายาม

attempt/try, to phá-yaa-yaam พยายาม

attend, to (a party/meeting, etc.) khâo rûam เข้าร่วม

at the latest, the latest lâa sùt ล่าสุด

attitude (opinion – formal) thàt sà ná khá tì ทัศนคติ

attractive (appealing to the eye) nâa dueng dùut น่าดึงดูด

aubergine/eggplant má-khǔea mûang มะเขือม่วง

auction, to (to tender) prà-muun ประมูล

auctioned off, to be prà-muun khăai ประมูลขาย

audience (looking at a

performance) phûu chom ผู้ ชม, or phûu fang (listening to a radio broadcast, etc.) ผู้ฟัง

August sĭng-hăa-khom สิงหาคม

aunt (elder sister of mother or father) pâa ป้า

aunt (mother's younger sister) náa น้า (also 'uncle' – mother's younger brother)

aunt (father's younger sister) aa อา (also 'uncle' – father's younger brother)

aunt (respectful address to a mature lady) khun pâa คุณป้า

Australia áwt sà treh lia ออสเตรเลีย

Australian khon áwt sà treh lia คนออสเตรเลีย

author *See* 'writer'

authority (official) jâo nâa thîi เจ้าหน้าที่

authority (power) amnâat อำนาจ

automobile/car rót yon รถยนต์; sedan rót kĕng รถเก๋ง

autumn rúeduu bai mái rûang ฤดูใบไม้ร่วง

available, to have (e.g. to sell/rent) mii มี

available, to make jàt hâi mii… จัดให้มี...

average, to (numbers) chàlìa เฉลี่ย

average, to feel (so-so, just OK) yang-ngán ยังงั้น

awake, to be (to have woken up) tùehn láew ตื่นแล้ว

awaken tùehn ตื่น

aware rúu tua รู้ตัว

awareness khwaam rúp rúu ความรับรู้

away: either the same word as 'go' pai ไป or 'leave' jàak pai จากไป

ax, axe khwăan ขวาน

B

baby thaa-rók ทารก (generally used in formal or written language; colloquially the term lûuk ลูก is used. This word is also used to refer to one's own or somebody else's children no matter their age)

back (part of body) lăng หลัง

11

back, rear lăng หลัง

back, to go klàp pai กลับไป

back ache pùat lăng ปวด
หลัง

back up/reverse, to thŏi pai
ถอยไป

backpack (bag) pêi เป้

backward thŏi lăng ถอยหลัง

bad lehw เลว, bad (e.g.
food that has gone off) sĭa
เสีย; no good mâi dii ไม่
ดี; awful/terrible/atrocious
(e.g. person, film, situation)
yâeh แย่

bad luck (unlucky, accursed)
suai ซวย, (alternatively)
chôhk ráai โชคร้าย

bag (paper or plastic) thŭng ถุง

bag (general term for bags;
also used for 'pocket' in a
garment) krà-păo กระเป๋า;
bag (suitcase) krà-păo
doehn thaang กระเป๋าเดินทาง

bake, to (to be baked) ò-p อบ

balance sŏm-dun สมดุล
(NOTE: the English word
'balance' is often used
with Thai pronunciation,
something like baa láan
บาลานซ์)

balcony, verandah rá biang
ระเบียง

bald hŭa láan (literally, 'head'-
'million') หัวล้าน

ball bawn บอล (also the
common colloquial word
used to refer to football/
soccer)

bamboo mái phài ไม้ไผ่

banana klûai กล้วย

band, a (of musicians) wong
don-trii วงดนตรี

bandage phâa phan phlǎeh
ผ้าพันแผล

Bangkok krung-thêp
กรุงเทพฯ

bank (financial institution) thá-
naa-khaan ธนาคาร

bank (of river) rim fàng mâeh
náam ริมฝั่งแม่น้ำ

bank account banchii thá-
naa-khaan บัญชีธนาคาร

banknote See 'note'

bankrupt, to go (a business)
lóm lá-laai ล้มละลาย, or
(COLLOQUIAL) jéng เจ๊ง (NOTE:
this is also used as a slang
term meaning to be 'broken/
worn out' as in 'my mobile/
cell phone is broken')

12

banquet ngaan líang งาน
เลี้ยง

bar (serving drinks) baa บาร์

barber châang tat phŏm ช่าง
ตัดผม

bargain, to tà-w rawng ต่อ
รอง

bark (dog bark) hào เห่า; to
howl hăwn หอน

barren (arid, dry environment)
hâeng-láeng แห้งแล้ง

base, foundation thăan ฐาน;
military base thăan tháp
ฐานทัพ

basic (the beginning level,
elementary) bûeang tôn เบื้อง
ต้น, or phúen-thăan พื้นฐาน

basis thăan ฐาน

basket, a tà-krâa ตะกร้า

basketball (from English)
báat-sàkèht-bawn บาสเก็ต
บอล, (COLLOQUIAL) báat บาส

bastard (as in 'you bastard!' –
the term given here is, in fact,
considerably stronger and far
more vulgar in meaning so
you can use your imagination)
âi-hîa ไอ้เหี้ย

bat (animal) kháang-khaaw
ค้างคาว

bathe/take a bath/have a
wash àap náam อาบน้ำ

bathrobe sûea khlum àap
náam เสื้อคลุมอาบน้ำ

bathroom hâwng náam
ห้องน้ำ

bathtub àang àap náam
อ่างอาบน้ำ

battery thàan ถ่าน, or
(from English) bàet-toeh-rîi
แบตเตอรี่, (COLLOQUIALLY SIMPLY)
bàet แบต

battle kaan sûu róp การสู้รบ

bay (or gulf) àaw อ่าว (NOTE:
the 'Gulf of Thailand' is àaw
thai อ่าวไทย)

be (at), to yùu thîi อยู่ที่

beach, a chaai hàat ชายหาด

bean(s) thùa ถั่ว

beancurd tâo hûu เต้าหู้

bear mĭi หมี

beard khraw เครา

beat (to defeat) ao cháná
เอาชนะ

beat (to strike) tii ตี

beat (as in music, rhythm)
jang-wà จังหวะ

beautiful (in appearance)
sŭai สวย

beauty parlour/beauty

13

salon ráan sŏehm sŭai (literally, 'shop/store'-'enhance'-'beauty') ร้านเสริมสวย

because phrá-w wâa เพราะว่า, or simply phrá-w เพราะ

become, to klaai pen กลายเป็น

bed tiang เตียง

bedbug rûet เรือด

bedding, bedclothes khrûeang nawn เครื่องนอน

bedroom hâwng nawn ห้องนอน

bedsheet phâa puu thîi nawn ผ้าปูที่นอน

bee phûeng ผึ้ง

beef, meat/flesh (in general) núea nûea เนื้อ (Note: also common slang word for marijuana)

beer bia เบียร์

before (in front of) khâang nâa ข้างหน้า

before (in time) kàwn ก่อน

beggar khăw-thaan (literally, 'request'-'things given') ขอทาน

begin, to rôehm เริ่ม

beginning, the tawn rôehm tôn ตอนเริ่มต้น; (COLLOQUIAL)

in the beginning/at first tawn râehk ตอนแรก

behave (FORMAL) prà-phrúet ประพฤติ; behaviour khwaam prà-phrúet ความประพฤติ

behind, to be (location) khâang lăng ข้างหลัง

belief, faith khwaam chûea ความเชื่อ

believe, to chûea เชื่อ

belly (stomach) tháwng ท้อง (Note: also the general way of referring to a woman falling pregnant/being pregnant; (SLANG/COLLOQUIAL) gut phung พุง (e.g. beer gut phung bia พุงเบียร์))

belongings (personal) khăwng sùan tua ของส่วนตัว, (COLLOQUIAL) khâaw khăwng (literally, 'rice/food'-'things') ข้าวของ

belonging to pen khăwng เป็นของ: e.g. 'it belongs to him/it's his' pen khăwng khăo (literally, 'belong'-'him') เป็นของเขา

below, downstairs khâang lâang ข้างล่าง

14

B

belt, a khěm khàt เข็มขัด;
　safety belt/seatbelt (in a car)
　khěm khàt níráphai เข็มขัด
　นิรภัย

beside khâang ข้าง, or
　khâang khâang ข้างๆ

besides (in addition, apart
　from) nâwk jàak… นอกจาก…

best (i.e the best) dii thîi sùt
　ดีที่สุด

best wishes dûai khwaam
　pràat-thà-nǎa dii ด้วยความ
　ปรารถนาดี

bet/gamble, to lên kaan
　phá-nan เล่นการพนัน, or
　simply lên phá-nan เล่นพนัน

betel nut màak หมาก

better (than something else)
　dii kwàa ดีกว่า

better, to get (improve) dii
　khûen ดีขึ้น

better, to get (from an illness)
　khôi yang chûa ค่อยยังชั่ว

between rá-wàang ระหว่าง

beverage (refreshment)
　khrûeng-dùehm เครื่องดื่ม

Bible, the (Christian) phrá
　kham-phii พระคัมภีร์

bicycle rót jàk-krà-yaan
　รถจักรยาน

big yài ใหญ่

bikini (from English) chút
　bì-ki-nîi ชุดบิกินี

bill (as in a restaurant – from
　English) bin บิล Also see
　under the entry 'pay'

billion phan láan (literally,
　'thousand'-'million') พันล้าน

billionaire sèht-thǐi phan
　láan เศรษฐีพันล้าน (the word
　sèht-thǐi เศรษฐี means a
　'wealthy man')

binoculars klâwng sǎwng
　taa กล้องสองตา

bird nók นก

birth, to give khlâwt lûuk
　คลอดลูก

birth certificate sǔu-ti-bàt
　สูติบัตร

birth control pill See
　'contraceptive pill'

birthday wan ko-eht
　(pronounced like 'one gurt')
　วันเกิด

biscuit, a (sweet, cookie)
　(from English) khúk-kîi คุกกี้

bit, a (just a bit, a little bit) nìt
　nòi นิดหน่อย

bite, to kàt กัด

bitter (taste) khǒm ขม

black sǐi dam สีดำ

black beans thùa dam ถั่วดำ (also part of a Thai slang expression meaning gay 'anal sex' àt thùa dam อัดถั่วดำ, àt อัด = 'stuff/compress')

black magic See 'voodoo'

blame, to thôht โทษ

bland/tasteless jùeht จืด

blanket phâa hòm ผ้าห่ม

bleed sǐa lûeat (literally, 'lose'- 'blood') เสียเลือด

blemish, a (flaw e.g. in a jewel, a person's complexion) tam ni ตำหนิ

blend/mix (a drink) phàsǒm ผสม

blind (person) taa bàwt ตาบอด

blog N, V (from English) bláwk บล็อก

blood lûeat เลือด

blood group mùu lûeat หมู่ เลือด

blood pressure khwaam dan lûeat ความดันเลือด, (COLLOQUIALLY, SIMPLY) khwaam dan ความดัน (NOTE: 'high blood pressure' is khwaam dan sǔung ความดันสูง; 'low

blood pressure' khwaam dan tàm ความดันต่ำ

blood test kaan trùat lûeat การตรวจเลือด

blouse sûea sà trii เสื้อสตรี

blow (the wind) phát พัด

blue (sky blue) sǐi fáa สีฟ้า Also see 'navy blue'

blunt (not sharp) thûeh ที่อ

board kràdaan กระดาน; **blackboard** kràdaan dam (literally, 'board'-'black') กระดานดำ Also see 'surfboard'

board, to (bus, train) khûen ขึ้น

boast (brag) ùat อวด, or ('talk big') khui móh คุยโม้

boat/ship rua เรือ

body, the râang kaai ร่างกาย

body, a (dead body, corpse) sòp ศพ

bodybuilding (COLLOQUIAL) lên klâam (literally, 'play'- 'muscle') เล่นกล้าม

boil, to tôm ต้ม (NOTE: also used as slang meaning 'cheat' or 'swindle')

boiling/boiled (e.g. water) dùeat เดือด

16

bomb/hand grenade N lûuk rá-bòet ลูกระเบิด

bon voyage! (Have a safe trip) doehn thaang plàwt phai ná เดินทางปลอดภัยนะ

bone krà-dùuk กระดูก

bong (bamboo water pipe for smoking tobacco or marijuana) bâwng บ้อง, or bâwng kan-chaa บ้องกัญชา

book năngsŭeh หนังสือ

bookshop ráan năngsŭeh ร้านหนังสือ

border, edge khàwp ขอบ

border (between countries) chaai daehn ชายแดน

bored, to be bùea เบื่อ

boring (a film, a person) nâa bùea น่าเบื่อ

born, to be kòeht (pronounced like 'gurt') เกิด

borrow, to khăw yuehm ขอยืม, or simply yuehm ยืม

boss, master N naai นาย

both (of them) tháng khûu ทั้งคู่

bother/disturb, to róp-kuan รบกวน

bother, disturbance kaan róp-kuan การรบกวน

bottle khùat ขวด

bottom (at the bottom) khâang tâi ข้างใต้

bottom (buttocks; also used in the broader sense to mean 'being at the bottom') kôn กัน

bowl chaam ชาม

box (general term) klàwng กล่อง

box (cardboard) klàwng krà-dàat กล่องกระดาษ

box, to/boxing (fighting) muai มวย; Thai boxing muai thai มวยไทย

boy dèk chaai เด็กชาย

boyfriend/girlfriend, a faehn แฟน

bra, brassiere yók song ยกทรง

bracelet kamlai mueh กำไล มือ

brag See 'boast'

brain sà-măwng สมอง

brake (in a vehicle) (from English) brèhk เบรก

brake, to yìap brèhk เหยียบ เบรก

branch (of a bank, business franchise) săa-khăa สาขา

branch (of a tree) kìng-mái กิ่งไม้

17

brand yîi-hâw ยี่ห้อ: also 'brand name' (from English) bran nehm แบรนเนม

brass thawng lŭeang (literally, 'gold'-'yellow') ทองเหลือง

brave/daring, to be klâa hăan กล้าหาญ

bread khànŏm pang ขนมปัง

break (glasses, plates) tàehk แตก; break (a leg, bones) hàk หัก

break apart, to tàehk yâehk แตกแยก

break down, to (car, machine) sĭa เสีย

breakfast, morning meal aa-hăan cháo อาหารเช้า

breakfast, to eat kin aa-hăan cháo กินอาหารเช้า

breast(s) (also chest, male or female) nâa òk หน้าอก; breasts/tits (COLLOQUIAL; also the word for 'milk') nom นม

breathe hăai-jai หายใจ; breathe in hăai-jai khâo หายใจเข้า; breathe out hăai-jai àwk หายใจออก

breed (of cat or dog) phan พันธุ์; 'what sort of breed is it (dog/cat etc.)?' phan àrai

breeze lom àwn àwn (literally, 'wind'-'gentle') ลมอ่อนๆ

bride jâo săaw เจ้าสาว

bridegroom jâo bàaw เจ้าบ่าว

bridge sà-phaan สะพาน (NOTE: the same word is used for 'bridge' in dental work); footbridge (over a busy road) sà-phaan loi (literally, 'bridge'-'float') สะพานลอย

brief sân-sân สั้นๆ

briefcase krà-păo tham ngaan กระเป๋าทำงาน

bright, to be (of light) sà-wàang สว่าง

bring, to ao maa (literally, 'take'-'come') เอามา (Often used like this: when the object, say an umbrella (rôm ร่ม), is understood. Otherwise if you wished to say the full sentence 'bring an umbrella' it would be ao rôm maa เอา ร่มมา, i.e. ao–'umbrella'– maa)

bring up/raise (children) líang เลี้ยง

bring up, to (e.g. a topic; submit plans) sà-nŏeh เสนอ

18

British angkrìt อังกฤษ; a British person khon angkrìt คนอังกฤษ

broad/wide/spacious, to be kwâang กว้าง

broadcast, program raai-kaan krà-jaai sĭang รายการกระจายเสียง

broadcast, to krà-jaai sĭang กระจายเสียง

broccoli (from English) bráwk-koh-lîi บรอกโคลี

broke, to be (SLANG; meaning 'to have no money') See 'money'

broken, does not work, spoiled sĭa เสีย, (COLLOQUIAL) jéng เจ๊ง

broken, shattered tàehk แตก

broken, snapped (of bones, etc.) hàk หัก

broken hearted (COLLOQUIAL) òk-hàk อกหัก

broken off or 'to break up' (relationship) lôehk kan เลิกกัน

bronze thawng sămrít ทองสัมฤทธิ์

broom, a mái kwàat ไม้กวาด

broth, soup náam súp น้ำซุป

brothel sâwng ซ่อง, or sâwng sŏh-pheh-nii ซ่องโสเภณี

brother (older) phîi chaai พี่ชาย

brother (younger) náwng chaai น้องชาย

brother-in-law (older) phîi khŏei พี่เขย

brother-in-law (younger) náwng khŏei น้องเขย

brown sĭi náamtaan สีน้ำตาล

bruise, to be bruised chám ช้ำ

brush (for scrubbing) praehng แปรง

brush (paint brush) phû-kan พู่กัน

bucket/bin, a thăng ถัง

Buddha (The Lord) phrá phút-thá-jâo พระพุทธเจ้า

Buddhism sàat-sà-năaphút ศาสนาพุทธ

Buddhist(s) chaaw phút ชาวพุทธ

buddy (friend) phûean เพื่อน

budget N ngóp prà-maan งบประมาณ

buffalo (water buffalo) khwaai ควาย

19

build, to sâang สร้าง

building, a (made of brick/stone) tùek ตึก

bull, a wua tua phûu วัวตัวผู้

bureaucrat/public servant khâa râat-chákaan ข้าราชการ

Burma phá-mâa พม่า; also Myanmar mian-mâa เมียนมาร์

Burmese (person) chaaw phá-mâa ชาวพม่า, or khon phá-mâa คนพม่า; Burmese (language) phaa-săa phá-mâa ภาษาพม่า

burn (injury) phlăeh mâi แผล ไหม้

burn, to phăo เผา

bus (the general term for bus, non-airconditioned, is either) rót meh รถเมล์ or rót bút (from the English 'bus') รถ บัส. An airconditioned bus or coach is commonly referred to as a rót thua รถทัวร์, or 'tour bus'.

bus station sá-thăa-nii rót meh สถานีรถเมล์. In colloquial Thai a bus station is khŏn-sòng (literally, 'transport'-'send') ขนส่ง

business thú-rá-kìt ธุรกิจ

businessperson nák thú-rá-kìt นักธุรกิจ

busy (bothersome – e.g. in a busy work environment where there is no let up) yûng ยุ่ง

busy (crowded and noisy) wûn waai วุ่นวาย

busy (telephone) săi mâi wâang สายไม่ว่าง

but tàeh แต่

butter noei เนย

butterfly phĭi sûea ผีเสื้อ

buttocks, bottom kôn ก้น

button krà-dum กระดุม

buy, to súeh ซื้อ

by (created by name of author/artist) dohy โดย

by means of dûai wíthii... ด้วยวิธี...

by the way, in addition nâwk jàak nii นอกจากนี้; furthermore ìik yàang nùeng อีกอย่างหนึ่ง

C

cab (taxi cab) rót tháek-sîi รถแท็กซี่

cabbage kàlàm plii กะหล่ำปลี

cabbage (Chinese cabbage) phàk kàat khăaw ผักกาดขาว

café ráan kaa-faeh (literally, 'shop'-'coffee') ร้านกาแฟ

cake khànŏm ná-khék (khék from English 'cake') ขนมเค้ก

calculate khamnuan คำนวณ

calculator a khrûeang khít lêhk เครื่องคิดเลข

calf (lower leg) nâwng น่อง

call, summon rîak เรียก

called, named chûeh ชื่อ

calm, peaceful sà-ngòp สงบ

Cambodia khà-mĕhn เขมร

Cambodian/Khmer chaaw khà-mĕhn ชาวเขมร, or khon khà-mĕhn คนเขมร, (language) phaa-săa khà-mĕhn ภาษาเขมร

camel ùut อูฐ

camera klâwng thàai rûup กล้องถ่ายรูป

can, be able to, capable să-mâat สามารถ

can/may àat jà อาจจะ

can/tin, a krà-pǎwng กระป๋อง

canal khlong คลอง

cancel yók lôehk ยกเลิก

cancer má-reng มะเร็ง

candle thian เทียน

candy, toffee, sweets (from English) táwp-fîi ทอฟฟี่; a sweet/lolly you suck on lûuk om ลูกอม

canvas phâa bai ผ้าใบ

cap mùak หมวก

capital (money, funds for investment) thun ทุน; capitalist/entrepreneur naay thun นายทุน

capitol (city of a country, state) mueang lŭang เมือง หลวง

capture, to (arrest) jàp จับ

car, automobile rót รถ

card (as in a credit card, name card, etc.) bàt บัตร (pronounced in a very similar way to the English word 'but'). *Also see* 'ID (identity card)'

cardboard krà-dàat khăeng กระดาษแข็ง

cards (game) phâi ไพ่; to play cards lên phâi เล่นไพ่

21

care for, to love and rák
láe ao-jai sài รักและเอาใจ
ใส่, also: take care ték khae
(from English; COLLOQUIAL)
เทคแคร์ (Also note: 'I don't
care' phŏm/chăn mâi khae
ผม/ฉันไม่แคร์)

care of (a child), to take
duu-laeh ดูแล

careful!, to be careful
ra-wang ระวัง

careless mâi rá-mát rá-wang
ไม่ระมัดระวัง, or sà-phrâo
สะเพร่า

carpet N phrom พรม

carrot (from English)
khaehràwt แครอต

carry, to (largish or heavy
objects e.g. suitcase) hîu หิ้ว

cart (street vendor pushcart,
supermarket trolley, pram) rót
khĕn รถเข็น

carve, to (a piece of meat)
cham-làe ชำแหละ, or simply
lâeh แล่

carve, to (a statue) kàe sàlàk
แกะสลัก

case (box) klàwng กล่อง

cash (money) ngoen sòt
เงินสด

cash a check, to lâehk chék
แลกเช็ค

cashew (nut) mét má-mûang
hĭm-má-phaan เม็ด
มะม่วงหิมพานต์; (COLLOQUIALLY)
mét má-mûang เม็ดมะม่วง

cat maeo แมว

catch, to (a ball; to arrest)
jàp จับ

catfish plaa-dùk ปลาดุก

cauliflower dàwk kà-làm
ดอกกะหล่ำ

cause (the cause of
something) sǎa-hèht สาเหตุ

cautious, careful rá-wang
ระวัง

cave, a thâm ถ้ำ

CD (from English) sii dii ซีดี

ceiling pheh-daan เพดาน

celebrate, to chà-lǎwng ฉลอง

celery ceh-loeh-rîi เซเลอรี

cell phone thoh-rá-sàp-
mueh thŭeh โทรศัพท์มือถือ,
commonly referred to in
speech as mueh thŭeh มือถือ
or moh-baai (from the
English 'mobile') โมบาย

center/centre, middle trong
klaang ตรงกลาง, or simply
klaang กลาง

22

center (of city) klaang mueang กลางเมือง

central sŭun klaang ศูนย์กลาง (Note the use of central in 'central Thailand' – i.e. the middle and most populous region of Thailand spreading out in all directions from Bangkok. The 'central region' as it is known is referred to as phâak klaang ภาคกลาง. *Also see* 'region'. It should be pointed out that Central Thai, also referred to as Bangkok Thai, is the official national language used in all forms of media and the education system. 'Central Thai' is known as phasăa klaang (literally, 'language'-'centre/middle') ภาษากลาง

century sàtà-wát ศตวรรษ

ceremony phí-thii พิธี

certain, sure nâeh jai แน่ใจ, or nâeh nawn แน่นอน

certainly! nâeh nawn แน่นอน

certificate prà-kàat-sànii-yábàt ประกาศนียบัตร

chain, a sôh โซ่

chair kâw-îi เก้าอี้

challenge tháa thaai ท้าทาย

champion (from English) cháehm-pîan แชมเปียน

chance, opportunity oh-kàat โอกาส

chance, by dohy bang-oen โดยบังเอิญ

change, small sèht sà-taang เศษสตางค์, (MORE COLLOQUIAL) sèht tang เศษตังค์

change, to (conditions, situations) plìan เปลี่ยน

change, exchange (money) lâehk plìan แลกเปลี่ยน (NOTE: for 'change or exchange money' you would say lâehk ngoen แลกเงิน, and for 'change clothes' plìan sûeàphâa เปลี่ยน เสื้อผ้า)

change (clothes, plans) plìan เปลี่ยน

change one's mind plìan jai เปลี่ยนใจ

character (personality) (FORMAL) bùk-khá-lík láksànà บุคลิกลักษณะ, (MORE COLLOQUIALLY) ní-săi นิสัย

character, letter (from an

23

alphabet) tua àksǎwn ตัว
อักษร, also (COLLOQUIALLY) tua
nǎngsǔeh ตัวหนังสือ
characteristic, qualities
láksanà ลักษณะ
charity kaan kùsǒn การกุศล
chase, to lâi taam ไล่ตาม
chase away/chase out, to
lâi pai ไล่ไป
chat, to khui คุย
cheap (in price) thùuk ถูก
cheat, to kohng โกง
cheat, a khon kohng คน
โกง; someone who habitually
cheats khon khîi kohng
คนขี้โกง
check/verify, to trùat sàwp
ตรวจสอบ
checked (pattern) laai màak
rúk ลายหมากรุก
cheek kâehm แก้ม
cheers! (Hooray!) chai yoh
ไชโย
cheese noei khǎeng เนยแข็ง
chef M phâw khrua (literally,
'father'-'kitchen') พ่อครัว F
mâeh khrua (literally,
'mother'-'kitchen') แม่ครัว
chemist (pharmacy) ráan
khǎai yaa ร้านขายยา;

chemist (proprietor of
pharmacy) phèhsàt-chá-
kawn เภสัชกร; **chemist**
(scientist) nák khehmii
นักเคมี
chess màak rúk หมากรุก
chest (box) hìip หีบ
chest (breast) nâa òk หน้าอก
chew, to khíao เคี้ยว; **chewing
gum** màak fàràng หมากฝรั่ง
(NOTE: the choice of words:
literally, 'betel nut'- 'foreign/
western' – i.e. 'foreign betel
nut')
chicken kài ไก่
child, a dèk เด็ก (NOTE:
also generally used to
refer to very junior staff in
a work environment i.e.
subordinates)
child (offspring) lûuk ลูก
chili (pepper) phrík พริก
chili sauce sáwt phrík
ซอสพริก
chilled, to be châeh yen
แช่เย็น
chilly (weather) nǎaw หนาว
chin khaang คาง
China mueang jiin (pronounced like 'jean') เมืองจีน

Chinese khon jiin คนจีน, (language) phaa-săa jiin ภาษาจีน

Chinese New Year (celebrated on differing dates from later January until around the middle of February) trùt jiin ตรุษจีน

chip (as in computer chip) (from English) chip ชิป

chip(s) See 'French fries'

chocolate (from English) cháwk-koh-láet ช็อกโกแลต

choke (on something) săm-lák สำลัก

choke, to (someone) bi-ip khaw (literally, 'squeeze'–'neck/throat') บีบคอ

cholera rôhk à-hì-waa โรค อหิวาต์, or khâi pàa (literally, 'fever'-'jungle') ไข้ป่า

cholesterol khăi man nai lûeat (literally, 'fat'-'in'-'blood') ไขมันในเลือด

choose, to lûeak เลือก; choice thaang lûeak ทางเลือก

chop/mince, to sàp ติบ

chopsticks tà-kìap ตะเกียบ

Christ, Jesus phrá yeh-suu พระเยซู

Christian khrítsian คริสเตียน; Christian(s) chaaw khrít ชาว คริสต์

Christianity sàatsà-năa khrít ศาสนาคริสต์

church bòht โบสถ์

cigar síkâa ซิการ์

cigarette bùrìi บุหรี่

cigarette lighter fai cháek ไฟแช็ค

cinema rohng năng โรงหนัง

cinnamon (spice) òb-choei อบเชย

circle (shape) wong klom วงกลม

circle (traffic) wong-wian วงเวียน

citizen prà-chaachon ประชาชน, or phon-lá-mueang พลเมือง

citrus: orange sôm ส้ม; lemon má-naaw มะนาว

city, large town mueang เมือง

civilization (from English) sìwílai ซิวิไลซ์, or aa-ráyá-tham อารยธรรม

class, category chán ชั้น, or prà-phêht ประเภท

clean, to be sà-àat สะอาด

25

clean, to (e.g. the bathroom) tham khwaam sà-àat ทำความสะอาด

cleanliness khwaam sà-àat ความสะอาด

clear (water, soup, liquid) săi ใส

clear (of weather) plàwt pròhng ปลอดโปร่ง

clearly (to see something clearly, to speak clearly) chát ชัด (NOTE: it is a genuine compliment in Thai when someone says you speak the language 'clearly' phûut thai chát (literally, 'speak'-'Thai' – 'clear[ly]') พูดไทยชัด)

clever chà-làat ฉลาด, or kèng เก่ง

client/customer, a lûuk-kháa ลูกค้า

climate ban-yaa-kàat บรรยากาศ

climb (a tree, a hill, a mountain) tài ไต่, or piin ปีน

clitoris mét lá-mút เม็ดละมุด, (SLANG) mét tháp-tim เม็ดทับทิม, (EXTREMELY VULGAR) tàet แตด

clock, a (or a watch) naalĭi-kaa นาฬิกา (Note: also term meaning 'hour' in the 24 hour system of time keeping i.e. 15 hours = 3 p.m.)

close/near, to be klâi ใกล้

close (to close a door), **cover** (to cover something, to put a lid on jar) pìt ปิด

close together, stuck together tìt gan ติดกัน

cloth phâa ผ้า

clothes, clothing sûea phâa เสื้อผ้า

cloud mêhk เมฆ

cloudy, overcast mûeht khrúem มืดครึ้ม, or simply mii mêhk (literally, 'have'-'cloud[s]') มีเมฆ

cloves kaan phluu กานพลู

club, association N sà-moh-săwn สโมสร

coarse (to the touch) yàap หยาบ, (vulgar, crude manner) yàap khaai หยาบคาย

coast (of the sea) chaai táleh ชายทะเล

coat, jacket sûea jáek-kêt เสื้อแจ็คเก็ต

coat, overcoat sûea nâwk เสื้อนอก

26

cockroach, a (COLLOQUIAL)
má-laehng-sàap แมลงสาบ
coconut má-phráo มะพร้าว;
young coconut má-phráo
àwn มะพร้าวอ่อน; coconut
milk/cream (used in curries)
kà-thí กะทิ
coffee kaa-faeh กาแฟ: black
coffee kaa-faeh dam (literally,
'coffee'-'black') กาแฟดำ;
white coffee kaa-faeh sài
nom (literally, 'coffee'-'put'-
'milk') กาแฟใส่นม
coin, a rĭan เหรียญ
cold (drink) yen เย็น
cold, a wàt หวัด; to have a
cold pen wàt เป็นหวัด
cold (weather) năaw หนาว
colleague, còworker
phûean rûam ngaan เพื่อน
ร่วมงาน
collect, to (a parcel, a present,
etc.) ráp รับ
college wít-thá-yaà-lai
วิทยาลัย
collide, to chon ชน
collision kaan chon การชน
color sĭi สี (also the word for
the noun 'paint')
comb wĭi หวี

combine ruam รวม; combine
with ruam kàp รวมกับ; join
together rûam kan ร่วมกัน
come, to maa มา
come back klàp maa กลับมา
come in (enter) khâo maa
เข้ามา
comedian tua tà-lòk ตัวตลก
comedy rûeang tà-lòk เรื่อง
ตลก, or simply tà-lòk ตลก
(which also means 'funny')
comfortable sàbaai สบาย
(a key Thai term which
means something like
'relaxed and comfortable', a
highly desirable state [often
also used with the implicit
sense of without worry or
concern]). Two very common
expressions meaning 'Are
you feeling comfortable/
Are you feeling well/How do
you feel? [generally asked
with the expectation that the
answer will be yes] are khun
sàbaai dii rŭeh คุณสบายดี
หรือ, khun sàbaai dii măi
คุณสบายดีไหม
command, order kham sàng
คำสั่ง

27

command, to (or, to order food in a restaurant) sàng sàng สั่ง สั่ง

common, ordinary tham-màdaa ธรรมดา

communicate (with someone) sùeh-săan สื่อสาร

company, firm bawrí-sàt บริษัท

compare, to prìap thîap เปรียบเทียบ

compared with prìap kàp เปรียบกับ

compel, to (to force) bangkháp บังคับ

compete, to khàeng แข่ง

competition, a (contest) kaan khàeng khăn การแข่งขัน

complain, to bòn บ่น; a grouchy/cranky person given to complaining khon khîi bòn คนขี้บ่น

complaint kham ráwng thúk คำร้องทุกข์

complete, to be (to have succeeded in completing a task) sămrèt สำเร็จ, or simply sèt เสร็จ

complete (thorough) dohy sîn choehng โดยสิ้นเชิง

complete, to be (whole)

sŏmbuun สมบูรณ์, or khróp thûan ครบถ้วน

complete, to tham hâi sèt ทำให้เสร็จ

completely yàang sŏmbuun อย่างสมบูรณ์

complicated/complex (a piece of machinery, a relationship) sáp sáwn ซับซ้อน

compose, write (letters, books, music) tàeng แต่ง, or khĭan เขียน

composition, writings kaan tàeng การแต่ง, kaan khĭan การเขียน

compromise, to prà-nii prà-nawm ประนีประนอม

compulsory/mandatory, to be bangkháp บังคับ

computer (from English) khawm-phiu-tôeh คอมพิวเตอร์, or (COLLOQUIALLY) khawm คอม (NOTE: a laptop computer is (from the English 'notebook') notèbúk โน้ตบุ๊ค.) Also see 'tablet PC'

concentrate, to (think) mii sà-maa-thí มีสมาธิ, or ao jai sài เอาใจใส่

28

concentrated (liquid, substance) khêm khôn เข้มข้น

concerning kìao kàp เกี่ยวกับ

condition/proviso, a ngûean-khǎi เงื่อนไข

condition (of a secondhand car) sà-phâap สภาพ

condition (symptom, indication, state, e.g. when discussing sickness, illness) aa-kaan อาการ

condom thǔng yang ถุงยาง, (from English) khawn-dâwm คอนดอม

condominium (condo) (from English) khawndo-mi-nîam (khondo) คอนโดมิเนียม (คอนโด)

confectionery/sweets khànǒm wǎan ขนมหวาน

confess (admit something) yawm ráp ยอมรับ

conference, a See 'meeting'

confidence khwaam mân-jai ความมั่นใจ

confidence, to have mii khwaam mân-jai มีความมั่นใจ

confident mân-jai มั่นใจ

Confucianism lát-thí khǒng júeh ลัทธิของจื๊อ

confuse, to (to be confusing) sàp sǒn สับสน

confused (in a mess) yûng yǒehng ยุ่งเหยิง

confused (mentally) ngong งง

confusing nâa sàpsǒn น่าสับสน

congratulations! (I congratulate you) khǎw sà-daehng khwaam yin-dii dûai ขอแสดงความยินดีด้วย

connect, to tàw ต่อ

connect (together) tìt tàw kan ติดต่อกัน

connection(s) (SLANG) sên เส้น, (COLLOQUIAL) to have connections with people of influence mii sên มีเส้น

conscious mii sà-tì มีสติ; be aware rúu tua rúu túa รู้ตัว

conscious of, to be rúu sǎmnúek รู้สำนึก

consider, to (consider an issue) phí-jaa-rá-naa พิจารณา

consider (to think over) phí-jaa-rá-naa พิจารณา, or trài trawng ไตร่ตรอง

29

constipation/to be constipated tháwng phùuk (literally, 'stomach'-'tie/tied') ท้องผูก

consult, talk over with prùek săa ปรึกษา

contact, get in touch with tìt tàw ติดต่อ

context bawrí-bòt บริบท

continent thá-wîip ทวีป

continue, to tham tàw pai ทำต่อไป

contraceptive (pill) (COLLOQUIAL) yaa khum ยาคุม

contract (legal) săn-yaa สัญญา (NOTE: the same word also means 'to promise')

control (something) khûap-khum ควบคุม

convenient, to be sà-dùak สะดวก

converse (FORMAL) sŏn-thá-naa สนทนา, (COLLOQUIAL) to 'chat' khui คุย

cook (person) khon tham aa-hăan คนทำอาหาร; also (from English) khúk กุ๊ก, or simply (COLLOQUIAL) M phâw krua พ่อครัว F mâeh krua แม่ครัว

cook, to tham aa-hăan ทำ อาหาร

cooked, to be (also, of fruit, 'to be ripe') sùk สุก

cooker (charcoal)/stove (oven) tao เตา

cookie, sweet biscuit (from English) khúkkîi คุกกี้

cool yen เย็น

cool, to (e.g. in a fridge) châeh yen แช่เย็น

cool (COLLOQUIAL – as in 'hip', 'trendy') têh เท่, or kèh เก๋

cop (police) tam-rùat ตำรวจ

copper (metal) thawng daehng ทองแดง

copy, to (imitate) lian bàep เลียนแบบ

copy N (e.g. a photocopy) sămnao สำเนา; v make a photocopy thài èkkà-săan ถ่ายเอกสาร, or simply (from English) 'copy' kóp-pîi ก๊อปปี้

coral hĭn pà-kaa-rang หิน ประการัง, or simply pà-kaa-rang ประการัง

coriander, cilantro phàk chii ผักชี

corn khâaw phôht ข้าวโพด

corner mum มุม

30

corpse (dead body) sòp ศพ

correct/to be right (answer to a question) thùuk tâwng ถูกต้อง

correct, to (a mistake/error) kâeh แก้

correspond (write letters, email) khǐan jòtmǎai เขียน จดหมาย, khǐan ii-mehl เขียนอีเมล

correspondent/reporter/ journalist phûu sùeh khàaw ผู้สื่อข่าว, or nák khàaw นักข่าว

corridor thaang doehn nai tùek ทางเดินในตึก

cosmetics See 'makeup'

cosmetic surgery See 'plastic surgery'

cost(s) (i.e. expenses) khâa chái jàai ค่าใช้จ่าย

cost (price) raa-khaa ราคา How much does it/this cost?/ What's the price? raa-khaa thâo-rài ราคาเท่าไหร่

cotton fâai ฝ้าย

cotton wool sǎm-lii สำลี

couch, sofa (from English) soh-faa โซฟา

cough, to ai ไอ

could, might àat jà อาจจะ: e.g. he could/might go khǎo àat jà pai เขาอาจจะไป

count, to náp นับ

country (nation) prà-thêht ประเทศ; Thailand prà-thêht thai ประเทศไทย

country/countryside (FORMAL) chon-ná-bòt ชนบท, (COLLOQUIAL) bâan nâwk บ้าน นอก

coup d'etat rát-prà-hǎan (literally, 'state' –'execute') รัฐประหาร

courgette, zucchini suu-kì-nii ซูกีนี

court (of law) sǎan ศาล

cousin lûuk phîi lûuk náwng ลูกพี่ลูกน้อง

cover, to pít ปิด, or khlum คลุม

cow, a wua tuamia วัวตัวเมีย

coworker, colleague phûean rûam ngaan เพื่อน ร่วมงาน

crab puu ปู

cracked, to be roi tàehk รอยแตก

cracker/salty biscuit khà-nǒmpang kràwp ขนมปัง กรอบ

31

crafts ngaan fǐi-much งานฝีมือ

craftsperson châang fǐi-much ช่างฝีมือ

cramp (muscle pain in arm/leg) tà-kriu ตะคริว; to have a cramp tà-kriu kin ตะคริวกิน; a stomach cramp tháwng jùk ท้องจุก

crash/bump (into) chon ชน; car crash rót chon รถชน; crash helmet/motorcycle helmet (COLLOQUIAL) mùak kan nók หมวกกันน็อก

crate lang mái ลังไม้

crazy, mad bâa-bâa baw-baw บ้าๆ บอๆ, or simply bâa บ้า, also (COLLOQUIAL TERM) ting-táwng ติงต๊อง (NOTE: a crazy/mad person is khon bâa คนบ้า)

cream (from English) khriim ครีม

create/build, to sâang สร้าง

criminal (FORMAL) àat-yaa-kawn อาชญากร, (COLLOQUIAL) phûu-ráai ผู้ร้าย

crocodile/alligator jawrá-khê จระเข้

crook (a cheat) khon khîi kohng คนขี้โกง

cross/angry, to be kròht โกรธ, or moh hòh โมโห

cross, go over (the road) khâam ข้าม

crow (bird) kaa กา

crowded/congested; tight (to grip someone's hand tightly, to feel stuffed after eating a lot of food, etc.) nâen แน่น

crown, a (as in dental work) khrâwp fan ครอบฟัน (NOTE: fan ฟัน or 'tooth' is pronounced like the English word 'fun')

cruel hòht ráai โหดร้าย

cry, to (out) ráwng ร้อง

cry, to (with tears) ráwng hâi ร้องให้

cry out, to (shout) tà-kohn ตะโกน

cucumber taehng kwaa แตงกวา

cuisine, food aa-hǎan อาหาร; style of cooking/cuisine, e.g. Chinese food/cuisine aa-hǎan jiin อาหารจีน

culture wát-thaná-tham วัฒนธรรม

cup, a thûai ถ้วย

32

cupboard, wardrobe, chest of drawers tûu ตู้

cure/treat (an illness) ráksǎa รักษา

cured, preserved, pickled (fruit) dawng ดอง

curious yàak rúu yàak hěn (literally, 'want know'-'want see') อยากรู้อยากเห็น

currency (FORMAL) ngoen traa เงินตรา, (SIMPLY COLLOQUIAL) ngoen 'money' เงิน

curly (as in 'curly hair') See 'frizzy'

curtains, drapes mâan ม่าน

cushion (pillow) mǎwn หมอน

custom/tradition prà-phehnii ประเพณี, or tham-niam ธรรมเนียม

customer/client lûuk kháa ลูกค้า

cut/slice hàn หั่น

cut, to tàt ตัด

cut (a wound)/cut by a knife See 'knife'

cute/appealing, to be nâa rák น่ารัก

D

dad/father (COLLOQUIAL) phâw พ่อ, (MORE FORMAL) bì-daa บิดา

daily (in the sense of a regular activity) prà-jam-wan ประจำวัน, (every day) thúk wan ทุกวัน

dam, a khùean เขื่อน

damage (i.e. to be damaged) chamrút ชำรุด, or sǐa hǎi เสียหาย, (SIMPLY COLLOQUIAL) phang พัง

damage, to tham hâi chamrút ทำให้ชำรุด

damp/humid, to be chúean ชื้น

dance, to tên ram เต้นรำ, or simply tên เต้น

dandruff rang-khaeh รังแค

danger/dangerous an-tà-raai อันตราย

dark, to be mûehd มืด

dark blue See 'navy blue'

dark skin (in colloquial Thai it is common to use the abbreviated word for 'black' dam ดำ even for someone many westerners would

33

consider to have a moderate tan) 'Dark skin' phĭu dạm ผิว ดำ or phĭu klám ผิวคล้ำ

darling/my love (expression of affection) thîi rák ที่รัก

date (of the month) wan thîi วันที่

date of birth wan duean pii kòeht (literally, 'day'-'month'-'year'-'birth') วันเดือนปีเกิด

daughter lûuk săaw ลูกสาว

daughter-in-law lûuk sà-phái ลูกสะใภ้

dawn cháo trùu เช้าตรู่

day wan วัน; **today** wan níi วันนี้; **yesterday** mûea waan (níi) เมื่อวาน(นี้)

day after tomorrow mà-ruehn (níi) มะรืน(นี้)

day before yesterday mûeawaan suehn níi เมื่อวานซืน (นี้)

daydream tọ̆ f̆an klaang wan ฝันกลางวัน

day off (also used for 'holiday', i.e. day off work) wan yùt วันหยุด

day time klaang wan กลางวัน

dead, to be (COLLOQUIAL) taai láew ตายแล้ว, **(MORE FORMAL)**

sĭa láew เสียแล้ว; **death** khwaam taai ความตาย

deaf, to be hŭu nùak หูหนวก

debt(s) nîi sĭn หนี้สิน

deceive, to làwk-luang หลอกลวง **(in colloquial speech the single word làwk** หลอก **is used)**

December than-waa-khom ธันวาคม

decide, to tàt-sĭn jai ตัดสินใจ

decision kaan tàt-sĭn jai การ ตัดสินใจ

decisive, to be (to act decisively) dèt-khàat เด็ดขาด

decline/decrease/get less lót long ลดลง

decline/refuse/deny, to pàtì-sèht ปฏิเสธ

decorate, to tòk tàeng ตกแต่ง

deejay (DJ or 'disk jockey' playing music on the radio or in a club etc.) dii jeh **(pronounced very similar to the English)** ดีเจ

deep lúek ลึก

defeat, to (someone else, i.e. to win) ao cháná เอาชนะ, or simply cháná ชนะ

defeated, to be (beaten, lose a contest) pháeh แพ้

defecate, to (POLITE) thàai ถ่าย, (COLLOQUIAL; the first of the following two terms is more appropriate in general) ùeh อี้, khîi ขี้ (Note: the word khîi ขี้ which is the common way of referring to faeces should not be thought of as equivalent to the English term 'shit'; khîi is not a vulgar word and such bodily functions are often talked of by Thai people in an unselfconscious, matter-of-fact way)

defect (or fault in something) khâw bòk phrâwng ข้อบกพร่อง

defend (in war), protect (oneself or somebody else), also to prevent (the outbreak of disease) pâwng kan ป้องกัน

definite nâeh nawn แน่นอน

deformed/crippled/disabled, to be phí-kaan พิการ

degree, level, standard (e.g. 'high standard') rá-dàp ระดับ

degree (awarded by college or university) pà-rin-yaa ปริญญา

degree(s) (temperature) ongsǎa องศา

delay tham hâi lâa cháa ทำให้ล่าช้า

delayed lâa cháa ล่าช้า

delete/rub out lóp àwk ลบ ออก

delicate (fine, detailed work/craftsmanship) lá-ìat ละเอียด, prà-nîit ประณีต

delicate (constitution, not strong) àwn-ae อ่อนแอ

delicious/tasty, to be àròi อร่อย

delinquent (SLANG) dèk wáen เด็กแว้น, or dèk skói เด็ก สก๊อย (young members of motorcycle gangs); jìk-kǒh จิ๊กโก๋ (more general types of delinquents), and kúi กุ๊ย (a distinct low-life variety)

deliver, to sòng ส่ง

demand, to rîak ráwng เรียกร้อง

democracy prà-chaa-thí-pà-tai ประชาธิปไตย

demonstrate (show how to)

35

săa-thít สาธิต

dental floss măi khàt fan
ไหมขัดฟัน

dentist (MORE FORMAL) thantà-
phâet ทันตแพทย์, (COMMON)
măw fan (literally, 'doctor'-
'tooth') หมอฟัน

depart, to àwk jàak ออก
จาก; departure àawk
doehn thaang ออกเดินทาง;
department (in bureaucracy)
phà-nàek แผนก

department store hâang
sàpphá-sĭn-kháa ห้างสรรพ
สินค้า, (SIMPLY COLLOQUIAL)
hâang ห้าง

depend (on somebody for
help) phôeng พึ่ง

depend (it depends on...)
khûen yùu kàp... ขึ้นอยู่
กับ..., or alternatively láew
tàeh แล้วแต่

deposit, to (money in a
bank, to leave something
somewhere) fàak ฝาก (NOTE:
it is also very common to
use this word in the following
sense – e.g. to ask somebody
going out to the shops to buy
something in particular for you

'Can you get (buy) me some
bread as well?' – fàak súeh [=
buy] khanŏm pang [= bread]
dûai ฝากซื้อขนมปังด้วย)

deposit, a (of payment on a
car, a house) ngoen mát jam
เงินมัดจำ, (money deposited
in the bank) ngoen fàak
เงินฝาก

depression (mental condition)
rôhk suem sâo โรคซึมเศร้า

depressed, to be klûm jai
กลุ้มใจ

descendant, heir/heiress
thaa-yâat ทายาท

describe, to banyaai
บรรยาย; description kham
banyaai คำบรรยาย, or kaan
banyaai การบรรยาย

desert (arid land) thá-leh saai
(literally, 'sea'-'sand') ทะเล
ทราย

desert, to (abandon) thíng ทิ้ง

design, to (a house) àwk
bàehp ออกแบบ

desire (to do something)
khwaam pràat-thànăa ความ
ปรารถนา; to desire (to do
something) yàak อยาก

desire (sexual) khwaam

khrâi ความใคร่, tan-hǎa
ตัณหา (NOTE: the word yàak
อยาก (previous entry) can
also convey this particular
meaning)

desk, table tó โต๊ะ

dessert khǎwng wǎan
(literally, 'thing'-'sweet')
ของหวาน

destination plaai thaang
ปลายทาง

destiny chôhk chá-taa โชค
ชะตา

destroy, to tham-laai ทำลาย

destroyed/ruined, to be
thùuk tham-laai ถูกทำลาย

detail(s) (e.g. in a contract –
'the fine print') raai-lá-ìat
รายละเอียด

detergent (washing powder)
phǒng sák fâwk ผงซักฟอก;
detergent (liquid – for washing
plates etc.) náam-yaa láang
jaan น้ำยาล้างจาน, (for
washing clothing) náam-yaa
sák phâa น้ำยาซักผ้า

**determined, intent on
getting something done/
accomplished** tâng-jai
ตั้งใจ

detour thaang âwm ทางอ้อม

develop, to phát-thá-naa
พัฒนา; **development** kaan
phát-thá-naa การพัฒนา

develop, to (grow) tòep toh
เติบโต

dial, to (telephone), **to spin**
mǔn หมุน

diabetes rôhk bao-wǎan โรค
เบาหวาน

dialect phaa-sǎa thìn ภาษา
ถิ่น

diamond, a phét เพชร

diaper (baby's diaper) phâa-
âwm ผ้าอ้อม

diarrhea, diarrhoea tháwng
sǐa ท้องเสีย, tháwng doehn
(literally, 'stomach'-'walk')
ท้องเดิน, tháwng rûang
ท้องร่วง

diary sà-mùt dai aa-rîi สมุด
ไดอารี่

dictionary phót-jà-
naànúkrom พจนานุกรม,
(COLLOQUIAL) dík (from English
'dictionary') ดิค

die, to (COLLOQUIAL) taai ตาย, or
(POLITE) sǐa เสีย

diesel (petrol, gasoline) (petrol
= náam-man) náam-man

dii-sel น้ำมันดีเซล

diet, to lót náamnàk ลดน้ำ
หนัก, (also from English) dai-
èt ไดเอท

difference (e.g. in quality)
khwaam tàehk tàang ความ
แตกต่าง

different tàehk tàang แตก
ต่าง; other ùehn อื่น

difficult (i.e. a difficult task)
yâak ยาก, difficult in the
sense of not being easy to do
things (e.g. going somewhere,
etc. or 'having a hard/difficult
life') lambàak ลำบาก

dig (a hole in the ground)
khùt ขุด

digest (food) yôi (aa-hǎan)
ย่อย (อาหาร)

dinner, to eat (POLITE) thaan
aa-hǎan yen ทานอาหารเย็น,
(COLLOQUIAL) kin khâaw yen
กินข้าวเย็น

diploma (from college or
school – also see 'degree')
à-nú-pàrin-yaa อนุปริญญา

dipper, ladle (implement used
when cooking stir-fry dishes)
tháp-phii ทัพพี

direct (directly, non-stop)

trong ตรง

direct, to (somebody to do
something) sàng สั่ง

direction (according to the
compass) thít thaang ทิศทาง

director (of company) phûu
jàt-kaan ผู้จัดการ

dirt din ดิน, (dust) fùn ฝุ่น

dirty, filthy sòkkapròk สกปรก

disagree (with someone) mâi
hěn dûai ไม่เห็นด้วย

disappear See 'vanish'

disappointed, to be phìt
wǎng ผิดหวัง

disaster phai phíbàt ภัยพิบัติ

disco (from English) dis-kô
ดิสโก้, (COLLOQUIAL) ték เทค;
nightclub (from English) nái-
khláp ไนท์คลับ

discount (in the price of
something) lót raa-khaa
ลดราคา

discover, to khón phóp
ค้นพบ

discuss, to (ways to solve a
problem) thòk panhǎa ถก
ปัญหา; discuss (exchange
ideas) lâek-plìan khwaam
khít hěn แลกเปลี่ยนความ
คิดเห็น

disease (general term) rôhk
โรค

disgusting nâa rangkìat น่า
รังเกียจ; to be disgusted
(COLLOQUIAL) màn sâi หมั่นไส้

dish/plate, a jaan จาน

disk (CD, DVD) phàen dís
แผ่นดิสก์

dislike, to mâi châwp
(literally, 'no'-'like') ไม่ชอบ

dissolve/melt, to lá-laai
ละลาย

display (a show, a
performance) kaan
sà-daehng การแสดง

display, to sà-daehng แสดง

distance (from one place to
another) rá-yá thang ระยะทาง

disturb, to róp-kuan รบกวน

disturbance khwaam mâi
sà-ngòp ความไม่สงบ

dive (into the sea, go diving)
dam náam ดำน้ำ

divide (up – e.g. between
different people) bàeng แบ่ง;
separate/split up yâehk แยก

divided by hăan dûai (e.g.
twenty divided by five, 20
hăan dûai 5) หารด้วย

divorce, to yàa หย่า

divorced, to be yàa láew
หย่าแล้ว

do, perform an action
tham ทำ

don't! (do something) yàa อย่า

don't mention it (or 'it
doesn't matter', 'that's OK,
don't worry about it') mâi
pen rai ไม่เป็นไร

do one's best tham dii thîi
sùt ทำดีที่สุด

doctor (COLLOQUIAL) măw หมอ,
(MORE FORMAL) phâeht แพทย์

document èhkkà-săan
เอกสาร

dog (COMMON, COLLOQUIAL) măa
หมา, (MORE GENTEEL, FORMAL)
sù-nák สุนัข

doll (toy) túkkà-taa ตุ๊กตา

dollar (from English) dawn-lâa
ดอลลาร์, (COLLOQUIAL) dawn ดอล

dolphin plaa-loh-maa ปลา
โลมา

donate bawrí-jàak บริจาค

done (cooked) sùk láew สุก
แล้ว

done (finished) sèt láew เสร็จ
แล้ว

donut (from English) doh-nát
โดนัท, khà-nŏm doh-nát

(khànŏm = a sweet) ขนม
โดนัท

door/gate, a prà-tuu ประตู

double (a pair, or as in 'double' bed) pen khûu เป็นคู่

double, twice the amount sǎwng thâo สองเท่า

doubt/suspect, to sŏng-sǎi สงสัย

down, downward long maa ลงมา

downstairs khâang lâang ข้างล่าง

down-to-earth (to be natural, unpretentious) pen tham-má-châat เป็นธรรมชาติ

downtown nai mueang ในเมือง

dozen lŏh โหล

dragon, a mang-kawn มังกร

drama (as in TV soap opera) lá-khawn ละคร; TV soap opera lá-khawn thii-wii ละครทีวี

drapes, curtains mâan ม่าน

draw, to (a picture) wâat วาด; draw a picture wâat rûup วาดรูป; a drawing rûup wâat รูปวาด

drawer, a (in a desk) línchák ลิ้นชัก

dream, a khwaam fǎn ความฝัน

dream, to fǎn ฝัน; Dream on! (as in 'In your dreams' or 'You must be kidding!') fǎn pai thóeh ฝันไปเถอะ

dress, frock chút krà-prohng ชุดกระโปรง

dressed, to get tàeng tua แต่งตัว

dressing gown sûea khlum เสื้อคลุม

drink, to dùehm ดื่ม

drink/beverage, a khrûeang dùehm เครื่องดื่ม

drive, to (a car) khàp ขับ

driver khon khàp คนขับ

driving license (for either car or motorcycle) (COLLOQUIAL) bai khàp khìi ใบขับขี่

drought (very dry weather conditions, land, etc.) hâehng láehng แห้งแล้ง

drown, to jom náam taai จม น้ำตาย

drug (medicine) yaa ยา, drug (narcotic) yaa sèhp tìt (literally, 'drug/medicine'-

'consume'-'stuck') ยาเสพติด

drugstore, pharmacy, chemist ráan khǎai yaa ร้านขายยา

drunk/intoxicated, to be mao เมา; a drunk (drunkard) khîi mao ขี้เมา. (NOTE: the word mao เมา is not only used to refer to someone being drunk on alcohol, it is also used to refer to someone being 'high' or 'stoned' on any type of drug. Stoned on marijuana, for example, is mao kan-chaa เมากัญชา. A habitual user of illegal drugs is referred to as khîi yaa ขี้ยา. The word khîi ขี้ in this instance means 'habitual', 'being prone to' some type of behaviour')

dry, to be hâehng แห้ง

dry (weather) hâehng láehng แห้งแล้ง

dry, to tham hâi hâehng ทำให้แห้ง, tàak ตาก; to dry clothing tàak phâa ตากผ้า

dry clean(ing) sák hâehng ซักแห้ง

dry out, to (in the sun) tàak

dàet ตากแดด

duck, a pèt เป็ด

dull (boring) nâa bùea น่าเบื่อ

dull (weather) khà-mùk-khà-mǔa ขมุกขมัว

dumpling (meat) saa lá pao ซาละเปา

durian (fruit) thú-rian ทุเรียน

during, in between nai rá-wàang ในระหว่าง

dusk klâi mûehd (literally, 'close'-'dark') ใกล้มืด

dust fùn ฝุ่น; dustbin/rubbish bin/garbage bin thǎng khà-yà ถังขยะ

duty (tax) phaa-sǐi ภาษี

duty (responsibility) nâa thîi หน้าที่

DVD (from English) dii wii dii ดีวีดี

dysentery rôhk bìt โรคบิด

41

E

each (as in 'each particular person', 'each particular book') tàeh lá แต่ละ; every... thúk... ทุก...

eagle nók in-sii นกอินทรี

ear hǔu หู; **earphone(s), headphones** hǔufang หูฟัง; **ear wax** khîi hǔu (literally, 'excrement'-'ear') ขี้หู

earlier, beforehand kàwn níi ก่อนนี้

early (i.e. to come earlier than usual) rew kwàa pàkàti เร็ว กว่าปกติ

early in the morning cháo trùu เช้าตรู่

earn, to (a wage) dâi khâa jâang ได้ค่าจ้าง

earrings tûm hǔu ตุ้มหู

earth, soil din din ดิน

Earth, the world lôhk โลก

earthenware khrûeng din-phǎo เครื่องดินเผา

earthquake phàen din wǎi แผ่นดินไหว

east (direction) tà-wan àwk ตะวันออก

easy ngâi ง่าย

eat, to — there are a number of words in Thai that mean 'to eat'. These range from the colloquial to more formal. They include: kin กิน or more fully kin khâaw (literally, 'eat'-'rice') กินข้าว (NOTE: the colloquial term kin กิน is also used as slang to refer to corrupt practices such as taking bribes); thaan (more polite, colloquial) ทาน; ráp prà-thaan (formal) รับประทาน; chǎn (for monks) ฉัน. When animals 'eat' another word is often used: dàek แดก. If dàek is used to refer to people eating, it is extremely rude and should be avoided. It is generally used in informal settings among intimate male friends, and rougher, rowdier elements of Thai society.

ecology níwêt-wít-thá-yaa นิเวศวิทยา; **ecologist** nák ní-wêht-wít-tháyaa นัก นิเวศวิทยา

economical/frugal, to be

42

prà-yàt ประหยัด

economy, the sèht-thà-kìt เศรษฐกิจ

ecstasy khwaam sùk mâak ความสุขมาก; **ecstasy (the drug)** yaa ii ยาอี

edge khàwp ขอบ

educate, to sùek-sǎa ศึกษา

education kaan sùek-sǎa การศึกษา

effect, result phǒn ผล

effort khwaam phá-yaa-yaam ความพยายาม

effort, to make an; try phá-yaa-yaam พยายาม

egg khài ไข่

eggplant, aubergine (general term) má-khǔea mûang มะเขือม่วง

eight (the number) pàet แปด

eighteen sìp pàet (literally, 'ten'-'eight') สิบแปด

eighty pàet sìp (literally, 'eight'-'ten') แปดสิบ

either...or mâi... kâw... ไม่...ก็...

ejaculate/to come
(COLLOQUIAL; used for both men and women) sèt เสร็จ, or sèt láew เสร็จแล้ว. (The

word sèt เสร็จ also means 'finished')

elbow khâw sàwk ข้อศอก

elder (i.e. 'older than') kàeh kwàa แก่กว่า

election kaan lûeak tâng การเลือกตั้ง

electric, electricity fai-fáa ไฟฟ้า

electrician châang fai-fáa ช่างไฟฟ้า

electronic (from English) i-lék thraw-ník อิเล็กทรอนิก

elephant cháang ช้าง; **a white elephant (regarded as auspicious in Thailand)** cháang phùeak (literally, 'elephant'-'albino') ช้างเผือก

elevator (from English 'lift') líp ลิฟต์

eleven sìp èt สิบเอ็ด

elite khon chán sǔung (literally, 'person/people'-'class/level'-'high') คนชั้นสูง

else (as in 'anything else?') àrai ìik อะไรอีก

email (message) (from English) ii-mehl อีเมล

email, to (send an email) sòng ii-mehl ส่งอีเมล

43

email address thîi yùu
ii-mehl ที่อยู่อีเมล

embarrassed/shy aai
(pronounced like 'eye') อาย

embarrassing, to be nâa
lá-aai น่าละอาย

embassy sà-thǎan thûut
สถานทูต

embrace/hug, to kàwt กอด

embroider(ed) pàk ปัก

embroidery yép pàk thàk rói
เย็บปักถักร้อย

emerald mawrá-kòt มรกต

emergency chùk chǒehn
ฉุกเฉิน

emotion, feeling khwaam
rúu-sèuk ความรู้สึก

emphasize/stress
something, to nén เน้น

employ (to hire someone)
jâang จ้าง

employee (generally used
with unskilled or lowly skilled
workers) lûuk jâang ลูกจ้าง

employer (boss) naai jâang
นายจ้าง

empty, to be wâang plào
ว่างเปล่า

end (ending) jòp จบ

end, to sèt sîn เสร็จสิ้น, also

jòp จบ

end (the tip, e.g. of the tongue,
nose, etc.) plaai ปลาย

enemy, an sàt-truu ศัตรู

energy phá-lang ngaan
พลังงาน

engaged (telephone) sǎai mâi
wâang สายไม่ว่าง

engaged (to be married) mân
หมั้น

engine/motor khrûeang yon
เครื่องยนต์, or (simply and
more colloquially) khrûeang
เครื่อง

engineer, an wítsà-wá-kawn
วิศวกร

England angkrìt อังกฤษ

English (people) khon angkrìt
คนอังกฤษ; (language) phaa-
sǎa angkrìt ภาษาอังกฤษ

engrave, to (to carve a piece
of stone, wood, etc.) kàe-sà-
làk แกะสลัก

enjoy, to (to be fun/
pleasurable) sà-nùk สนุก
(This is a quintessential Thai
word and the full sense of the
term is not really adequately
conveyed by the English
word 'enjoy.' In Thai being

44

sà-nùk is highly desirable)

enjoyable nâa sà-nùk น่าสนุก

enjoy oneself, to tham tua hâi sà-nùk ทำตัวให้สนุก (sometimes the English word 'enjoy' is also used in Thai: en-joy เอนจอย)

enlarge, to khà-yǎai ขยาย

enough, sufficient phaw พอ

enquire/ask, to thǎam ถาม

enter, to khâo เข้า (NOTE: this word is frequently used in conjunction with either the word 'come' maa มา, or 'go' pai ไป; e.g. 'come in [here]' khâo maa เข้ามา, or 'go in [there]' khâo pai เข้าไป)

entire, whole tháng mòt ทั้งหมด

entrance, way in thaang khâo ทางเข้า

entrepreneur/business person nák thurá-kìt นักธุรกิจ

envelope, an sawng ซอง

environment, the sìng wâeht láwm สิ่งแวดล้อม

envy ìtchǎa อิจฉา; **envious** nâa ìtchǎa น่าอิจฉา

equal thâo thiam เท่าเทียม

equality khwaam thâo thiam ความเท่าเทียม

equipment/implement ù-pà-kawn อุปกรณ์

error, mistake khwaam phìt ความผิด

escalator bandai lûean บันได เลื่อน

escape/flee, to nǐi หนี

especially dohy chà-phá-w โดยเฉพาะ

essay (e.g. term essay at university) riang khwaam เรียงความ, or **(essay/article in a newspaper)** bòt khwaam บทความ

establish, set up kàw tâng ก่อตั้ง

estimate, to prà-maan ประมาณ; **estimate the price/ give a quote** tii raa-khaa ตี ราคา

ethnic group, minority group chon klùm nói ชนกลุ่มน้อย

Eurasian (the offspring of an Asian and European/ Caucasian parent) lûuk khrûeng (literally, 'child'- 'half') ลูกครึ่ง

45

Euro (currency) ngoen yuù-roh เงินยูโร

Europe yú-ròhp ยุโรป

even (e.g. even young people like it) máeh tàeh แม้แต่

even (smooth) rîap เรียบ

even (evenly matched, equal in a race/competition, e.g. a tie in a football game) sà-mŏeh kan เสมอกัน

evening tawn yen ตอนเย็น

event hèht kaan เหตุการณ์

ever (e.g. 'have you ever been to…?') khoei เคย (Note: for fuller description of how this word is used *see* 'have'.)

every thúk ทุก

everybody, everyone thúk khon ทุกคน (Note: common idiom – 'everybody for themselves/every man for himself' tua khrai tua man ตัวใครตัวมัน

every day thúk wan ทุกวัน

every kind of… thúk chá-nít ทุกชนิด

everything thúk sìng ทุกสิ่ง

every time thúk khráng ทุกครั้ง

everywhere thúk thîi ทุกที่

evidence, proof làk thăan หลักฐาน

evil, to be chûa rái ชั่วร้าย N khwaam chûa ความชั่ว

exact, to be (COLLOQUIAL) trong péh ตรงเป๊ะ, (or in short) péh เป๊ะ

exactly! just so! (COLLOQUIAL) nân lâe นั่นแหละ

exam, test (knowledge or skill) sàwp สอบ

examine, inspect, to trùat-sàwp ตรวจสอบ

example, an tua yàang ตัวอย่าง

example, for chên… เช่น…

excellent yâwt yîam ยอดเยี่ยม; **great,** (COLLOQUIAL) 'that's great!' sùt yâwt สุดยอด

except, to be exempt (e.g. 'everyone can go except him') yók wéhn ยกเว้น; **an exception** khâw yók wéhn ข้อยกเว้น

except (i.e. in the sense of being 'apart from' or 'in addition to') nâwk jàak นอกจาก

exchange, to (money,

46

opinions) lâehk plìan แลกเปลี่ยน

exchange rate àttraa lâek plìan อัตราแลกเปลี่ยน

excited tùehn tên ตื่นเต้น

exciting nâa tùehn tên น่าตื่นเต้น

excrement/faeces (FORMAL MEDICAL TERM) ùt-jàgàrá อุจจาระ, (COLLOQUIAL) khîi ขี้ (in English the common colloquial for this is 'shit' of course, but the Thai word does not have the same type of crude/vulgar sense to it and, while not exactly polite, is not particularly rude. Thus khîi ขี้ is not used in situations, common with English, when someone is angry or has made a mistake, etc.)

excuse me! (attracting attention) used as an apology, e.g. 'I'm sorry' (for bumping into you) khǎw thôht ขอโทษ (literally, 'request/ask for'- 'punishment')

excuse me! (said trying to get past someone in a crowded place) khǎw thaang nòi ขอ

ทางหน่อย

excuse, an khâw kâe tua ข้อแก้ตัว

exercise, to àwk kamlang kaai ออกกำลังกาย

exist (to be alive) mii chiiwít yùu มีชีวิตอยู่

exit, way out thaang àwk ทางออก

expand, grow larger khà-yǎai ขยาย

expect, to khâat wâa… คาดว่า...

expense(s) raai jàai รายจ่าย

expenses, expenditure khâa chái jàai ค่าใช้จ่าย

expensive, to be phaehng แพง

experience pràsòp-kaan ประสบการณ์

experience, to (to have experienced something) mii pràsòp-kaan มีประสบการณ์

expert (have expertise) cham-naan ชำนาญ; an expert (in a particular field) phûu chîao-chaan ผู้เชี่ยวชาญ

expire, to (e.g. a driving license) mòt aa-yú หมดอายุ

explain, to à-thí-baai อธิบาย

(NOTE: the first two syllables of this word à and thí are very short; '(I) can't explain' à-thí-baai mâi dâi อธิบายไม่ ได้; explanation kham à-thí-baai คำอธิบาย

explode, to (e.g. a bomb) rá-bòet ระเบิด

export, to sòng àwk ส่งออก

express, urgent dùan ด่วน

express (emotion, one's feelings) sà-daehng แสดง

expressway, freeway thaang dùan ทางด่วน

extend (make larger/longer, add to) tàw ต่อ; **extension** (telephone) tàw ต่อ (NOTE: to 'extend a visa' is tàw wii-sâa ต่อวีซ่า)

extra, increase phôehm เพิ่ม

extraordinary (special) phí-sèht พิเศษ

extravagant (spendthrift) fûm fueai ฟุ่มเฟือย

extremely (COLLOQUIAL) sùt khìit สุดขีด, or (in short) sùt sùt สุดๆ (e.g. 'extremely hot' ráwn sùt sùt ร้อนสุดๆ, 'hot' = ráwn ร้อน)

eye taa ตา

eyebrow khíu คิ้ว (it is pronounced like 'cute' in English)

eyeglasses, glasses, spectacles wâen taa แว่นตา

F

fable/legend, a ní-thaan นิทาน

fabric/textile/cloth phâa ผ้า

face nâa หน้า; **lose face** (dignity, to be embarrassed) khǎai nâa (literally, 'sell'-'face') ขายหน้า, or sǐa nâa (literally 'ruined/spoiled'-'face') เสียหน้า

face/confront, to phà-choehn nǎa เผชิญหน้า

fact, facts khâw thét jing ข้อเท็จจริง

factory rohng ngaan โรงงาน

fail, to (to be unsuccessful) mâi sǎmrèt ไม่สำเร็จ; **to fail a test/exam** sàwp tòk (literally, 'test'-'fall') สอบตก

failure khwaam lóm lěuo ความล้มเหลว

faint/swoon, to pen lom เป็นลม

48

fair (to be just)/fair-minded
yút-tì-tham ยุติธรรม (NOTE:
the English word 'fair' is
commonly used in Thai but
generally in the negative
sense, i.e. something that is
'not fair' mâi fae ไม่แฟร์)

fake, a (an imitation) plawm
ปลอม, e.g. referring to a fake
Rolex – 'it's a fake!' khǎwng
plawm ของปลอม

fall, autumn (season) rúeduu
bai mái rûang ฤดูใบไม้ร่วง

fall, to (drop, decrease) tòk
ตก

fall/fell over hòk-lóm หกล้ม,
or simply lóm ล้ม

false, artificial thiam เทียม

false (not true) mâi jing ไม่
จริง; wrong phìt ผิด

family khrâwp khrua
ครอบครัว

famine khwaam òt yàak
ความอดอยาก

famous mii chûeh sǐang
(literally, 'have'-'name'-
'sound/voice') มีชื่อเสียง,
(COLLOQUIAL) 'to be famous'
dang ดัง; a famous/well
known person khon dang คน

ดัง (NOTE: dang ดัง is also the
word for a 'loud' sound/noise)

fan (of a singer/movie star)
faehn แฟน (from English:
also colloquial term for either
girl or boyfriend)

fan (for cooling) phát-lom
พัดลม

fancy/luxurious/opulent
rǔùràa หรูหรา

far/distant klai ไกล See
'note' under the entry for
'near' to help differentiate
these two terms

fare khâa dohy-sǎan
ค่าโดยสาร (for buses and
minivans), or simply, and
more colloquially khâa rót
ค่ารถ

farmer chaaw naa (literally,
'people'-'rice field') ชาวนา

fart N, V (COLLOQUIAL) tòt ตด

fashion (clothing) In Thai the
English word is commonly
used but with slightly
different pronunciation
faèshun (NOTE: unfashion-
able/old-fashioned/out-of
date choei เชย)

fast, rapid rew เร็ว; the

49

expression to tell someone
to 'go faster' or 'hurry up' is
rew-rew เร็วๆ

fast, to (go without food) òt
aa-hǎan อดอาหาร

fat, grease khǎi man ไขมัน
(NOTE: the word for
cholesterol is khǎi man
nai lûeat (literally, 'fat'-'in'-
'blood') ไขมันในเลือด)

fat, plump, obese ûan อ้วน
(NOTE: the word 'fat' does
not quite have the same
negative connotations in Thai
conversation as it does in the
west, although this could be
changing. A more polite word
to refer to someone who is
carrying a few extra kilograms
is sǒmbuun สมบูรณ์ which
means 'healthy', 'complete',
'perfect')

father (COLLOQUIAL) phâw พ่อ,
(FORMAL) bì-daa บิดา

father-in-law phâw taa พ่อตา

favourite (to like the most)
châwp mâak thîi sùt ชอบ
มากที่สุด

fax (machine/message) fáek(s)
แฟกซ์; to send a fax sòng

fáek(s) ส่งแฟกซ์

fear N khwaam klua ความกลัว

February kum-phaa-phan
กุมภาพันธ์

fee (generally for a public sector
service) khâa tham-niam ค่า
ธรรมเนียม; service fee khâa
bawrí-kaan ค่าบริการ

feed, to hâi aa-hǎan ให้อาหาร

feel, to rúu-sùek รู้สึก

feeling khwaam rúù-sùek
ความรู้สึก

feeling cold (i.e. to feel cold)
nǎaw หนาว

feet/foot (for humans) tháo
เท้า, foot/feet (for animals)
tiin ตีน (NOTE: in central Thai
the word tiin, when applied
to people, is extremely rude)

female (human being) yǐng
หญิง, female (animal) tua
mia ตัวเมีย

fence rúa รั้ว

feng shui huang jûi ฮวงจุ้ย

ferry ruea khâam fâak เรือ
ข้ามฟาก

fertile (of land) ù-dom
sǒmbuun อุดมสมบูรณ์

festival, a (very common
in Thailand) thêht-sàkaan

50

เทศกาล; also 'temple fair' (similarly very common) ngaan wát งานวัด

fetch, to (to go and get) pai ao maa (literally, 'go'-'take'-'come') ไปเอามา

fever khâi ไข้; to have a fever pen khâi เป็นไข้...

few mâi kìi... ไม่กี่...

few, a săwng săam (literally, 'two'-'three') สองสาม

fiancé, fiancée khûu mân คู่หมั้น

field, a (a sporting field, a parade ground) sà-năam สนาม; a rice field thûng naa ทุ่งนา, or simply naa นา

fierce, vicious (to describe either an animal or person) dù ดุ

fifteen sìp hâa (literally, 'ten'-'five') สิบห้า

fifty hâa sìp (literally, 'five'-'ten') ห้าสิบ

fight, to (physically) sûu สู้

fight over, to (e.g. the control of a piece of land, a child, etc.) yâehng แย่ง

figure (number) tua lêhk ตัวเลข

figure (body shape) hùn หุ่น: e.g. 'a good figure' hùn dii หุ่นดี

fill, to (e.g. up a car with petrol) toehm เติม

fill out (a form) kràwk กรอก (also see 'form')

film, movie (COLLOQUIAL) năng หนัง, (MORE FORMAL) phâap-phá-yon ภาพยนตร์

filthy See 'dirty'

final sùt tháai สุดท้าย

finally ...nai thîi sùt ...ในที่สุด (in Thai, usually used at the end of a sentence)

find, to phóp พบ; trying to find/ to look for something hăa หา

fine (okay) dii ดี, OK (from English) oh-kheh โอเค

fine, a (for some type of infringement) khâa pràp ค่าปรับ. (In the 'entertainment scene' in Thailand there is also something known as a 'bar fine' – the English words pronounced in the Thai manner. This is the 'fee' a patron has to pay to take a woman (dancer, hostess) out

51

of the premises. A separate
'fee' for 'services rendered'
is negotiated between these
two individuals)

finger níu นิ้ว; fingernail lép mueh เล็บมือ

finish sèt เสร็จ

finish off, to (a job/task) tham hâi sèt ทำให้เสร็จ

finished (complete) sèt láew เสร็จแล้ว

finished (none left) mòt láew หมดแล้ว

fire fai ไฟ; 'there's a fire (burning)!' fai mâi ไฟไหม้

fire someone, to lâi àwk ไล่ออก

fireworks prà-thát ประทัด

firm, company bawrí-sàt บริษัท

firm (skin, muscles) nâen แน่น; firm (mattress) khǎeng แข็ง; firm (secure) mânkhong มั่นคง

first râehk แรก; at first thii râehk ทีแรก, or tawn râehk ตอนแรก

first, earlier, beforehand kàwn ก่อน

fish plaa ปลา

fish, to (to go fishing) tòk plaa ตกปลา

fish sauce náam plaa (literally, 'water'-'fish') น้ำปลา

fit, to (clothing; 'it fits perfectly') sài phaw dii ใส่พอดี

fitting, suitable, appropriate mà-w sǒm เหมาะสม

five hâa ห้า

fix, to (a time, appointment) nát นัด

fix, to (repair) kâeh แก้, sâwm ซ่อม

flag, a thong ธง; national flag thong châat ธงชาติ

flame, a pleow fai เปลวไฟ

flashlight/torch, a fai chǎi ไฟฉาย

flat, apartment (from English) flàet แฟลต

flat, smooth (e.g. the sea) rîap เรียบ; flat (e.g. a flat tire/ tyre) baehn แบน

flesh, meat núea เนื้อ

flexible/adaptable, to be yûet yùn ยืดหยุ่น

flight, a (on an airline) thîao bin เที่ยวบิน

flip flops/thongs *See* 'slipper'

52

flippers (fins – used for snorkeling, diving, etc.) tiin kòp (literally, 'feet'-'frog') ตีนกบ, also (from English) fin ฟิน

flirt, to jìip (pronounced like the word 'jeep' with a low tone) จีบ

float, to loi ลอย

flood N, v náam thûam น้ำท่วม

floor phúehn พื้น

flour pâehng แป้ง (NOTE: the same word pâehng แป้ง also means 'face powder', 'baby powder' etc.)

flower, a dàwk mái ดอกไม้

flu/influenza khâi wàt yài ไข้หวัดใหญ่

fluent (to do something – e.g. speak a language – fluently) khlâwng คล่อง

fluid/liquid khăwng lĕhw ของเหลว

flute, a khlùi ขลุ่ย

fly (insect) má-laehng-wan แมลงวัน

fly, to bin บิน

fog màwk หมอก

fold, to (e.g. a piece of paper) pháp พับ

follow along, to taam ตาม

follow behind, to taam lăng ตามหลัง

fond of, to be (to like someone) châwp ชอบ

food aa-hăan อาหาร (NOTE: the word 'rice' khâaw ข้าว is often colloquially used to refer to 'food')

foot/feet tháo เท้า (NOTE: the word used for animals' foot/ feet is tiin ตีน. It is extremely rude and inappropriate to use this term when referring to humans in polite, or even informal, conversation)

for sămràp สำหรับ, also pûea เพื่อ

forbid, to hâam ห้าม

forbidden tâwng hâam ต้อง ห้าม, or simply hâam ห้าม

force, energy kamlang กำลัง

force/compel, to bangkháp บังคับ

forecast/predict (as in weather forecast) phá-yaa-kawn พยากรณ์

forehead nâa phàak หน้าผาก

foreign/overseas tàang prà-thêht ต่างประเทศ

53

foreigner chaaw tàangchâat ชาวต่างชาติ. Also the common word fàràng ฝรั่ง. This can be an ambiguous term (meaning 'foreigner – westerner-caucasian') that, for some, has negative connotations. The term chaaw tàangchâat ชาวต่าง ชาติ – noted above – does not have such connotations.

forest, jungle pàa ป่า

for ever tà-làwt pai ตลอดไป

forget, to luehm ลืม

forgive, to hâi à-phai ให้อภัย

forgiveness, mercy kaan hâi à-phai การให้อภัย

forgotten, to be thùuk luehm ถูกลืม

fork (utensil) sâwm ส้อม

form (shape) rûup râang รูปร่าง

form (to fill out a form) kràwk bàehp fawm กรอกแบบ ฟอร์ม, or simply kràwk fawm กรอกฟอร์ม

formal, official, officially thaang kaan ทางการ

fortress, fort pâwm ป้อม

fortunately/luckily… chôhk dii thîi… โชคดีที่…

fortune teller măw duu หมอดู; to have one's fortune told (COLLOQUIAL) duu măw ดูหมอ

forty sìi sìp สี่สิบ

forward, to go pai khâang nâa ไปข้างหน้า

foul-mouth(ed) (to speak rudely/coarsely) pàak ráai ปากร้าย, (SLANG; very rude, best left unsaid) pàak măa (literally, 'mouth'–'dog') ปาก หมา

four sìi สี่

fourteen sìp sìi สิบสี่

fraction (a fraction of something) sèht-sùan เศษส่วน (NOTE: to make fractions in Thai the 'formula' is sèht เศษ (top number), sùan ส่วน (bottom number), e.g. ¾ – three quarters sèht săam sùan sìi เศษสามส่วน สี่. Also see the entry under a 'quarter')

France (country) prà-thêht fà-ràngsèht ประเทศ ฝรั่งเศส; **French** (person) khon fà-ràngsèht คน

54

ฝรั่งเศส; (language) phaa-săa
fà-ràngsèht ภาษาฝรั่งเศส

frame (e.g. picture frame)
kràwp กรอบ

fraud kaan kohng การโกง;
a fraud/fraudster khon khîi
kohng คนขี้โกง

free (of charge) mâi khít ngoen
ไม่คิดเงิน, (also commonly
used – from English) frii ฟรี

free of commitments mâi
mii khâw phùuk mát ไม่มี
ข้อผูกมัด

free/independent, to be
ìtsàrà อิสระ

freedom ìtsàrà-phâap
อิสรภาพ

freeze, to (as with frozen food)
châeh khăeng แช่แข็ง

French fries/chips (from
English) frén fraai เฟรนช์-
ฟราย, or man fàràng thâwt
มันฝรั่งทอด

frequent bòi บ่อย; frequently
bòi-bòi บ่อยๆ

fresh sòt สด

Friday wan sùk วันศุกร์

fried (deep fried), fry thâwt
ทอด; stir-fry/stir fried phàt
ผัด

friend phûean เพื่อน. NOTE:
friends phûean-phûean
เพื่อนๆ; a close friend phûean
sànìt เพื่อนสนิท, (COLLOQUIAL/
SLANG) phûean síi เพื่อน
ซี้. Also note the following
idiomatic expressions:
phûean kin เพื่อนกิน (casual,
fair-weather friends) (literally,
'friend'-'eat'); phûean taai
เพื่อนตาย (friends who will
do anything for you) (literally,
'friend'-'die')

friendly, outgoing pen kan
ehng เป็นกันเอง (This expression also means 'take it easy,
make yourself at home')

frightened tòk jai ตกใจ (NOTE:
often said as tòka jai)

frizzy/curly/kinked (hair)
phŏm yìk ผมหยิก

from jàak จาก: e.g. 'what
country do you come from?'
khun maa jàak prathêht
arai (literally, 'you'-'come'-
'from'-'country'-'what'?) คุณ
มาจากประเทศอะไร

front (in front of) khâang nâa
ข้างหน้า

frost náam kháang khăeng

55

น้ำค้างแข็ง, or **mâeh khá-**
níng แม่คะนิ่ง

frown, to **khà-mùat khíu**
ขมวดคิ้ว

frozen **châeh khǎeng** แช่แข็ง

frugal See 'economical'

fruit **phǒnlá-mái** ผลไม้

fry, to See 'fried'

fulfill (to complete something
successfully) **sǎmrèt** สำเร็จ

full **tem** เต็ม

full, to have eaten one's fill
ìm อิ่ม; to be full already **ìm**
láew อิ่มแล้ว

fun, to have **sà-nùk** สนุก

function/work, to **tham**
ngaan ทำงาน

funds, funding, capital
thun ทุน

funeral **ngaan sòp** งานศพ

fungus/mould **chúea raa** เชื้อ
รา; to be mouldy (COLLOQUIAL)
raa khûen ราขึ้น

funny **tà-lòk** ตลก, or **khǎm khǎm** ขำ

furniture (from English) **foeh-**
ní-jôeh เฟอร์นิเจอร์

further, additional **phôehm**
toehm เพิ่มเติม

fussy (COLLOQUIAL) **rûeang**
mâak (literally, 'issues'-

'many') เรื่องมาก, or
(alternatively) **jûu jîi** จู้จี้

future, the **à-naà-khót**
อนาคต; in (the) future **nai**
à-naàkhót ในอนาคต

G

gallstone **kâwn nìu** ก้อนนิ่ว;
gallstones **nìu** นิ่ว

gamble, to **lên kaan phá-nan**
เล่นการพนัน

game (from English) **kehm** เกม

garage (for car repairs) **ùu**
sâwm rót อู่ซ่อมรถ

garage (for parking) **rohng**
rót โรงรถ

garbage/rubbish/trash **khà-**
yà ขยะ

garden, yard (also
'plantation') **sǔan** สวน

gardens (public), park **sǔan**
sǎa-thaa rá-ná สวนสาธารณะ

garland (garlands of flowers
are very common in Thailand)
phuang maa-lai พวงมาลัย
(NOTE: the same word is also
used for 'steering wheel'),
garland – also simply **maàlai**
มาลัย

garlic kra-thiam กระเทียม

garment, clothing sûea phâa เสื้อผ้า

gas (from English, for cooking etc.) káet แก๊ส

gasoline, petrol náam-man น้ำมัน

gasoline/gas/petrol station pám náam-man ปั๊มน้ำมัน

gate, door prà-tuu ประตู

gather, to rûap ruam รวบรวม

gay (homosexual) (from English) keh เกย์, (SLANG) effeminate homosexual tút ตุ๊ด

German, a (person) khon yoeh-rá-man คนเยอรมัน; German (language) phaa-săa yoeh-rá-man ภาษาเยอรมัน; Germany (the country) prà-thêht yoeh-rá-má-nii ประเทศเยอรมนี

gender (sex – i.e. male/female) phêht เพศ

general, all-purpose thûa pai ทั่วไป

generally, in general dohy thûa pai โดยทั่วไป

generation (used for people, the particular year/vintage of a car etc.) rûn รุ่น

generous jai kwâang (literally, 'heart'-'broad/wide') ใจกว้าง

gentle, graceful (behaviour, movement) àwn yohn อ่อน โยน; to do something (e.g. like a massage) gently bao-bao เบาๆ

gentleman sù-phâap bùrùt สุภาพบุรุษ

genuine/authentic/real (the opposite of an imitation/ fake) tháeh แท้; the genuine article/the real thing khǎwng tháeh ของแท้

gesture, manner, expression, bearing, attitude (i.e. the way one appears to another – friendly, unfriendly, disinterested) thâa thaang ท่าทาง

get, to (receive) dâi ได้, or dâi ráp ได้รับ

get off (e.g. a bus) long ลง

get on (e.g. a bus) khûen ขึ้น

get up/stand up lúk khûen ลุกขึ้น

get well soon! hăai wai-wai หายไวๆ

ghost, a phǐi ผี

gift/present, a khǎwng khwǎn ของขวัญ

ginger khǐng ขิง

girl (child) dèk phûu yǐng เด็ก ผู้หญิง, or simply dèk yǐng เด็กหญิง

girlfriend/boyfriend (steady) faehn แฟน; (SLANG) a casual girlfriend, mainly for sex and a bit of fun without much, if any, commitment kík กิ๊ก

give, to hâi ให้ (NOTE: this important word is also used in a variety of ways with various meanings – see the Thai-English section)

give in/give up IDIOM (as in 'I give in, you can go out if you want to' or, 'I give up, I can't fix it') yawm pháeh (literally, 'allow/permit'-'defeat') ยอม แพ้

glad dii jai ดีใจ

glass (for drinking) kâew แก้ว

glass (material – as in a window or the windscreen of a car. It is also the Thai word for 'mirror') krà-jòk กระจก

glasses, spectacles wâen taa แว่นตา

glue/paste N kaaw กาว

glutinous (or sticky) **rice** khâaw nǐaw ข้าวเหนียว

go, to pai ไป – a common greeting in Thai is 'Where are you going?' pai nǎi (literally, 'go'-'where')ไปไหน. To ask 'where have you been?' is pai nǎi maa (literally, 'where'-'come') ไปไหนมา

go along, join in pai dûai ไปด้วย

go around, visit pai yîam ไปเยี่ยม

go back/return klàp pai กลับ ไป, or simply klàp กลับ

go for a walk pai doehn lên ไปเดินเล่น

go home klàp bâan กลับบ้าน

go out, exit àwk pai ออกไป

go out (for fun) (pai) thîaw (ไป)เที่ยว (NOTE: the word thîaw is another quintessential Thai term and used in various ways – e.g. to go to a friend's house (for fun) is thîaw bâan phûean เที่ยวบ้านเพื่อน; to go to the beach (for fun) is thîaw chaai hàat เที่ยวชายหาด; to go to a bar (for fun) is thîao baa เที่ยวบาร์; (for men) to go out and fool around with loose women is thîao phûu-yĭng เที่ยวผู้หญิง; and someone (invariably male) who is habitually interested in going out on the town at night is a nák thîao นักเที่ยว

go out, to (fire, candle, electricity – as in a blackout) dàp ดับ (also slang meaning 'to die')

go to bed pai nawn ไปนอน

goal, objective pâo măi เป้าหมาย

goal, a goal (in football/ soccer) prà-tuu ประตู (Note: the same word for 'door' or 'gate')

goat pháe แพะ

God phrá phûu pen jâo พระ ผู้เป็นเจ้า, or simply phrá jâo พระเจ้า

goddess jâo mâeh เจ้าแม่

gold (precious metal) thawng kham ทองคำ, or simply thawng ทอง; the Golden Triangle (the area in northern Thailand where the borders

of Burma, Laos, and Thailand meet) săm lìam thawng kham สามเหลี่ยมทองคำ

gold (colour) sĭi thawng สีทอง

golf (from English) káwp กอล์ฟ; to play golf lên káwp เล่นกอล์ฟ

gone, finished (i.e. there is none left/sold out) (of the soap/ is all used up) mòt láew หมดแล้ว

gonorrhea (VD) rôhk năwng nai (literally, 'disease'-'pus'-'in') โรคหนองใน

good dii ดี; very good dii mâak ดีมาก

goodbye laa kàwn ลาก่อน, (MORE COLLOQUIALLY) pai kàwn ná ไปก่อนนะ

good luck! chôhk dii โชคดี

goodness (me)! ôh hoh โอ้โฮ

goose, a hàan ห่าน

gossip súp síp ninthaa ซุบซิบ นินทา, or simply (to talk behind one's back) ninthaa นินทา

government rát-thà-baan รัฐบาล

GPO (General Post Office, i.e. the main post office or,

59

following the Thai, the central post office) prai-sànii klaang ไปรษณีย์กลาง (klaang กลาง means 'central/middle')

GPS (navigation system – from English; pronounced very similar to the English 'GPS') จีพีเอส

grab/snatch, to yâeng แย่ง

gradually, bit by bit thii lá nít ทีละนิด

gram (weight) (from English) kram กรัม

grand, great yîng yài ยิ่งใหญ่, yài toh ใหญ่โต

grandchild lăan หลาน

granddaughter lăan săaw หลานสาว

grandfather (maternal) taa ตา

grandfather (paternal) pùu ปู่

grandmother (maternal) yaay ยาย

grandmother (paternal) yâa ย่า

grandparents pùu yâa taa yaai ปู่ย่าตายาย

grandson lăan chaai หลานชาย

grapes à-ngùn องุ่น

grass yâa หญ้า

grave lŭm sòp หลุมศพ

gray, grey sĭi thao สีเทา

grease (as used in cars/trucks etc.) jaa-rá-bii จารบี

greasy See 'oily'

great/impressive, to be prà-tháp jai ประทับใจ

great (COLLOQUIAL - as in 'that's great/fantastic'/'tops!') sùt yâwt สุดยอด

Greater vehicle of Buddhism – the Mahayana doctrine lát-thí máhăa-yaan ลัทธิมหายาน

green (colour) sĭi khĭao สีเขียว

green beans thùa fàk yaaw ถั่วฝักยาว

greens (green vegetables) phàk sĭi khĭao ผักสีเขียว, or simply phàk khĭao ผักเขียว

greet/welcome, to thák thaai ทักทาย, or tâwn ráp ต้อนรับ

greetings kaan thák thaai การทักทาย

grill/toast, to pîng ปิ้ง, or yâang ย่าง

ground, earth, soil, dirt din ดิน; ground, earth phúehn din พื้นดิน

60

group, a klùm กลุ่ม, phûak พวก, (COLLOQUIAL) group of friends/mates/buddies/ entourage phák phûak พรรคพวก

grow, plant plùuk ปลูก

grow, to toh โต

grow larger, to toh khûen โตขึ้น

grown up, to be (e.g. from a child to an adolescent) toh láew โตแล้ว

guarantee, to (insure) prà-kan ประกัน, also làk prà-kan หลักประกัน

guard, to fâo yaam เฝ้ายาม; **a guard** (nightwatchman) yaam ยาม

guess, to dao เดา

guest (visitor in one's home, hotel guest) khàehk แขก (NOTE: this word is also used to refer to swarthy people with darker complexions such as Indians, Pakistanis, and Arabs in general)

guesthouse ruean ráp-rawng khàek เรือนรับรอง แขก (NOTE: the English word 'guesthouse' is commonly

used in Thai, pronounced something like 'guest-how')

guest of honour khàek phûu kìat แขกผู้มีเกียรติ

guide/lead, to nam นำ

guidebook nángsǔeh nam thîao หนังสือนำเที่ยว

guilty (of a crime), **to be wrong** phìt ผิด

guilty, to feel rúu-sùek phìt รู้สึกผิด

gun (general term) peuhn ปืน; **pistol/handgun** peuhn phók ปืนพก; **rifle** peuhn yaaw (literally, 'gun'-'long') ปืนยาว; **shotgun** peuhn lûuk sǎwng ปืนลูกซอง; **machine gun** peuhn kon ปืนกล; **gunman/ hitman/hired killer** mueh-peuhn (literally, 'hand'-'gun') มือปืน

gym (from English) yim ยิม; (COLLOQUIAL) **to work out in the gym/go to the gym** lên yim (literally, 'play'-'gym') เล่นยิม

61

H

habit (habitual behaviour, often used to refer to a person's character – what sort of person they happen to be) ní-sǎi นิสัย

hacker, a (i.e. computer hacker – from English) háek-kôeh แฮกเกอร์

hail (hailstones) lûuk hép ลูกเห็บ

hair (on the head – humans) phǒm ผม, (hair on rest of the human body apart from the head; also for animals, i.e. fur) khǒn ขน

half, a khrûeng ครึ่ง *Also see* 'Eurasian'

hall, a (or large room) hâwng thǒhng ห้องโถง

hammer, a kháwn ค้อน

hammock, a pleh yuan เปล ยวน, (COLLOQUIAL) pleh เปล

hand mueh มือ

handcuffs kun-jaeh mueh (literally, 'key'-'hand') กุญแจมือ

handicap/handicapped/

disabled phí-kaan พิการ

handicraft ngaan fǐi-mueh งานฝีมือ, or (FORMAL) hàt-thà-kam หัตถกรรม

handle (of an object, e.g. a knife) dâam ด้าม

hand out, distribute jàehk แจก

hand over mâwp hâi มอบให้

handsome làw หล่อ; (COLLOQUIAL) a good-looking, handsome man rûup làw รูปหล่อ

hang, to (a painting) khwǎehn แขวน; to hang down/dangle (e.g. fruit hanging down from a tree) hôi ห้อย

happen/occur, to kòeht khûen เกิดขึ้น

happened (as in 'what happened?') kòeht àrai khûen เกิดอะไรขึ้น

happy, to be mii khwaam sùk มีความสุข

happy birthday! sùksǎn wan kòeht สุขสันต์วันเกิด (or simply the expression 'happy birthday' pronounced in the Thai way – something like 'háeppîi bértday')

happy new year! sùksăn
wan pii mài สุขสันต์วันปีใหม่

harbor, pier, port thâa ruea
ท่าเรือ

hard (to be difficult) yâak ยาก

hard (solid, stiff) khăeng แข็ง

hard disk (from English)
háad-dís ฮาร์ดดิสก์; (from
English) hard drive háad-drái
ฮาร์ดไดรฟ์

**hardly (e.g. able to do
something, any left, etc.)**
thâehp jà mâi… แทบจะไม่…

**hardship (difficult
circumstances)** khwaam
lambàak ความลำบาก, or
simply lambàak ลำบาก

**hardworking, industrious,
diligent** khà-yăn ขยัน

**harmonious (e.g. relations
with others)** râap rûehn
ราบรื่น

hat, cap mùak หมวก; *also
see* entry under 'helmet'

hate, to klìat เกลียด

hatred khwaam klìat ความ
เกลียด

have, to have… mii… มี…
(the Thai word is used in
various ways, e.g. to have

available, to own, there is…)

have been somewhere
khoei pai เคยไป: e.g. If
someone asks you 'have you
ever been to Chiang Mai?' –
in Thai the question is khun
khoei pai chiang mài măi
คุณเคยไปเชียงใหม่ไหม. If
you have, the answer 'yes' is
khoei pai เคยไป, or simply
just khoei เคย. To answer in
the negative 'I've never been'
is mâi khoei pai, or simply
mâi khoei ไม่เคย.

have done something khoei
tham เคยทำ: e.g. If some
asks you 'have you ever
ridden a horse?' – in Thai the
question is khun khoei khìi
máa măi คุณเคยขี่ม้าไหม. If
you have, the answer 'yes' is
khoei khìi เคยขี่, or simply
just khoei เคย. To answer in
the negative see the previous
entry.

have to, must tâwng ต้อง

he, him (also she, her and the
third person plural pronoun
'they') khăo เขา

head (COLLOQUIAL) hŭa หัว, (the

63

more formal medical term is) sĭi-sà ศีรษะ

head (the boss, person in charge) hŭa nâa หัวหน้า

head for, toward mûng pai มุ่งไป

headdress khrûeang prà-dàp sĭi-sà เครื่องประดับศีรษะ

health sùk-khà-phâap สุขภาพ

healthy sŏmbuun สมบูรณ์; to be healthy sùk-khà-phâap dii สุขภาพดี, or khăeng raehng แข็งแรง (which normally would be translated as 'strong', but also means 'healthy and well')

hear, to dâi-yin ได้ยิน; listen to (the radio) fang ฟัง

heart, the hŭa jai หัวใจ (NOTE: in a more metaphorical sense i.e. 'my heart is not in it' just the word jai ใจ is used. In Thai there are numerous compound words that incorporate jai ใจ: e.g. to 'feel sorry' as in 'feeling sorry on hearing bad news' is sĭa jai (literally, 'spoiled'-'heart') เสียใจ)

heart attack hŭa jai waai หัวใจวาย

heat, to v tham hâi ráwn ทำให้ร้อน

heat N khwaam ráwn ความร้อน

heaven/paradise sà wăn สวรรค์

heavy nàk หนัก; also see 'weight'

heel (of the foot) sôn tháo ส้นเท้า

height khwaam sŭung ความสูง

hell ná-rók นรก

hello, hi (greeting used at any time of the day) sàwàt dii สวัสดี

hello! (answering the phone, from English) hallŏh ฮัลโหล

helmet (as in crash helmet/motorcycle helmet) mùak kan nók หมวกกันน็อก

help, to chûai ช่วย or chûai lŭea ช่วยเหลือ

help! ('Please help!') chûai dûai ช่วยด้วย

help, to chûai ช่วย

hepatitis rôhk tàp àk-sèhp (literally, 'disease/illness'-

64

'liver'-'inflamed') โรคตับ
อักเสบ

her, his, their khǎwng kháo
ของเขา; hers, his, theirs
khǎwng kháo ของเขา

here thîi nîi ที่นี่

hereditary kammá-phan
(pronounced 'gum-àpun')
กรรมพันธุ์

herpes (STD) rôhk roem
โรคเริม

hero phrá-èk (e.g. in a film
– 'leading man') พระเอก;
wii-rá bù-rùt (e.g. in a war,
in a disaster saving lives)
วีรบุรุษ, hii-rôh (from English)
ฮีโร่; heroine naang-èk (e.g.
in a film – 'leading woman')
นางเอก, wii-rá sà-trii (e.g. in
a conflict etc.) วีรสตรี

heroin (narcotic) (from English)
heroh-iin เฮโรอีน, (COLLOQUIAL)
phǒng khǎaw (literally,
'powder'-'white') ผงขาว

hidden, to be sâwn yùu
ซ่อนอยู่

hide, to (from someone) (do
something furtively) àehp
แอบ; hide something/to be
hidden sâwn wái ซ่อนไว้

high (mountain, prices etc.),
tall (person, tree) sǔung สูง

hill noehn khǎo เนินเขา, or
simply noehn เนิน

hill tribe chaaw khǎo (literally,
'people'-'mountain') ชาวเขา

hinder/obstruct, to kìit
khwǎang กีดขวาง

hindrance sìng kìit khwǎang
สิ่งกีดขวาง

hire/rent, to châo เช่า (NOTE:
to hire/rent a car is châo rót
เช่ารถ, while a rental car is
rót châo รถเช่า)

his (or 'hers' or 'their(s)')
khǎwng kháo ของเขา

history prà-wàt-ti-sàat
ประวัติศาสตร์; one's own
personal history prà-wàt
sùan tua ประวัติส่วนตัว

hit, strike, beat (for a person
to hit, strike, or beat another
person or object) tii ตี; to hit
or collide with.... chon ชน

HIV (also see 'AIDS' – from
English) etch-ai-wii เอชไอวี

hobby/pastime ngaan à-dì-
rèhk งานอดิเรก

hold, grasp, to thǔeh ถือ or
jàp จับ

hold back yùt wái หยุดไว้

hole, a (but not of the 'hole in the ground' variety) ruu รู; hole in the ground lǔm หลุม

holiday (festival) wan yùt thêht-sà-kaan วันหยุด เทศกาล

holiday (vacation) wan yùt phák phàwn วันหยุดพักผ่อน

holiday (public) wan yùt râatchá-kaan วันหยุดราชการ, or simply wan yùt วันหยุด

holy, sacred sàksìt ศักดิ์สิทธิ์

home, house bâan บ้าน

homework (from school, college) kaan bâan การบ้าน; housework ngaan bâan งาน บ้าน

homosexual See 'gay'

honest sûeh-sàt ซื่อสัตย์

honey náam phûeng (literally, 'water'-'bee') น้ำผึ้ง

Hong Kong hâwng kong ฮ่องกง

hoodlum/tough guy/thug, a anthá-phaan อันธพาล, or (MORE COLLOQUIALLY) nák-leng นักเลง

hooker, whore (prostitute) (POLITE) sǒhphehnii โสเภณี,

(COLLOQUIAL) phûu-yǐng hǎa kin (literally, 'woman'-'look for'-'eat') ผู้หญิงหากิน, phûu-yǐng hǎa ngoen (literally, 'woman'-'look for'-'money') ผู้หญิงหาเงิน

hope, to wǎng หวัง, or 'to hope that....' wǎng wâa... หวังว่า...

hope N khwaam wǎng ความ หวัง

hopefully dûai khwaam wǎng ด้วยความหวัง

horny (desirous of sex) (SLANG, RUDE) ngîan เงี่ยน; also yàak อยาก (which, in general usage, means 'want')

horrible (frightening) nâa klua น่ากลัว

hors d'oeuvre(s), entrée, starter khǎwng wâang ของว่าง

hospital rohng phá-yaa-baan โรงพยาบาล

host N jâo phâap เจ้าภาพ

hostess (in an entertainment establishment) phûu-yǐng bawrí-kaan (literally, 'woman'-'service') ผู้หญิง บริการ

hot (spicy) phèt เผ็ด

hot (temperature) ráwn ร้อน

hot (as in 'sexy' – from English)
hàwt ฮอท (NOTE: the word
'sexy' is also commonly used
in Thai sék-sîi เซ็กซี่)

hotel rohng-raehm โรงแรม
(NOTE: in Thailand there are
many 'short-time' hotels with
'canvas curtains' so a car can
be parked discreetly. These
are known as rohng-raehm
mâan rûut (literally, 'hotel'-
'curtain'-'zip') โรงแรมม่านรูด

hot spring náam phú ráwn
น้ำพุร้อน

hour chûa-mohng ชั่วโมง

house See 'home'

houseboat See 'raft'

housekeeper (servant),
room maid (in hotel) mâeh
bâan (literally, 'mother'-
'house/home') แม่บ้าน

how? yàang-rai อย่างไร, or
yang-ngai ยังไง: e.g. 'how do
you do it?' tham yàang-rai
ทำอย่างไร, or (in colloquial
speech like this) tham
yang ngai ทำยังไง (NOTE: in
contrast to the English form

this question tag comes at
the end of the sentence)

how are you? sa-baai dii
rŏeh? (NOTE: the word rŏeh
here, although spelled
with an 'r', is commonly
pronounced lŏeh) สบายดี
หรือ, also sa-baai dii mǎi
สบายดีไหม

however yàang-rai kâw
taam อย่างไรก็ตาม

how long (does it take)?/for
how long? naan thâo-rài
นานเท่าไหร่ (the word naan
means 'a long time' so the
question – naan thâorài
has the following pattern
'long time' – 'how much?')

how long? (length) yaaw
thâorài ยาวเท่าไร (the word
yaaw means 'long' with
the question yaaw thâorài
having the following pattern
'long' – 'how much?')

how many...? kìi... กี่...

how much? thâo rài เท่าไหร่
– to say 'how much is it?',
'what's the price?', or 'what
does it cost?' (the word for
price/cost is raa-khaa ราคา)

the pattern is raa-khaa thâorài i.e. 'price/cost' – 'how much?' ราคาเท่าไหร่

how old? aa-yú thâo-rài อายุ เท่าไหร่ (the word for 'age' is aa-yú อายุ – again the pattern is the same as above i.e. 'age' – 'how much?')

huge yài ใหญ่

human/human being má-nút มนุษย์

humid chúehn ชื้น

humorous, funny, amusing khòp khǎn ขบขัน, or tà-lòk ตลก

hundred rói ร้อย

hundred thousand sǎehn แสน

hungry, to be hungry hǐu หิว: the common expression for 'I'm hungry' is hǐu khâaw (literally, 'hungry'-'rice/food') หิวข้าว; for 'I'm thirsty' the expression is hǐu náam (literally, 'hungry'-'water') หิวน้ำ

hurry up! rew-rew เร็วๆ

hurt (injured), to be sore jèp เจ็บ

hurt, to (cause pain) tham hâi

jèp ทำให้เจ็บ

husband (POLITE) sǎa-mii สามี, (SLANG) phǔa ผัว (in more educated circles considered rude, generally seen as low class language – referring to the sexual partner of a woman, the couple not being formally married)

hut, shack, shed krà-thâwm กระท่อม, or krà-táwp กระต๊อบ

hybrid car ('hybrid' from English) rót-yon hai-brìd รถยนต์ไฮบริด

hygiene/cleanliness khwaam sà-àat ความสะอาด

I

I, me (NOTE: there are numerous first person pronouns, i.e. the words for 'I' and 'me', and other ways to refer to oneself in Thai. This issue is too complex to be discussed here. For our purposes the following common polite terms will suffice: for males phǒm (the same word as 'hair on the head') ผม; for females dìchǎn ดิฉัน, or simply chǎn ฉัน)

ice náam khǎeng น้ำแข็ง (literally, 'water'-'hard')

ice cream (from English) ai-sà-khriim ไอศกรีม

ICU (from the English abbreviation of the term 'Intensive Care Unit' – in common usage in Thai hospitals and used by the general public) ai-sii-yuu ไอซียู

ID (in this entry referring to 'Identity card' which all Thai citizens possess) bàt prà-chaachon (literally, 'card'-'people/populace') บัตร ประชาชน

idea khwaam khít ความคิด

identical, alike, the same as mǔean-kan เหมือนกัน, or simply mǔean เหมือน

identity (as in 'national identity/characteristics) èkkàlák เอกลักษณ์; Thai identity èkkàlák thai เอกลักษณ์ไทย

idiom (figure of speech) sǎm-nuan สำนวน

idiot, an (a fool) khon ngô (literally, 'person'-'stupid') คนโง่

if (used in much the same way as English) thâa ถ้า

ignorant (to be unaware of something, not to know what's going on) (COLLOQUIAL) mâi rúu rûeang ไม่รู้เรื่อง; ignorant ('unschooled' or 'uneducated') khàat sùek-sǎa (literally, 'missing/ without'-'education') ขาดการ ศึกษา or mâi mii kaan sùek-sǎa (literally, 'no'-'have'-'education') ไม่มีการศึกษา

ignore, to lá loei ละเลย, or mâi sǒn-jai (literally, 'no'-'interest') ไม่สนใจ

ill/sick pùai ป่วย, or simply mâi-sàbaai ไม่สบาย

illegal/illicit phìt kòt-mǎai ผิดกฎหมาย

illness khwaam jèp pùai ความเจ็บป่วย

image phâap ภาพ, or rûup phâap รูปภาพ

imagination jin-tà-naa-kaan (NOTE: the first syllable jin is pronounced like the English word 'gin') จินตนาการ

imagine, to (visualize an image) néuk phâap นึกภาพ

imagine (in the sense 'imagine/suppose that....?') sŏm-mút wâa สมมุติว่า

immediately than thii ทันที

immigration (as in the Immigration Bureau where visas are extended, etc.) sam nák ngaan trùat khon khâo mueang สำนักงานตรวจคน เข้าเมือง, (colloquially referred to by the abbreviation taw maw [pronounced like 'tore more', from the words trùat ตรวจ - 'check/inspect' and mueang เมือง - 'country'] ตอมอ)

immoral phìt sǐin ผิดศีล

impatient jai ráwn (literally, 'heart'-'hot') ใจร้อน

impolite, rude mâi sù-phâap ไม่สุภาพ

import, an (imported goods) sǐn-kháa nam khâo สินค้า นำเข้า

import, to nam khâo นำเข้า

importance khwaam sǎmkhan ความสำคัญ

important sǎmkhan สำคัญ

impossible pen pai mâi dâi เป็นไปไม่ได้

impression, to make/create an sâang khwaam prà-tháp jai สร้างความประทับใจ

impressive, to be prà-tháp jai ประทับใจ

in nai ใน

in (time, years, e.g.'in ten years' time') phaai nai ภายใน

incense (joss sticks) thûup ธูป

income, wages, salary raai dâi รายได้, (MORE COLLOQUIAL) ngoen duean เงินเดือน

incident, an hèht kaan เหตุการณ์

include ruam รวม; including... ruam tháng... รวมทั้ง...

incompatible, to be (e.g. two people who do not get on) khâo kan mâi dâi เข้า กันไม่ได้

inconvenient mâi sà-dùak ไม่สะดวก

increase, to phôehm เพิ่ม, or phôehm khûen เพิ่มขึ้น

incredible (as in 'amazing!', 'unbelievable!') mâi nâa chûea ไม่น่าเชื่อ

indeed! (to emphasize something as in 'really, it's true!') jing-jing จริงๆ

independent (to be free, not to be controlled by others) ìtsàrà อิสระ

indifferent/blasé, to be chŏei-chŏei เฉยๆ (Note: a very commonly used expression in Thai)

indigenous (person) chaaw phúehn mueang ชาวพื้น เมือง; for something that is indigenous to a particular place simply – phúehn mueang พื้นเมือง

Indonesia (the country) indohnii-sia อินโดนีเซีย (in colloquial speech Indonesia is often referred to simply as indo อินโด)

Indonesian chaaw indohnii-sia ชาวอินโดนีเซีย, or khon indohnii-sia คนอินโดนีเซีย; Indonesian (language) phaa-săa indohnii-sia ภาษา อินโดนีเซีย

industry N (factories etc.) ùt-săhà-kam อุตสาหกรรม

inexpensive mâi phaehng ไม่แพง

infant thaa rók ทารก

infect tìt chúea ติดเชื้อ, or tìt rôhk ติดโรค

infection kaan tìt chúea การติดเชื้อ, kaan tìt rôhk การติดโรค

influence ìt-thí-phon อิทธิพล

influence, to (to have influence – in Thai this generally means to have 'connections' enabling one to engage in 'extra legal' activities) mii ìt-thí-phon มีอิทธิพล (There is also the expression ìt-thí-phon mûehd อิทธิพลมืด which means 'dark influence(s)' or, more correctly in English, 'dark force(s)' which is used to refer to well-placed individuals involved behind the scenes in political intrigue, extortion, bribery, murder)

influenza (the flu) khâi wàt yài ไข้หวัดใหญ่

inform, to (e.g. the police about a problem) jâehng แจ้ง; **inform** (tell) bàwk บอก

information, data khâw-muun ข้อมูล; **knowledge** khwaam rúu ความรู้

information booth/ hotel reception (where information about various things is available)/**public relations** prà-chaa sămphan ประชาสัมพันธ์

ingredient(s) (in a recipe) sùan prà-kàwp ส่วนประกอบ

inhabit/live, to yùu aa-săi อยู่อาศัย, or simply yùu อยู่

inhabitant phûu yùu aa-săi ผู้อยู่อาศัย

inject, to chìit ฉีด; **an injection** of medicine/vaccine/drug chìit yaa ฉีดยา

injured, to be dâi ráp bàat jèp (literally, 'receive/get'-'injury') ได้รับบาดเจ็บ

injury bàat jèp บาดเจ็บ

ink mùek หมึก

innocent bawrí-sùt บริสุทธิ์ (NOTE: the English word 'innocent' – in-noh-sén อินโนเซนท์ – is also used in

Thai. Additionally, the Thai term bawrí-sùt is also used to refer to a virgin)

innovation ná-wát tà-kam นวัตกรรม

in order that, so that phûea thîi เพื่อที่

inquire sàwp thăam สอบถาม

insane rôhk jìt โรคจิต; (or simply the word for) mad/ crazy bâa บ้า – a simple slang expression to express the same thing is to refer to such a person as mâi tem (literally, 'not'-'full') ไม่เต็ม

insect (general term for insects) má-laehng แมลง

insert, to sâek แทรก

inside khâang nai ข้างใน

inspect, to trùat ตรวจ

inspector, an phûu trùat sàwp ผู้ตรวจสอบ

inspire ban-daan jai บันดาลใจ; **inspiration** raeng ban-daan jai แรงบันดาลใจ

instead of thaen thîi แทนที่, or simply thaen แทน

instrument/tool khrûeang mueh เครื่องมือ

instruct, to (give advice) hâi

kham náe-nam ให้คำแนะนำ

insult someone/to look
down on someone duu
thùuk ดูถูก

insure, to prà-kan ประกัน;
insurance prà-kan phai
ประกันภัย

intellect pan yaa ปัญญา, or
sàti-pan yaa สติปัญญา

intelligent mii sàti-pan yaa
มีสติปัญญา, (MORE COLLOQUIAL)
chà-làat ฉลาด

intend, to tâng-jai ตั้งใจ

intended for sǎmràp สำหรับ

intention kwaam tâng-jai
ความตั้งใจ

interest (on money) dàwk
bîa ดอกเบี้ย, (or colloquially,
simply) dàwk ดอก

interest (personal) khwaam
sǒn-jai ความสนใจ

interested in, to be sǒn-jai
สนใจ

interesting nâa sǒn-jai น่าสนใจ

international naa-naa châat
นานาชาติ

Internet, the (from English)
inthoehnèt อินเทอร์เน็ต,
(COLLOQUIAL) nèt เน็ต

interpret/translate plaeh

แปล (NOTE: one common way
to ask 'what does this/that
mean?' is plaeh wâa àrai
แปลว่าอะไร

interpreter, an lâam ล่าม

intersection (i.e. four-way
intersection) sìi yâehk สี่แยก
(the word yâehk แยก means
'to separate'); a five-way intersection hâa yâehk ห้าแยก

intimate, to be (to be close
to, a close friend) sà-nìt สนิท;
also see 'friend'

into, to go into khâo pai
khâang nai (literally, 'enter'-
'go'-'inside') เข้าไปข้างใน

introduce oneself, to náe-
nam tua ehng แนะนำตัวเอง

introduce someone, to náe-
nam tua แนะนำตัว

invent, to prà-dìt ประดิษฐ์

invest (in a business etc.) long
thun ลงทุน

investigate sùep สืบ

invitation kham choehn
คำเชิญ

invite, to (ask along) chuan
ชวน

invite, to (formally) choehn
เชิญ

73

J

invoice, receipt bai kèp
ngoen ใบเก็บเงิน, (COLLOQUIAL)
bai sèht ใบเสร็จ

involve, to/to be concerned
with kìao khâwng เกี่ยวข้อง

iron, steel lèk เหล็ก

iron, an (to iron clothing) tao
rîit เตารีด

iron, to (clothing) rîit sûea
รีดเสื้อ

Islam (the religion of Islam)
sàat-sà-nǎa ìt-sàlaam ศาสนา
อิสลาม

island kàw (pronounced very
short like 'oh!' in 'Oh! Ooh'
with a 'g' sound in front) เกาะ

it man (the an pronounced
like 'un' in 'unlucky') มัน
(used for things, animals, an
event, an issue, etc. – NOTE:
when used to refer to a
person it is extremely rude;
at times some Thai people
may use this to refer to
foreigners which reflects a
contemptuous attitude)

itch khan คัน; to be itchy
aa-kaan khan อาการคัน

item, individual thing sìng สิ่ง

ivory ngaa cháang งาช้าง

jacket (from English) jáekkêt
แจ็คเก็ต

jade yòk หยก

jail/gaol khúk คุก; to be in jail/
gaol/incarcerated tìt khúk
ติดคุก

jam (from English, e.g.
'strawberry jam') yaehm แยม

January má-ká raa-khom
มกราคม

Japan yîipùn ญี่ปุ่น

Japanese chaaw yîipùn ชาว
ญี่ปุ่น, or khon yîipùn คน
ญี่ปุ่น

jar (i.e. a large water jar) òhng
โอ่ง; a (very) small jar (e.g.
containing face powder/
ointment etc.) krà-pùk กระปุก

jaw kraam กราม

jealous/envious ìt-chǎa
อิจฉา; jealous (a jealous
boyfriend, wife etc.) hǔeng
หึง; someone who is
extremely jealous khîi hǔeng
ขี้หึง

jealousy khwaam ìt-chǎa
ความอิจฉา

jeans (from English) kaang keng yiin กางเกงยีน

jelly wún วุ้น

jellyfish maehng-kà-phrun แมงกะพรุน

jet ski (from English) jét sà-kii เจ็ตสกี

jewel phét phloi เพชรพลอย

jewellery khrûeang phét phloi เครื่องเพชรพลอย

job, work ngaan งาน (Note: the same word also means 'a party' or 'a festive occasion')

join, go along pai dûai ไปด้วย

join together/participate, to khâo ruâm เข้าร่วม

joint (in the body) khâw ข้อ

joke, to (with someone) phûut lên พูดเล่น

journalist nák khàaw นักข่าว

journey kaan doehn thaang การเดินทาง

judge See 'magistrate'

judge/decide, to tàt-sǐn ตัดสิน

jug (of beer), pitcher yùeak เหยือก

juice (i.e. fruit juice) náam phǒnlá-mái น้ำผลไม้

July kà-rákàdaakhom กรกฎาคม

jump, to krà-dòht กระโดด

June mí-thù-naayon มิถุนายน

jungle pàa ป่า

just, only thâonán เท่านั้น; 'only/just ten baht' sìp bàat thâonán สิบบาทเท่านั้น (Note: a very useful and common expression meaning 'just this/that amount' is khâe níi (this) แค่นี้, or khâe nán (that) แค่นั้น. And for the sentence 'I just want this much' you say '(I' is understood) – ao khâe níi (literally, 'want'-'just'-'this') เอาแค่นี้)

just/fair, to be yúttì-tham ยุติธรรม

just now dǐao níi ehng เดี๋ยวนี้เอง, or phaw dii พอดี

K

kangaroo jing-jôh จิงโจ้

karaoke khaa-raa oh-kè คาราโอเกะ

Karen (ethnic group living in different areas along the Thai-

75

Burmese/Myanmar border) kà-rìang กะเหรี่ยง

karma kam (pronounced like 'gum' as in 'chewing gum') กรรม

keep, to kèp เก็บ, also kèp wái เก็บไว้ (NOTE: wái ไว้ is an important word in Thai. In conjunction with other words it serves a number of functions. In a broader sense it means to 'preserve/conserve/ uphold' and to 'place/leave/ replace, restore/wear') See Thai-English section.

kettle (hot water jug) kaa náam กาน้ำ

key, a (to a room) kunjaeh กุญแจ

key (i.e. on computer keyboard) pâehn แป้น

keyboard (of computer – from English) khii-bàwt คีย์บอร์ด

Khmer See 'Cambodia'

kick, to tèh เตะ

kickboxing (i.e. Thai boxing) muai thai มวยไทย

kid (child) dèk เด็ก

kidnap/abduct lák phaa ลักพา

kidney(s) tai ไต

kidney beans thùa daehng (literally, 'beans'-'red') ถั่วแดง

kill/murder, to khâa ฆ่า

kilogram kì-loh kram กิโลกรัม, or simply kì-loh กิโล

kilometer kì-loh mêht กิโลเมตร, or simply ki-loh กิโล

kind, good (of persons) jai dii ใจดี

kind (type) prà-phêht ประเภท

kindergarten rohng rian à-nú-baan โรงเรียนอนุบาล

king phrá-má-hǎa kà-sàt พระ มหากษัตริย์ (NOTE: in everyday speech the Thai monarch is referred to as nai lǔang ในหลวง)

kingdom aà-naa-jàk อาณาจักร

kiss, to jùup (pronounced 'joop') จูบ

kitchen hâwng khrua ห้อง ครัว, or simply khrua ครัว

kitten, a lûuk maeo ลูกแมว

knee hǔa khào หัวเข่า or simply khào เข่า

kneel khúk khào คุกเข่า

knife, a mîit มีด; to be cut by a knife (i.e. wound inflicted

by knife) mîit bàat มีดบาด;
similarly 'cut by a piece of
glass' kâeo bàat แก้วบาด

knock, to (on a door) kháw
(pronounced with a very short
vowel – similar to the first
part of the exclamation 'oh!
ooh' preceded by a 'k' sound)
เคาะ; knock on the door
kháw prà-tuu เคาะประตู

know, to rúu รู้ (somewhat
more formal, and in certain
contexts more polite, is the
word sâap ทราบ)

know, be acquainted with
rúu-jàk รู้จัก

knowledge khwaam rúu
ความรู้

koala (bear) khoh-aa-lâa
โคอาล่า

Korea (North) kao-lǐi nǔea
เกาหลีเหนือ

Korea (South) kao-lǐi tâi
เกาหลีใต้

Korean (person) khon kao-lǐi
คนเกาหลี

kungfu muai jiin (literally,
'boxing'-'Chinese') มวยจีน

L

label pâai ป้าย, or khrûeang
mǎai เครื่องหมาย

labour/labor N raehng ngaan
แรงงาน

labourer/laborer (unskilled
construction worker) kam-
má-kawn กรรมกร

lack, to khàat khlaehn
ขาดแคลน; lacking khàat ขาด

ladder, a bandai บันได

ladle, dipper krà-buai
กระบวย

lady sù-phâap sà-trii สุภาพ
สตรี

lake thá-leh sàap ทะเลสาบ

lamb (mutton) núea kàe เนื้อ
แกะ

lamp tà-kiang ตะเกียง

land, plot, lot, property thîi
din ที่ดิน

land/go down, to (plane)
long ลง

landlord jâo khǎwng bâan
châo (literally, 'owner'-
'house'-'rent') เจ้าของบ้านเช่า

lane (of a highway – from
English) lehn เลน

77

lane, a (anywhere in size from a small lane to what many would consider a significant road) soi ซอย

language phaa-săa ภาษา; sign language phaa-săa bâi ภาษาใบ้

Laos (country) prà-thêht lao ประเทศลาว, (COLLOQUIAL) lao láo ลาว

Laotian khon lao คนลาว

laptop/notebook computer See 'computer'

large, big yài ใหญ่

laser săeng leh-sôeh แสง เลเซอร์

last (e.g. last piece of cake; to be last in a race) sùt tháai สุดท้าย

last name (i.e. surname) naam sà-kun นามสกุล

last night mûea khuehn níi เมื่อคืนนี้

last week aa thít thîi láew อาทิตย์ที่แล้ว

last year pii thîi láew ปีที่แล้ว

late, to be sǎai สาย

late at night dùek ดึก

lately/recently mûea rew-rew níi เมื่อเร็วๆ นี้

later thii lăng ทีหลัง

laugh, to hǔa rá-w หัวเราะ

laugh at, to hǔa rá-w yá-w หัวเราะเยาะ

lavatory/toilet hâwng náam (literally, 'room'-'water') ห้องน้ำ

lawn, oval, playing fields sà-nǎam yáa สนามหญ้า

law, legislation kòtmǎai กฎหมาย

lawyer thá-naai-khwaam ทนายความ, (COLLOQUIAL) thá-naai ทนาย

lay (to lay/put something down i.e. 'to put a book on the table') waang วาง

lay (as in 'lay down on the bed') nawn long นอนลง; to lay/sleep on one's stomach nawn khwâm นอนคว่ำ; to lay/sleep on one's back nawn ngǎai นอนหงาย; to lay/sleep on one's side nawn tà-khaehng นอนตะแคง

lay or set the table (i.e. before dinner) jàt tó จัดโต๊ะ

layer, floor in a building (e.g. on the tenth floor) chán ชั้น

78

lazy, to be khîi kìat ขี้เกียจ

lead (metal) tà kùa ตะกั่ว

lead, to (or take someone somewhere) nam นำ, or phaa พา

lead (to guide someone somewhere) nam pai นำไป

leader phûu nam ผู้นำ

leaf bai mái ใบไม้

leak, to rûa รั่ว

learn/study, to rian เรียน

lease/let, to (a property) hâi châo ให้เช่า

least (smallest amount) nói thîi sùt น้อยที่สุด

least (at least) yàang nói อย่างน้อย

leather năng หนัง

leave, depart àwk pai ออกไป

leave behind by accident (i.e. forget) luehm ลืม

leave behind on purpose thíng wái ทิ้งไว้

leave behind for safe-keeping (deposit, store, leave something somewhere to be picked up later) fàak ฝาก

lecture, a kaan banyaai การบรรยาย

left (opposite of 'right') sáai ซ้าย; on the left khâang sáai ข้างซ้าย; left-hand side sáai mueh ซ้ายมือ; to be left-handed thà-nàt mueh sáai ถนัดมือซ้าย

left, remaining thîi lǔea ที่เหลือ

leg(s) khǎa ขา

legal taam kòtmǎai ตามกฎหมาย

legend tam naan ตำนาน

leisure (free time) wehlaa wâang เวลาว่าง

lemon (citrus) má-naaw มะนาว

lemongrass tà-khrái ตะไคร้

lend, to hâi yuehm ให้ยืม

length khwaam yaaw ความยาว

lens (i.e. a camera lens – from English) len เลนส์

lesbian **(SLANG/COLLOQUIAL)** feminine lesbian – from the English word 'lady') dîi ดี้, (butch lesbian – from the English word 'tom') tawm ทอม

less (a lesser amount) nói kwàa น้อยกว่า

lessen, reduce lót long ลด

ลง, or simply lót ลด (as in 'reduce the price') lót raa-khaa ลดราคา)

Lesser vehicle of Buddhism, Hinayana latthí hǐnnáyaan ลัทธิหินยาน

lesson, a (at school; also used in the sense as a 'lesson' learned through experience) bòt rian บทเรียน

let, allow, permit v à-nú-yâat อนุญาต, let (someone do something etc.) hâi ให้ (NOTE: this is an important word in Thai used in a variety of ways – see the Thai-English section)

let someone know, to (i.e to tell someone) bàwk บอก

letter (as in a 'letter in the mail') jòt mǎai จดหมาย

letter (in the alphabet) àk-sǎwn อักษร, tua àk-sǎwn ตัวอักษร, or tua nǎng-sǔeh ตัวหนังสือ

lettuce phàk salàt (literally, 'vegetable'-'salad') ผักสลัด

level (even, flat) rîap เรียบ, or râap ราบ

level (or storey in a tall building) chán ชั้น

level (standard as in 'high level', 'low level' etc.) rá-dàp ระดับ

lewd (crude, obscene) laa-mók ลามก

library hâwng sà-mùt ห้องสมุด

license (for driving) bai khàp khìi ใบขับขี่

license, permit bai à-nú-yâat ใบอนุญาต

lick, to lia เลีย

lid (of a jar etc.) fǎa ฝา

lie, tell a falsehood koh-hòk โกหก, (COLLOQUIAL/SLANG) taw-lǎeh ตอแหล; a liar khon koh-hòk คนโกหก

lie down, to nawn นอน

life chii-wít ชีวิต

life (as in 'this life', 'this incarnation') châat níi ชาตินี้

lifejacket (on a boat) sûea chuùchîip เสื้อชูชีพ

lifetime (throughout one's life) tà-làwt chii-wít ตลอดชีวิต

lift, elevator (from English) líp ลิฟท์

lift (to give someone a lift in a car) pai sòng ไปส่ง

lift, raise yók ยก

80

light (light a match) jùt จุด;
  light a fire jùt fai จุดไฟ
light (not heavy) bao เบา
light, to be (bright) sà-wàang
  สว่าง
light (lamp) fai ไฟ
light bulb làwt fai หลอดไฟ
lighter, a (cigarette lighter) fai
  cháek ไฟแช็ค
lightning fáa phàa ฟ้าผ่า
like, to be (to be the same)
  mǔean เหมือน
like/be pleased by, to
  châwp ชอบ
like this (COLLOQUIAL) (i.e. in this
  way/in this manner) bàehp
  níi แบบนี้; 'do it like this' (e.g.
  holding chopsticks) tham
  bàehp níi ทำแบบนี้
like-minded; to have the
  same ideas/tastes mii jai
  trong kan (literally, 'have'-
  'heart/mind'-'straight/direct'-
  'together') มีใจตรงกัน
likewise mǔean kan เหมือน
  กัน
lime/lemon má naaw มะนาว
limited/restricted, to be (in
  time, space) jam-kàt จำกัด
line, a (mark) sên เส้น

line (queue – from English)
  khiu คิว
line up, to (enter the queue)
  khâo khiu เข้าคิว
lineage (ancestry) trà-kuun
  ตระกูล
lion sǐng-toh สิงโต, or simply
  sǐng สิงห์
lip(s) rim fǐi pàak ริมฝีปาก
liquor, alcohol lâo เหล้า
list, a raai kaan รายการ
listen to fang ฟัง
listening, to be (to someone
  talking, the radio) fang yùu
  ฟังอยู่
literature wanná-khá-dii
  วรรณคดี
little (not much) nói น้อย; a
  little bit nít nòi นิดหน่อย
little (small) lék เล็ก
live (be alive) mii chii-wít yùu
  มีชีวิตอยู่
live, to be located (stay in a
  place) yùu อยู่
lively/full of life, to be chii-
  wít chii-waa ชีวิตชีวา
liver tàp ตับ
load, burden (i.e. responsibility) phaa-rá ภาระ
load, to (up/pack a suitcase)

81

banjù บรรจุ

loan, to v hâi yuehm ให้ยืม

loan, a (of money) ngoen kûu เงินกู้; go and get a loan (from a bank/money lender) kûu ngoen กู้เงิน

loathe/dislike/despise rang kìat รังเกียจ

lobster kûng mangkawn (literally, 'prawn/shrimp'- 'dragon') กุ้งมังกร

located, to be tâng yùu ตั้ง อยู่, or simply yùu อยู่

location/site (e.g. a good/bad location for a home, business, etc.) tham-leh ทำเล

lock, a mâeh kunjaeh (literally, 'mother'-'key') แม่กุญแจ (NOTE: colloquially the word for 'key' kunjaeh กุญแจ is also used to refer to a lock)

lock, to (from English) láwk ล็อก

locked, to be láwk láew ล็อกแล้ว

lodge, bungalow (from English) bang-kà-loh บังกะโล

logical mii hèt-phŏn (literally, 'have'-'reason') มีเหตุผล

lonely, to be ngǎo เหงา

long (length of something other than distance) yaaw ยาว

long/far (distance) klai ไกล

long (time) naan นาน

look! (look at that!) duu sí ดูซิ

look after (e.g. children) duùlaeh ดูแล

look at, to duu ดู

look for/search/look up (find in book) hǎa หา

look(s) like duu mǔean ดูเหมือน

look out! (be careful) rá wang ระวัง

loose (not tight) lǔam หลวม

lose, be defeated pháeh แพ้

lose, mislay tham hǎai ทำ หาย

lose (for someone 'to lose their life/to die') sǐa chii-wít เสียชีวิต

lose money, to (on a business venture) (COLLOQUIAL) khàat thun; lose money (on something and get nothing in return) sǐa ngoen frii (literally, 'waste'-'money'- 'free') เสียเงินฟรี

lost (missing) hăi หาย

lost (can't find way) lŏng (thaang) หลง (ทาง)

lost property khăwng hăi ของหาย

lots of (COLLOQUIAL) yóe yáe (both words pronounced very short) เยอะแยะ, or yóe mâak เยอะมาก

lottery (from English) láwt toeh rîi ล็อตเตอรี่, (COLLOQUIAL) hŭai หวย; (COLLOQUIAL) to win the lottery thùuk hŭai ถูกหวย

loud, to be dang ดัง (also colloquial term for 'famous')

lounge room/living room hâwng ráp khàek (literally, 'room'-'receive'-'guest[s]') ห้องรับแขก, or hâwng nâng lên (literally, 'room'-'sit'- 'play') ห้องนั่งเล่น

love N khwaam rák ความรัก

love, to v rák รัก

lovely/adorable (of a person/ cute behaviour) nâa rák น่ารัก

lovely/beautiful (e.g. view) sŭai-ngaam สวยงาม

low (opposite of 'high') tàm ต่ำ

luck chôhk โชค

lucky chôhk dii โชคดี

luggage/bag/suitcase krà păo กระเป๋า

lump (e.g. of rock; also a lump/ growth on the body) kâwn ก้อน

lunch, midday meal aa-hăan klaang wan อาหารกลางวัน

lunch, to eat khâaw thîang ทานข้าวเที่ยง, (MORE COLLOQUIAL) kin khâaw thîang กินข้าวเที่ยง

lung(s) pàwt ปอด

lust/desire tanhăa ตัณหา

luxury khwaam rŭu răa ความ หรูหรา; luxurious rŭu răa หรูหรา

lychee (fruit) lín-jìi ลิ้นจี่

machine, a khrûeang jàk เครื่องจักร

mad See 'crazy/insane'

madam, ma'am (term of address) maà-daam มาดาม, mâem แหม่ม

Mafia maàfia มาเฟีย (NOTE: this term is commonly used

in Thailand to refer to local criminal organizations or foreign gangs operating in Thailand)

magazine waa-rá-săan วารสาร

magic (with spells, incantations – not stage magic) khaa-thăa aa-khom คาถาอาคม

magistrate/judge phûu-phí phâak-săa ผู้พิพากษา

magnet mâeh lèk (literally, 'mother'-'iron/steel') แม่เหล็ก

mahout (elephant keeper/ handler) khwaan cháang ควาญช้าง

maid (female servant in a private residence) săaw chái (literally, 'woman'-'use') สาวใช้; room maid (in a hotel/ private residence) mâeh bâan แม่บ้าน

mail, post (from English) mehl เมล

mail, to sòng ส่ง

mailman/postman bùrùt praisànii บุรุษไปรษณีย์

main, most important sămkhan สำคัญ

mainly, for the most part

sùan yài ส่วนใหญ่, or sùan mâak ส่วนมาก

major/big (something important/significant) yài ใหญ่

make/do, to tham ทำ

make-up (cosmetics) khrûeang săm-aang เครื่อง สำอาง

Malaysia maàlehsia มาเลเซีย

Malaysian (people) chaaw maàlehsia ชาวมาเลเซีย

male (human being) chaai ชาย; male (animal) tua phûu ตัวผู้

mama-san (brothel keeper, female bar keeper) mâe láo แม่เล้า (Note: the word 'mama-san' is also commonly used)

man/men phûu chaai ผู้ชาย

manage/organize, to jàt-kaan จัดการ

manager phûu jàt-kaan ผู้จัดการ

Mandarin (official language of China) phaa-săa jiin klaang ภาษาจีนกลาง

mango má-mûang มะม่วง

mangosteen (fruit) mang-khút มังคุด

maniac *See* 'crazy/insane'

mankind/humans/humanity
má-nút มนุษย์

manners (etiquette/behaviour)
maa-rá-yâat มารยาท

manual (to work with one's hands) tham dûai mueh (literally, 'do'-'by/with'-'hand') ทำด้วยมือ

manual (instructional book, e.g. instructions on how to operate a DVD player) khûu mueh คู่มือ

manufacture, to phà-lìt ผลิต

many, much, a lot mâak มาก

map, a phǎehn thîi แผนที่

March mii-naakhom มีนาคม

market tà-làat ตลาด (NOTE: in Thailand there are markets that move from one location to another in the same town. For example on a Monday the market may be in one place, the next day somewhere else, and so on. Markets of this variety are referred to as tà-làat nát ตลาดนัด. The word nát นัด means 'appointment', 'to arrange to meet', 'to set a date')

marijuana/marihuana kan-chaa (pronounced 'gun-jar') กัญชา (NOTE: common slang for marijuana is núea (the normal word for 'meat/beef/flesh') เนื้อ)

married, to be tàehng-ngaan láew แต่งงานแล้ว

marry/get married, to tàehng-ngaan แต่งงาน

mask, a nâa kàak หน้ากาก

massage, to nûat นวด

massage (Thai traditional style) nûat thai นวดไทย, or nûat phǎehn bohraan แผนโบราณ

massage parlour (these establishments, while generally offering normal straight massages, are primarily geared towards providing customers with sexual services) àab òb nûat อาบอบนวด

masturbate (COLLOQUIAL/SLANG) for men chák wâaw (literally, 'to pull/draw'-'kite') ชักว่าว; the equivalent for women tòk bèt ตกเบ็ด (which normally means 'to go fishing')

mat (e.g. a woven floor mat) sùea เสื่อ

match/game, a (from English) kehm เกม

matches (COLLOQUIAL) mái-khìit ไม้ขีด, (or more fully) mái-khìit-fai ไม้ขีดไฟ

material (e.g. building material) wát-thù วัตถุ (NOTE: the syllable thù here is pronounced very short), or wàtsà-dù วัสดุ

matter, issue (as in 'a matter/issue of great importance') rûeang เรื่อง

matter (as in the common Thai expression which can be translated into English as – 'it doesn't matter', or 'it's all right, don't worry about it', or 'that's fine', or also 'my pleasure') mâi pen rai ไม่เป็นไร

mattress, a thîi nawn ที่นอน

maximum/the most mâak thîi sùt มากที่สุด

May (month) phrúet-sà-phaa-khom พฤษภาคม

may àat jà อาจจะ: e.g. I (male speaking) may go phŏm àat

jà pai ผมอาจจะไป

maybe àat jà อาจจะ, also baang thii บางที (which may also be translated as 'sometimes')

me *See* the entry under 'I'

meal, a múeh มื้อ

mean, to be (stingy) (COLLOQUIAL) khîi nĭao (literally, 'faeces/shit'-'sticky', i.e. someone who is so tight they want to keep their own excrement) ขี้เหนียว – also refers to 'cruel' jai-ráai ใจร้าย

mean, to (intend) mii jehttà-naa มีเจตนา

mean, to (word) măai khwaam หมายความ (NOTE: the expression 'What does it/this/do you mean is?' is măai khwaam wâa àrai หมายความว่าอะไร *Also see* 'interpret/translate')

meaning (the 'meaning' of something) khwaam măi ความหมาย

meanwhile (in the meantime/at the same time) nai wehlaa diao kan ในเวลาเดียวกัน

measure, to wát วัด

meat/flesh núea เนื้อ

meatball (which, in fact, may either be beef, pork, or fish) lûuk chín ลูกชิ้น

mechanic (the general term for a skilled tradesman is châang ช่าง followed by the particular area of expertise: note motor vehicle = rót รถ; engine = khrûeang เครื่อง). The full word for a motor mechanic is either châang rót ช่างรถ, or châang khrûeang ช่างเครื่อง

meddle, to (interfere in some-one else's affairs) yûng ยุ่ง

media, the (mass media, radio, television, Internet etc.) sùeh muanchon สื่อมวลชน, (COLLOQUIAL) sùeh สื่อ

medical thaang kaan phâeht ทางการแพทย์

medicine/drug yaa ยา

medium (size – neither big nor small) khà-nàat klaang ขนาดกลาง

meet, to phóp พบ

meeting, a (e.g. a conference) pràchum ประชุม

melodious (pleasing to the ear, a beautiful sound) phai-rá-w ไพเราะ, (or simply and more commonly) phrá-w เพราะ

melon (i.e. fruit/vegetables in the melon family) taehng แตง: e.g. watermelon taehng moh แตงโม; cucumber taehng kwaa แตงกวา

melt, to lá-laai ละลาย (the same word also means 'dissolve')

member (e.g. of a Club) sà-maa-chík สมาชิก

memory (one's memory) khwaam song jam ความ ทรงจำ

mend/fix/repair, to sâwm ซ่อม

menstruate, to (a woman's period) mii prà-jam duean มีประจำเดือน, (COLLOQUIAL) pen men เป็นเมนส์

mentally retarded panyaa àwn (literally, 'intellect'- 'weak/tender/soft') ปัญญาอ่อน

mention, to klàaw thŭeng กล่าวถึง

menu (from English) mehnuu

เมนู, or raai-kaan aa-hăan รายการอาหาร

merchandise (commercial products, goods) sĭn-kháa สินค้า

merely/only phiang เพียง

mess, in a rók รก; **a messy house** bâan rók บ้านรก

message khâw khwaam ข้อความ; **SMS message** (from English) es-em-es เอส เอ็มเอส

metal (COLLOQUIAL) lèk เหล็ก (NOTE: this term actually means 'iron' or 'steel'; the proper word for 'metal' is loh-hà โลหะ)

method (of doing something) wí-thii วิธี

metre/meter (length – from English) méht เมตร

microwave (oven) (COLLOQUIAL – from English) wéhf (pronounced similar to 'wave') เวฟ

midday thîang wan เที่ยงวัน

middle/centre, the sŭun klaang ศูนย์กลาง

middle (as in middle of the day) klaang กลาง

midnight thîang khuehn เที่ยงคืน

migrate, to v òp-phá-yóp อพยพ; **a migrant** n phûu òp-phá-yóp ผู้อพยพ

mild (not spicy) mâi phèt ไม่ เผ็ด

mild (not severe – as in a storm, a protest, etc.) mâi run raehng ไม่รุนแรง, (not strong) àwn อ่อน

mile (distance – from English) mai ไมล์

milk nom นม (also the common word for a woman's breasts)

million láan ล้าน

millionaire (or a general term for a wealthy person) sèht-thĭi เศรษฐี

mince, to (meat/pork etc.) sàp สับ

mind (i.e. the physical brain) sà-măwng สมอง

mind (i.e. as in one's mind) jìt-jai จิตใจ, or simply jai ใจ

mind, to be displeased/ offended rang kìat รังเกียจ, (COLLOQUIAL) as in to 'hold something against someone else/consider something inappropriate' tŭeh ถือ

mine, a (i.e. diamond mine) mŭeang เหมือง, or mŭeang râeh เหมืองแร่

minibus/van, a rót tûu รถตู้

ministry, a (as in a government ministry) krà-suang กระทรวง

minor (not important) mâi sămkhan ไม่สำคัญ

minority, a (group) chon klùm nói ชนกลุ่มน้อย

minus (-) lóp ลบ

minute naa thii นาที

mirror, a krà-jòk กระจก

miscellaneous (misc) bèt tà-lèt เบ็ดเตล็ด

miser/skinflint/tightwad, a khon khîi nĭao คนขี้เหนียว

misfortune chôhk ráai โชค ร้าย

miss, to (a bus, a flight) phlâat พลาด

miss, to (somebody) khít thŭeng คิดถึง

Miss (title for an unmarried woman) naang săaw นางสาว

missing (to disappear) hăi หาย, or hăi pai หายไป

mist, fog màwk หมอก

mistake, a khwaam phìt ความผิด

mistaken (to be incorrect) phìt phlâat ผิดพลาด

mistress/minor wife (a complex and significant area of Thai social life) mia nói เมียน้อย (NOTE: a man's 'major wife' is known colloquially as a mia lŭang เมียหลวง) *Also see* entry under 'wife'

misunderstand(ing) khâojai phìt เข้าใจผิด

mix/blend, to phà-sŏm ผสม

mobile/cell phone (*also see* 'telephone') thoh-rá-sàp mueh tŭeh โทรศัพท์มือถือ, (COLLOQUIAL) mueh tŭeh มือถือ, (or from English) moh-baai (moh pronounced as in 'mow the lawn', and bai as in 'buy shares!') โมบาย; smartphone (from English) sà-márt fohn สมาร์ทโฟน

mock/make fun of yá-w yóei เยาะเย้ย

modern than sà-măi ทันสมัย

modest, simple, ordinary tham-má-daa ธรรมดา

89

moment (instant) chûa khànà ชั่วขณะ

moment (in a moment, just a moment) dĭao (COLLOQUIAL) เดี๋ยว (in a more formal environment – e.g. office/ surgery etc. a receptionist would say 'please wait a moment' raw sák khrûu รอ สักครู่)

moment ago (i.e. just a moment/second/minute ago) mûea kîi níi เมื่อกี้นี้

Monday wan jan วันจันทร์

money ngoen เงิน (this word also means 'silver') (MORE COLLOQUIAL) tang ตังค์ (shortened from another old Thai term for 'money' sà-taang สตางค์: 100 sàtaang = one baht); to have no money/to be broke (SLANG) mâi mii tang ไม่มี ตังค์, or thǎng tàehk (literally, 'bucket'-'broken') ถังแตก

monitor (of computer)/**screen** jaw (pronounced like the English word 'jaw') จอ

monk (a Buddhist monk) phrá พระ

monkey ling ลิง

month duean เดือน

monument, a ànù-sǎ-wárii อนุสาวรีย์

mood See 'passion' (NOTE: 'to be in a bad mood' aa rom sĭa อารมณ์เสีย)

moody/irritable, to be ngùt-ngìt หงุดหงิด

moon duang jan ดวงจันทร์

morality sǐin-lá-tham ศีล ธรรม

more (comparative) kwàa กว่า: e.g. better dii kwàa (literally, 'good'-'more') ดีกว่า

more of (things)/**more than** mâak kwàa มากกว่า

more or less mâi mâak kâw nói ไม่มากก็น้อย

morning (time), the cháo เช้า, or tawn cháo ตอนเช้า

moron/stupid person khon ngôh คนโง่

mosque sù-rào สุเหร่า

mosquito yung ยุง

most (superlative) thîi sùt ที่สุด: e.g. the most expensive phaehng thîi sùt แพงที่สุด

most (the most) mâak thîi sùt มากที่สุด

mostly, for the most part
sùan yài ส่วนใหญ่

mother (COMMON/COLLOQUIAL)
mâeh แม่, (MORE FORMAL) maan
daa มารดา; stepmother mâeh
líang แม่เลี้ยง

mother-in-law (wife's
mother) mâeh yaai แม่ยาย;
(husband's mother) mâeh
să-mii แม่สามี

motor/engine, a khrûeang
yon เครื่องยนต์, or simply
khrûeang เครื่อง

motorcycle maw-toeh-sai
มอเตอร์ไซค์, (MORE COLLOQUIAL)
rót khrûeang รถเครื่อง (also
see 'taxi' for 'motorcycle taxi')

motor vehicle (specifically 'a
car') rót yon รถยนต์

mountain phuu khǎo ภูเขา

mouse/rat (rodent) nǔu หนู

mouse (computer – from
English) máo เมาส์

moustache, a nùat หนวด

mouth pàak ปาก

mouthwash (i.e. Listerine)
náam yaa bûan pàak น้ำยา
บ้วนปาก

move, to khlûean thîi
เคลื่อนที่

move from one place to
another (e.g. to move house)
yáai ย้าย

movement, motion khwaam
khlûean wăi ความเคลื่อนไหว

movie, a nǎng หนัง

movie house/cinema rohng
nǎng โรงหนัง

mow, cut (the lawn/grass)
tàt ตัด

Mr (title) naai นาย

Mrs (title) naang นาง

MSG/msg (flavour enhancer)
phǒng chuu rót (literally,
'powder'-'boost/lift/elevate'-
'taste') ผงชูรส

much, many, a lot mâak
มาก, (COMMON COLLOQUIAL) yóe
(pronounced something like
'yer!' very short with a high
tone) เยอะ

muscle klâam núea กล้ามเนื้อ

museum phíphít-tháphan
พิพิธภัณฑ์

mushroom(s) hèt เห็ด

music dontrii ดนตรี

musician, a nák don trii นัก
ดนตรี

Muslim múslim มุสลิม

must tâwng ต้อง: e.g. (I) must

go (chǎn) tâwng pai ต้องไป

mute (unable to speak) bâi
ใบ้; to be mute pen bâi เป็น
ใบ้ *See* 'language' (for 'sign
language')

my, mine (male speaking)
khǎwng phǒm ของผม;
(female) khǎwng dìchǎn/
chǎn ของดิฉัน/ฉัน

Myanmar *See* 'Burma'

N

nail (finger, toe), claws of an
animal lép เล็บ

nail (used in carpentry/
building) tà-puu ตะปู

naked plueai เปลือย; a naked
body/to be in the nude
(FORMAL) plueai kaai เปลือย
กาย, or (SIMPLE COLLOQUIAL)
póh โป๊

name chûeh ชื่อ; 'what's your
name?' khun chûeh àrai
(literally, 'you'-'name'-'what'?)
คุณชื่ออะไร

narcotic(s) yaa sèp tìt
(literally, 'drug'-'consume'-
'stuck/addicted') ยาเสพติด

narrow khâehp แคบ; to be

narrow-minded/petty jai
khâehp (literally, 'narrow'-
'heart') ใจแคบ

nation, country châat ชาติ

national hàeng châat แห่ง
ชาติ

national anthem phlehng
châat เพลงชาติ

national park, a ùt-thá-yaan
hàeng châat อุทยานแห่งชาติ

nationality sǎnchâat สัญชาติ:
e.g. Thai nationality sǎnchâat
thai สัญชาติไทย

native (indigenous) phúen
mueang พื้นเมือง

natural pen thammá-châat
เป็นธรรมชาติ

nature thammá-châat
ธรรมชาติ

naughty son (pronounced like
the English word 'on' with 's'
in front) ซน

navel (belly button) sà dueh
สะดือ

navy, the kawng tháp ruea
กองทัพเรือ

navy blue/dark blue/royal
blue sǐi náam-ngoen
สีน้ำเงิน

near, nearby klâi ใกล้ (NOTE:

the Thai words 'near' **klâi**
ใกล้ and 'far' **klai** ไกล are
perhaps the most significant
examples of the importance
of getting the tones correct as
they convey the completely
opposite meaning. Hint: the
word for 'near' has a falling
tone and when said, is shorter
than the mid-tone word for
'far' **klai** ไกล. To say 'very
near' simply repeat the word
twice **klâi-klâi** ใกล้ๆ)

nearly kùeap เกือบ

neat, orderly, well-behaved
rîap rói เรียบร้อย – This term
is widely used and conveys
the notion of ideal behaviour
and deportment. (NOTE: this
term is also commonly used
to express the idea that a job/
task has been successfully
completed, something like
'done!')

necessary jam-pen (jam
จำ is pronounced like 'jum'
in the English word 'jump')
จำเป็น

neck khaw คอ

necklace sôi khaw สร้อยคอ

necktie (from English) nékthai
เน็คไท

need khwaam jam-pen ความ
จำเป็น

need, to jam-pen จำเป็น

needle, a khěm เข็ม

neighbour phûean bâan
เพื่อนบ้าน

nephew lǎan chaai หลานชาย

nerve, a sên prà-sàat เส้น
ประสาท

nervous/anxious kang-won
jai กังวลใจ

nest (e.g. bird's nest) rang รัง;
bird's nest rang nók รังนก

net (mosquito net) múng มุ้ง

network khruea khàai เครือ
ข่าย; social network khruea
khàai sǎngkhom เครือข่าย
สังคม

neutral (impartial) pen klaang
เป็นกลาง

never mâi khoei ไม่เคย (NOTE:
for a fuller description of how
the word khoei เคย is used
see 'have')

never mind! mâi pen rai ไม่
เป็นไร

nevertheless (FORMAL) yàang-
rai kâw taam อย่างไรก็ตาม,

or (COLLOQUIAL) yang-ngai kâw taam ยังไงก็ตาม

new, to be mài ใหม่

news khàaw ข่าว

newspaper năng sǔeh phim หนังสือพิมพ์

New Year pii mài ปีใหม่, (the expression) 'Happy New Year' sàwàt dii pii mài สวัสดีปีใหม่ (NOTE: the traditional Thai new year (13–15 April) is called sǒng-kraan สงกรานต์)

New Zealand niu sii-laehn นิวซีแลนด์

next (in line, sequence) tàw pai ต่อไป

next to thàt pai ถัดไป

next week aa-thít nâa อาทิตย์หน้า

next year pii nâa ปีหน้า

nice/good dii ดี

nickname (NOTE: most Thai people have both a first name and a nickname – frequently a shortened version of their first name – or something else, invariably short, altogether) chûeh lên (literally, 'name'-'play') ชื่อเล่น

niece lăan săaw หลานสาว

night klaang khuehn กลางคืน

nightclothes/nightdress/ pyjamas chút nawn ชุดนอน

nightclub (from English) nái-khláp ไนท์คลับ

nightly thúk khuehn ทุกคืน

nine kâo เก้า

nineteen sìp kâo สิบเก้า

ninety kâo sìp เก้าสิบ

no, not, none mâi mii ไม่มี (used with nouns. NOTE: there are many ways of expressing 'no' – this being dependent on the form of the question asked), e.g. 'to have no friends' mâi mii phûean ไม่มีเพื่อน

no, not mâi ไม่ (used with verbs and adjectives), e.g. 'it's not hot' mâi ráwn ไม่ร้อน

nobody (as in 'there is nobody here') mâi mii khrai ไม่มีใคร

noise, a sound sĭang เสียง

noisy, loud noise sĭang dang เสียงดัง

nonsense (to be meaningless) rái săa rá ไร้สาระ, or lěow-lăi เหลวไหล

noodles (rice noodles) kŭai tĭao ก๋วยเตี๋ยว, or (egg noodles) bà-mìi บะหมี่

94

noon tawn thîang ตอนเที่ยง

normal pà-kà-tì ปกติ

normally (dohy pà-kà-tì โดย
ปกติ

north nŭea เหนือ

north-east tàwan àwk chĭang
nŭea ตะวันออกเฉียงเหนือ
(NOTE: in Thailand the north-
east region of the country is
referred to as iisăan – this is
written in English in various
ways: Isarn/Isan/Isaan – อีสาน)

north-west tà-wan tòk chĭang
nŭea ตะวันตกเฉียงเหนือ

nose jà-mùuk จมูก; (colloquial
word for) 'mucous' khîi
mûuk (literally, 'excrement'-
shortened word for 'nose')
ขี้มูก

nostril ruu jà-mùuk รูจมูก

not mâi ไม่ (NOTE: 'not' may
be expressed in other ways
depending on the form of
question asked, or nature of
statement being made)

note (i.e. banknote) (COLLOQUIAL)
(from the English 'bank')
báeng แบงค์

notebook sà-mùt สมุด

note down, to jòt nóht จด

โน้ต, or (more colloquially –
the equivalent to) 'jot it down'
jòt wái จดไว้

nothing (as in 'nothing is
going on') mâi mii arai
ไม่มีอะไร (NOTE: in certain
instances, e.g. in response to
the question 'What did you
say?' to answer 'Nothing!' is the
word plàaw เปล่า [which also
means 'empty/vacant/plain/
bare'] is commonly used)

notice, to (to notice
something) săngkèht สังเกต

notify (e.g. the police) jâehng
khwaam แจ้งความ

novel, a ná-wá ní-yaai
นวนิยาย, or simply ní-yaai
นิยาย

November phrúet-sà-jì-kaa-
yon พฤศจิกายน

noun (part of speech) kham-
naam (pronounced 'narm') คำ
นาม, or simply naam นาม

now dĭao níi เดี๋ยวนี้, or tawn
níi ตอนนี้

nowadays/these days
sà-măi níi สมัยนี้

no way (COLLOQUIAL) (e.g. there
is 'no way' to get there, or

'Can I go with you?' – 'No way!') mâi mii thaang ไม่มี ทาง

nowhere (as in a sentence such as 'there is nowhere like home') mâi mii thîi năi ไม่มี ที่ไหน (literally, 'no'-have'- 'where?')

nude plueai เปลือย, or 'naked body/nude' plueai kaai เปลือยกาย, or (SIMPLE COLLOQUIAL) póh โป๊

numb, to be chaa ชา

number (from English; most commonly used when asking for a telephone number) boeh เบอร์; (general term for 'number' is) măai lêhk หมายเลข

nurse N phá-yaa-baan พยาบาล

nut (food i.e. nuts in general) thùa ถั่ว

nylon (from English) nai lâwn ในลอน

O

oar/paddle mái phaai ไม้พาย

obese *See* 'fat'

obey, to/to be obedient

chûea fang เชื่อฟัง

object, thing sìng khăwng สิ่งของ

object, to (to oppose) khát kháan คัดค้าน

obstinate/stubborn, to be dûeh ดื้อ

obstruct/block, to khàt khwăang ขัดขวาง

obtain/get dâi ráp ได้รับ, or simply dâi ได้

occasion/opportunity oh-kàat โอกาส

occasionally pen khráng khraaw เป็นครั้งคราว; once in a while (COLLOQUIAL) naan-naan thii นานๆ ที

occupation (profession – term often, but not always, used to refer to someone with professional qualifications) aa-chîip อาชีพ; (colloquially the word for 'work' – ngaan งาน – is used): 'What (work) do you do?' (khun) tham ngaan àrai ทำงานอะไร

occur (for something to happen) kòeht khêun เกิดขึ้น

ocean má-hăa sà-mùt มหาสมุทร (*also see* 'sea')

o'clock naa lí kaa นาฬิกา
(NOTE: this word is used in the
24 hour system of telling the
time such as in official Thai
news broadcasts and more
generally at sea/by aircraft/
the military etc.: e.g. 13 naa
lí kaa = 1 p.m.). The everyday
Thai system of telling the time
is somewhat more complex
and cannot be outlined here.

October tù-laa-khom ตุลาคม

odour (i.e. to smell not so
good) mii klìn มีกลิ่น

of course nâeh nawn แน่นอน

off (to turn something off) pìt
ปิด; turned off already pìt
láew ปิดแล้ว

off, to be (gone bad) sĭa เสีย;
also nâo เน่า (rotten)

offend (e.g. break the law)
tham phìt ทำผิด

offend (i.e. to displease
someone/to be offensive)
tham hâi mâi phaw jai
ทำให้ไม่พอใจ

offer sà-nŏeh เสนอ; suggest
náe nam แนะนำ

office thîi tham ngaan
ที่ทำงาน, (also commonly –

from English) áwp-fít ออฟฟิศ

official(s) (i.e. government
servants, bureaucrats) khâa
râat-chá-kaan ข้าราชการ, or
jâo nâa thîi เจ้าหน้าที่

often bòi บ่อย; very often bòi-
bòi บ่อยๆ

oil (general term for 'oil', and
common word for petrol/
gasoline) náam-man น้ำมัน

oily/greasy (food) lîan เลี่ยน;
e.g. greasy food aa-hăan lîan
อาหารเลี่ยน

ointment (from English
'cream') kriim ครีม

okay tòk-long ตกลง (the
English word OK is also
widely used oh-keh โอเค)

old (of people) kàeh แก่; an old
person khon kàeh คนแก่

old (of things) kào เก่า

olden times, in (i.e. 'in the
past....') sà-măi kàwn สมัย
ก่อน

older brother (or sister) phîi
พี่ (NOTE: an important word
in Thai with a far broader
meaning than simply 'older
brother/older sister'; it is used
by a junior or younger person

97

to mean 'you' when speaking to an older or higher status person in various, mainly less formal, contexts. In addition the term is also commonly used to mean 'he/she' when talking about another older or higher status individual)

on (i.e. on top) bon บน

on (a particular date) wan thîi วันที่

on (to turn something on) pòeht เปิด

on fire, to be fai mâi ไฟไหม้

on foot (e.g. came [here] on foot/walked [here]) doehn maa เดินมา; (e.g. went [there] on foot/walked [there]) doehn pai เดินไป

on the whole/generally dohy thûa pai โดยทั่วไป

on time, to be trong weh laa ตรงเวลา

once (i.e. one time) khráng nùeng ครั้งหนึ่ง; a single time khráng diao ครั้งเดียว; once in a while – see 'occasionally'

one nùeng หนึ่ง

one-way ticket tŭa thîao diao (literally, 'ticket'-'trip'- 'single') ตั๋วเที่ยวเดียว

one who, the one who (did something etc.) khon thîi… คนที่…

onion hăwm yài หอมใหญ่

only thâonán เท่านั้น

open, to pòeht เปิด (same word as 'turn on')

opinion khwaam hĕn ความ เห็น

opium fìn ฝิ่น

opportunity/chance oh kàat โอกาส

oppose, to tàw tâan ต่อต้าน

opposed, to be kháan ค้าน; opposition (in government) fàai trong khâam ฝ่ายตรง ข้าม

opposite (to be facing) yùu trong khâam อยู่ตรงข้าม

opposite (contrary) trong khâam ตรงข้าม

option/alternative thaang lûeak ทางเลือก

optional lûeak dâi เลือกได้

or rŭeh (commonly pro- nounced [incorrectly] with an 'l' sound – lŭeh) หรือ

oral dûai pàak (literally, 'with'-'mouth') ด้วยปาก, or oral sex chái pàak ใช้ปาก (NOTE: for such delicate subject matter the terms given are the least crude and offensive of the possibilites) (fellatio – sucking) om อม, (cunninglis – licking) lia เลีย

orange, an sôm ส้ม

orange (colour) sǐi sôm สีส้ม

orchid klûai mái กล้วยไม้

order (command) kham sàng คำสั่ง

order (a written form for food, goods, medicine, etc.) bai sàng ใบสั่ง

order (as in – in order/in sequence) taam lam dàp ตามลำดับ

order something (e.g. in a restaurant), command, to (someone to do something) sàng สั่ง

orderly/organized, to be pen rá-bìap เป็นระเบียบ

ordinary tham-má-daa ธรรมดา: e.g. 'ordinary person' khon tham-má-daa คนธรรมดา (NOTE: ordinary

folk/householders – both in the city and rural areas – are colloquiallly known by the term chaaw bâan ชาวบ้าน)

organization, an ong-kaan (pronounced 'ong-garn') องค์การ, or ong-kawn องค์กร

organize/arrange, to jàt kaan จัดการ

origin jùt rôehm tôn จุดเริ่ม ต้น; source (the source of something, e.g. bootlegged DVDs) làeng แหล่ง

original (an original of something, the real thing) tua jing ตัวจริง, or khǎwng jing ของจริง; the original of a document is tôn chà-bàp ต้นฉบับ

originate, come from maa jàak มาจาก: e.g. 'what country do you come from?' khun maa jàak prà-thêht àrai คุณมาจากประเทศอะไร

ornament (for the home) khrûeang prà-dàp เครื่อง ประดับ

other ùehn อื่น: e.g. 'other person' khon ùehn คนอื่น

ought to, should khuan ควร

our(s) khǎwng rao ของ
เรา: e.g. our house bâan
khǎwng rao บ้านของเรา,
(COLLOQUIAL AND EVEN SIMPLER)
bâan rao บ้านเรา (NOTE: This
is a very common idiomatic
way in which Thai people
refer to their own country or
hometown – i.e. 'our home')

out (i.e. take something out –
'a plate out of the cupboard')
àwk ออก; **to take out/
withdraw** thǎwn ถอน: e.g.
take out a tooth/pull a tooth
out thǎwn fan ถอนฟัน

**out-of-date/outdated/old-
fashioned** láa sà-mǎi ล้า
สมัย, (COLLOQUIAL) choei เชย

outfit (matching set of
clothing) chút ชุด

outing (to go out for fun/
pleasure) (pai) thîao (ไป)
เที่ยว (NOTE: an important
Thai word – thîao – is used in
a wide range of ways to refer
to a pleasant/enjoyable visit
somewhere – to a friend's
house, the beach, a disco,
bar, another country, etc.)

outside khâang nâwk ข้างนอก

oval (shape) rûup khài รูปไข่

oven tao òp เตาอบ

over (to be), finished,
completed sèt เสร็จ

over (e.g. to turn over a fish
when frying it)/**around** (as in
to turn a car around) klàp กลับ

overcast, cloudy mii mêhk
มีเมฆ

overdose, an (of a drug) yaa
koen khà-nàat ยาเกินขนาด

overlook (not to notice)
mawng khâam มองข้าม

overpass (a pedestrian
overpass) sà-phaan loi
(literally, 'bridge'-'float')
สะพานลอย

overseas tàang prà-thêet
ต่างประเทศ

overtake/pass (another
vehicle) saeng แซง

over there thîi nôhn ที่โน่น

overturned/capsized (boat)
lôm ล่ม

overturned (vehicle following
an accident – on its roof)
ngǎi tháwng หงายท้อง

owe, to pen nîi เป็นหนี้

own, on one's (just one
person), alone khon diao

คนเดียว; to come alone/on one's own maa khon diao มาคนเดียว

own, personal (belongings) khǎwng sùan tua ของ ส่วนตัว

own, to (owner) pen jâo khǎwng เป็นเจ้าของ

oxygen (from English) áwk-sì-jên (jen pronounced like 'gen' in the English word) ออกซิเจน

oyster (general term) hǒi หอย; a large succulent type of oyster hǒi naang rom หอย นางรม (Note: the word hǒi is also a common slang term for a woman's vagina)

P

pack, to (luggage) kèp khǎwng เก็บของ

package hàw khǎwng ห่อ ของ, or simply hàw ห่อ

packet hàw lék (literally, 'package'-'small') ห่อเล็ก (a small packet, or sachet, is also referred to as a sawng ซอง)

page (in a book) nâa หน้า

pagoda/stupa (spire shaped solid structure with no interior space, not a temple though located in temple grounds) jeh-dii เจดีย์

paid, to have jàai láew จ่าย แล้ว

pain/painful jèp เจ็บ; very painful jèp mâak เจ็บมาก

painkiller, a yaa kâeh pùat ยาแก้ปวด

paint ɴ sǐi สี (Note: sǐi สี is also the word for 'colour')

paint, to (house, furniture) thaa sǐi ทาสี

painting, a phâap wâat ภาพ วาด

pair of, a khûu nùeng คู่ หนึ่ง (Note: one pair is nùeng khûu หนึ่งคู่)

pajamas/pyjamas chút nawn ชุดนอน

palace (royal) wang วัง, or (more formally) phrá-râat-chá-wang พระราชวัง

pale (as in a pale face of someone unwell or in a state of shock) sǐit ซีด: e.g. a pale face nâa sǐit หน้าซีด

palm (of hand) *See* 'sole'

pan (frying pan/wok) krà-thá กระทะ (NOTE: both syllables are very short)

pancake (from English; the word 'pancake' is widely understood)

panda (animal) mǐi phaen-dâ (literally, 'bear'-'panda') หมี แพนด้า

panorama phâap kwâang (literally, 'picture'-'wide') ภาพ กว้าง

panties (female)/**underpants** (male) kaang-kehng nai กางเกงใน

pants/trousers kaang-kehng กางเกง

papaya má-lá-kaw มะละกอ

paper krà-dàat กระดาษ; **sandpaper** krà-dàat saai (literally, 'paper'-'sand') กระดาษทราย

parade/procession khà-buan hàeh ขบวนแห่ (NOTE: a common event as part of cultural life, especially in rural Thailand)

paradise/heaven sà-wǎn สวรรค์

parallel, to be khà-nǎan ขนาน

paralysis/to be paralyzed am-má-phâat อัมพาต

parcel, a hàw ห่อ, or hàw phát-sà-dù ห่อพัสดุ

pardon me? what did you say? (a most useful expression) àrai ná? อะไรนะ

parents phâw mâeh (literally, 'father'-'mother') พ่อแม่

park (a public park/garden) sǔan sǎa-thaa rá-ná สวน สาธารณะ

park, to (car) jàwt rót จอดรถ

parliament rát-thà-sà-phaa รัฐสภา

parrot, a nók kâew นกแก้ว; **parrot fish** (common in southern Thailand) plaa nók kâew ปลานกแก้ว

part, a (of something/not the whole) sùan ส่วน; for the most part/the majority sùan mâak ส่วนมาก; a part/one part (of something) sùan nùeng ส่วนหนึ่ง

part, spare part (of car/machine) à-lài อะไหล่

participate, to mii sùan rûam มีส่วนร่วม

102

particular, particularly, especially dohy cha phá-w โดยเฉพาะ

partner (in business) hûn sùan หุ้นส่วน

partner (spouse) khûu sŏmrót คู่สมรส

party (birthday party etc.) ngaan งาน (NOTE: the same word also means the opposite – 'work')

party (political) phák พรรค; political party phák kaan mueang พรรคการเมือง

pass, go past phàan ผ่าน

pass, to (exam) sàwp phàan สอบผ่าน (NOTE: to fail an exam is sàwp tòk สอบตก)

passenger phûu dohy săan ผู้โดยสาร

passion/mood (with feeling – this term can be used in either a positive or negative sense. NOTE: it also has 'sexual' overtones) aa-rom อารมณ์; passionate mii aa-rom mâak มีอารมณ์มาก

passionfruit (not particularly common in Thailand) sàò-wá-rót เสาวรส

passport năngsŭeh doehn thaang (literally, 'book'-'travel') หนังสือเดินทาง, (COLLOQUIAL) (from English) páat-sà-pàwt พาสปอร์ต

password/pin number rá-hàt รหัส

past, former à-dìit อดีต; 'in the past' nai à-dìit ในอดีต

pastime/hobby ngaan à-dìrèhk งานอดิเรก

patient (the ability to wait/ endure)/ to have patience òt thon อดทน

patient (sick person in hospital) khon khâi คนไข้

patron (client/customer) lûuk kháa ลูกค้า

pattern, design, style bàehp แบบ

patterned (i.e. to have a pattern – material, etc.) mii laai มีลาย

pavilion (common in Thailand – an airy, open structure where one can sit and relax) săa-laa ศาลา

pawn, to jam-nam (pronounced 'jum' as in 'jumble', and 'num' as in 'number')

103

จำนำ; a pawnshop rohng jam-nam โรงจำนำ

pay, to jàai จ่าย; to pay a bill jàai bin จ่ายบิล (Note: the word bin บิล is from English as is the word chék เช็ค given below). In higher class restaurants to ask to 'pay the bill' it is usual to say chék bin เช็คบิล. On the other hand when paying for a meal at a street stall, or at an ordinary cheap restaurant it is usual to say kèp tang dûai เก็บตังด้วย

pay attention to/ concentrate (on something) ao jai sài (literally, 'take'-'heart/mind'-'put') เอาใจใส่, tâng-jai ตั้งใจ

pay off (a debt) chái nîi ใช้หนี้

payment, a jàai ngoen จ่ายเงิน

peace (not war) sǎnti-phâap สันติภาพ

peaceful, to be sà-ngòp สงบ

peak, summit yâwt ยอด (Note: common colloquial usage – the word yâwt is used when checking the

balance of credit on one's mobile/cell phone. The expression for 'the balance' in such a case is yâwt ngoen ยอดเงิน)

peanut thùa lí-sǒng ถั่วลิสง

pearl khài múk ไข่มุก

pea(s) thùa ถั่ว

peasant (peasant farmer/rice farmer) chaaw naa ชาวนา

pedestrian crossing thaang máa laai ทางม้าลาย (Note: máa laai ม้าลาย means 'zebra')

pee/piss/urinate N, V (COLLOQUIAL) yîao เยี่ยว, or chìi ฉี่

peel, to (a piece of fruit) pàwk ปอก

pen, a pàak-kaa ปากกา

pencil, a din-sǎw ดินสอ

penis (COLLOQUIAL; extremely vulgar – equivalent of the English 'cock/dick/prick') khuai ควย, (COLLOQUIAL; but significantly less vulgar – the equivalent of something like 'willy') jǔu จู๋ (pronounced similar to the word 'Jew' but with a rising tone)

pension, a (government payment to retired workers) bîa bam-naan เบี้ยบำนาญ, or simply bam-naan บำนาญ

people/person khon คน, **(more broadly as in) 'the people/public'** prà-chaa-chon ประชาชน

pepper (i.e. black pepper) prík thai พริกไทย

pepper (chili pepper) prík พริก

percent/percentage (from English) poeh-sen เปอร์เซ็นต์

perfect sŏm-buun สมบูรณ์, or dii lôeht ดีเลิศ

perform, to (work/do work) (FORMAL) pàtìbàt ngaan ปฏิบัติ งาน (NOTE: the word 'do' tham is colloquially used – e.g. 'perform work/do work/ work' tham ngaan ทำงาน)

perfume náam hăwm **(literally, 'water'-'fragrant')** น้ำหอม

perhaps, maybe àat jà อาจ จะ, **(a common alternative is)** baang thii บางที

period (full stop - .) jòp จบ

period (menstrual) prá-jam duean ประจำเดือน, **(COLLOQUIAL) (from English – menstruation)** men เมนส์; **to be having one's period** pen men เป็นเมนส์

period (of time) ráyá wehlaa ระยะเวลา

permanent, to be thăa-wawn ถาวร

permit, a bai à-nú-yâat ใบ อนุญาต

permit/allow, to à-nú-yâat อนุญาต

person, a khon คน

personality bùk-khá-lík-kà-phâap บุคลิกภาพ

perspire/sweat, to ngùea àwk เหงื่อออก

pet (animal) sàt líang สัตว์เลี้ยง

petrol/gasoline náam man น้ำมัน

petrol station See 'gasoline/ gas'

pharmacy, drugstore, chemist ráan khăai yaa ร้านขายยา

Philippines fí líp-pin ฟีลิปปินส์

phlegm (mucous) sĕm-hà เสมหะ

phone *See* 'telephone'

photocopy, a săm-nao สำเนา

photocopy, to thăai săm-nao ถ่ายสำเนา

photograph rûup thàai รูปถ่าย

photograph, to thàai rûup ถ่ายรูป

pick, choose lûeak เลือก

pick up, to (e.g. to pick someone up from the airport) ráp รับ

pickpocket, a khà-mohy lúang krà-păo ขโมยล้วง กระเป๋า

pickpocket, to lúang krà-păo ล้วงกระเป๋า

picky *See* 'fussy'

picture, a (movie) năng หนัง

picture (general term used for both photographic and non-photographic images) rûup phâap รูปภาพ

piece, portion, section tawn ตอน (NOTE: commonly used in 'time expressions': e.g. tawn cháo ตอนเช้า '[in] the morning', tawn yen ตอน เย็น '[in] the evening')

piece (a piece or item) chín ชิ้น

pierce, penetrate thîm ทิ่ม

pig, a mŭu หมู

pigeon nók phí-râap นกพิราบ

pigtail (hairstyle) hăng pia หางเปีย; ponytail hăng máa (literally, 'tail'-'horse') หางม้า

pile, a (e.g. a pile of rubbish) kawng กอง

pill(s) mét yaa (literally, 'pill'-'medicine/drug') เม็ดยา

pillion (to ride – i.e sit behind the rider on a motorcycle) (COLLOQUIAL) sáwn tháai ซ้อน ท้าย

pillow/cushion, a măwn หมอน

pimp, procurer (SLANG) maehng-daa แมงดา

pimple(s) *See* 'acne'

pin number/PIN *See* 'password'

pinch (e.g. to pinch someone on the arm) yík หยิก

pineapple sap-pà-rót สับปะรด

pink sĭi chomphuu สีชมพู

pitcher, jug yùeak เหยือก

pity (to feel pity/sorry for someone) nâa sŏngsăan น่าสงสาร

106

place, a thîi ที่ (used in
conjunction with the name
of a particular place, e.g.) at
home thîi bâan ที่บ้าน; at a/
the store thîi ráan ที่ร้าน. Or
it can be used as follows: 'He
has a place' [this could refer
to a home/a piece of land,
etc.] khǎo mii thîi เขามีที่)

place/put (on) waang วาง

plain (clothing – not fancy)
rîap เรียบ

plain (level ground) thîi râap
ที่ราบ

plan, a (from English) N
phǎehn แผน

plan, to waang phǎehn
วางแผน

plane, a khrûeang bin เครื่อง
บิน

plant, a (general term covering
everything from a small plant
to a large tree) tôn mái ต้นไม้

plant, to plùuk ปลูก

plastic (from English;
pronounced either) pláat-
sàtìk or pláasòtìk พลาสติก

plastic or cosmetic
surgery sǎn-lá-yá-kam
ศัลยกรรม (in colloquial

speech often pronounced
sǎn-yá-kam)

plate, a jaan (pronounced
'jarn') จาน

play, to lên เล่น

playful, to be khîi lên ขี้เล่น

plead, to âwn wawn
อ้อนวอน

plead, to (in court – present
one's side of a case) hâi
kaan ให้การ

pleasant (in the sense of a
'pleasant atmosphere' –
somewhere where one feels
'relaxed and comfortable')
sà-baai jai สบายใจ

please (go ahead – 'come
in', 'sit down' etc.) choehn
(pronounced similar to the
word 'churn') เชิญ

please (request for help) chûai
ช่วย

please (request for something)
khǎw ขอ

please (to please someone/
attend to someone's needs/
wishes) ao jai sài (literally,
'take'-'heart'-'put') เอาใจใส่,
or simply ao jai เอาใจ

pleased, to be dii jai ดีใจ

pleasing, to be (to hit the spot) thùuk jai ถูกใจ; (colloquial; to be pleasing in the sense of) meeting all one's 'requirements', or 'specifications' thùuk sà-pék ถูกสะเป็ก (NOTE: the word here sà-pék สะเป็ก is from English)

pleasure khwaam sùk ความสุข

plenty (a lot) mâak maai มากมาย

plug (bath) plák ปลั๊ก

plug (electric) plák fai ปลั๊กไฟ

plus (as in '2 plus 2', or 'the price of the ticket, plus the hotel, plus the rental car') bùak บวก

pocket (also the word for 'bag' as in 'suitcase' or 'overnight travel bag', etc.) krà-pǎo กระเป๋า

point/dot, a jùt จุด

point (out), to chíi ชี้

poison yaa phít ยาพิษ

poisonous mii phít มีพิษ; a poisonous snake nguu mii phít งูมีพิษ

police tam-rùat ตำรวจ, (SLANG) chà-lǎam bòk (literally, 'shark'-'land' or 'land shark') ฉลามบก

police station sà-thǎa-nii tamrùat สถานีตำรวจ, (COLLOQUIAL) rohng phák โรงพัก

policy (i.e. government policy, the policy of a company) ná-yoh-baai นโยบาย

polish, to khàt ngao ขัดเงา, or simply khàt ขัด (pronounced like the English word 'cut', but with a low tone)

politics kaan mueang การเมือง; to be involved in politics lên kaan mueang (literally, 'play'-'politics') เล่นการเมือง; a politician nák kaan mueang นักการเมือง

polite, to be sù-phâap สุภาพ

poor, to be jon จน

ponytail (hairstyle) See 'pigtail'

popular pen thîi níyom เป็นที่นิยม

population (i.e. 'what is the population of Thailand?') prà-chaakawn ประชากร

porch/verandah rá-biang ระเบียง

pork núea mǔu เนื้อหมู

pornographic/porno/
porn (abbreviated from
English; colloquial) pó:h โป๊;
a pornographic film/DVD
etc. nǎng pó:h หนังโป๊; a
pornographic magazine/
book, etc. nǎngsǔeh pó:h
หนังสือโป๊ (NOTE: the word
pó:h is also commonly used
to describe someone who is
scantily dressed or revealing
more skin/flesh than
appropriate in public)

port/wharf/habour thâa ruea
ท่าเรือ

portion, serve thîi ที่; (e.g. in
a restaurant when ordering)
'two cups of coffee' kaa-faeh
sǎwng thîi กาแฟสองที่

pose, to (to pose for the
camera/strike a pose) waang
thâa วางท่า

position (in a organization)
tam-nàeng ตำแหน่ง;
position/posture (a bodily
position – e.g. yoga posture)
thâa ท่า

possess, to pen jâo khǎwng
เป็นเจ้าของ

possessions sǒmbàt สมบัติ,
(COLLOQUIAL) khâaw khǎwng
(literally, 'rice'-'thing(s)') ข้าว
ของ, or sìng khǎwng สิ่งของ

possible pen pai dâi เป็นไป
ได้ (NOTE: 'impossible' is pen
pai mâi dâi เป็นไปไม่ได้)

possibly See 'perhaps/
maybe'

post, pole, column sǎo เสา

post, mail jòt-mǎai จดหมาย

postcard prai-sà-nii-yá-bàt
ไปรษณียบัตร, or (from English)
pó:ht-sà-káat โปสการ์ด

post office prai-sà-nii
ไปรษณีย์

postpone, to lûean เลื่อน

postponed, delayed lûean
weh-laa เลื่อนเวลา

posture See 'position'

pot, a (for cooking) mâw หม้อ
(NOTE: also used as a slang
term for 'vagina')

potato man fàrang มันฝรั่ง, or
simply man มัน

poultry (i.e. chicken) kài ไก่

pour, to (a drink) rin ริน; to
pour water or some other
liquid over something râat
ราด (NOTE: this word is used,

109

for example, when food, such as curry, is served over/on top of rice – so, rather than having two dishes – one of rice and one of curry/or a stir-fry – there is but one dish [often translated in a menu] as râat khâaw ราดข้าว)

poverty (*also see* 'hardship') khwaam yâak jon ความยากจน

power am-nâat อำนาจ

powerful mii am-nâat มีอำนาจ

practice, to fùek hàt ฝึกหัด, or simply just fùek ฝึก

praise (COLLOQUIAL) chom ชม (the same word is also translated as 'admire')

praise/extol, to yók yâwng ยกย่อง

pram/stroller (for a baby/young child) rót khĕn dèk รถเข็นเด็ก

prawn/shrimp kûng กุ้ง

pray, to (Buddhist style) sùat mon สวดมนต์

pray, to (Christian style) à-thít-thăan อธิษฐาน

prayer, a bòt sùat mon บท สวดมนต์

precious/valuable mii khâa (literally, 'have'-'value') มีค่า

predict *See* 'forecast'

prefer, to châwp mâak kwàa (literally, 'like'-'more than') ชอบมากกว่า

pregnant tháwng ท้อง (NOTE: same word as 'stomach')

prejudice à-khá-tì อคติ, (COLLOQUIAL) 'to look down on someone' duu thùuk ดูถูก

prepare, make ready triam เตรียม

prepared/ready, to be (to do something) phráwm พร้อม

prescription, a (from a doctor) bai sàng yaa ใบสั่งยา

present (gift) khǎwng khwǎn ของขวัญ

present, to (a formal request, ideas – in a formal context) sà-nǒeh เสนอ

present moment, at the khà-nà ní ขณะนี้

presently, nowadays (formal – for colloquial see 'now') pàt-jù-ban-ní ปัจจุบันนี้

president (of a republic) prà-thaa-na thíp-baw-dii ประธานาธิบดี

press, to kòt กด

pressure khwaam kòt dan ความกดดัน Also see 'blood pressure'

pretend, to klâehng แกล้ง (NOTE: this is an interesting Thai word that also means 'to do something to someone else out of spite or malice', 'to annoy or tease')

pretty (of places, things) sǔai สวย

pretty, cute nâa rák น่ารัก

prevent, to pâwng kan ป้องกัน

previous/before kàwn ก่อน: e.g. to come/arrive before someone else maa kàwn มา ก่อน; previously tàeh kàwn แต่ก่อน

price raàkhaa ราคา

pride/dignity sàk-srǐi ศักดิ์ศรี

priest (Christian) bàat lǔang บาทหลวง

primary school rohng rian prà-thǒm โรงเรียนประถม; primary (school) education pràthǒm sèuk-sǎa ประถม ศึกษา

prime minister naàyók rát-

thà-montrii นายกรัฐมนตรี

prince jâo chaai เจ้าชาย

princess jâo yǐng เจ้าหญิง

print, to phim พิมพ์ (NOTE: the English word 'print' is now widely used – e.g. to print a document/photograph etc.) prín ปรินท์

prison (COLLOQUIAL) khúk คุก; to be imprisoned/jailed tìt khúk (literally, 'stuck'-'prison') ติดคุก

prisoner nák thôht นักโทษ

private (not public) sùan tua ส่วนตัว

prize/reward, a raang-wan รางวัล

probably See 'perhaps'

problem pan-hǎa ปัญหา, (COLLOQUIAL) 'no problem(s)/ no worries' mâi mii pan-hǎa ไม่มีปัญหา

procession See 'parade'

produce/manufacture, to phà-lìt ผลิต

profession aa-chîip อาชีพ; a professional mueh aa-chîip มืออาชีพ

professor sàat-traa-jaan ศาสตราจารย์

profit (on the sale of something) kam-rai ทำไร

profound (to have a deep meaning) léuk-séung ลึกซึ้ง, or (more colloquially simply) séung ซึ้ง

program (e.g. television progam, list of items – also see 'menu') raai-kaan รายการ

prohibit See 'forbid', 'forbidden'

project, a khrohng-kaan โครงการ

promise, to sănyaa สัญญา (Note: used as a noun this word means a 'contract')

pronounce, to àwk sĭang ออกเสียง

proof/evidence làk-thăan หลักฐาน

propaganda See 'advertise'

property sáp-sĭn ทรัพย์สิน Also see 'possessions'

prosper (develop) jà-roehn เจริญ; progress (in the sense of development to more complex, advanced society) khwaam jà-roehn ความ เจริญ

prosper (to do well) râm-ruai (râm pronounced like the English word 'rum') ร่ำรวย

prostitute sŏh-pheh-nii โสเภณี; also see 'hooker'

protest, to prà-thúang (Note: the syllable pra is very short) ประท้วง; a 'protest march' is doehn prà-thúang (literally, 'walk'-'protest') เดินประท้วง

proud, to be phuum-jai ภูมิใจ

prove, to phí-sùut พิสูจน์

province (administrative unit; there are presently 76 provinces in Thailand outside the Bangkok area) jang-wàt จังหวัด

prude/prudish – a 'fuddy-duddy' (i.e. to be opposed to liberal social ideas/ behaviour) châo rá-bìap เจ้าระเบียบ

psychiatrist jìt-tà-phâet (literally, 'mind/spirit'-'doctor') จิตแพทย์

pub (from English) phàp (pronounced similar to the English word 'pup') ผับ

pubic hair/pubes (VULGAR) mŏi หมอย

112

public săa-thaa rá-ná
สาธารณะ; a public place thîi
săa-thaa rá-ná ที่สาธารณะ

public relations prà-chaa
săm-phan ประชาสัมพันธ์
(NOTE: the same term is used
for both an 'information
booth/tourist information' and
'reception' in a hotel)

publish, to phim พิมพ์

pull, to dueng ดึง

pump, to v sùup สูบ; a pump
N khrûeang sùup เครื่องสูบ
(NOTE: the word sùup is also
used to mean 'smoke' as
in 'smoke a cigarette' sùup
bùrìi สูบบุหรี่)

punch (as in to 'punch'
someone) tòi ต่อย, or chók
ชก

punctual/on time trong
weh-laa ตรงเวลา

punish, to long thôht ลงโทษ

pupil/student nák rian
นักเรียน

pure/innocent bawrí-sùt
บริสุทธิ์

purple sĭi mûang สีม่วง

purpose (i.e. 'the purpose
is to increase literacy') jùt

mûng măai จุดมุ่งหมาย

purse (for money) krà-păo
ngoen กระเป๋าเงิน

pus (in a wound) năwng หนอง

push, to phlàk ผลัก, or dan
(pronounced like the word
'done') ดัน

put, place (as in 'put it on the
table') waang วาง

put off, delay, postpone
lûean เลื่อน

put on (clothes) sài ใส่

puzzled/confused, to be
ngong งง

pyjamas See 'pajamas'

Q

qualification khun-ná-
sŏmbàt คุณสมบัติ

quality (as in 'good quality
merchandise') khun-ná-
phâap คุณภาพ: e.g. 'good
quality' khun-ná-phâap dii
คุณภาพดี

quantity jam-nuan จำนวน

quarrel See 'argue'

quarter, a (¼) sèht nùeng
sùan sìi เศษหนึ่งส่วนสี่

queen prá raa-chí-nii พระ

113

ราชินี, or simply raa chí-nii ราชินี

question kham thăam คำถาม

queue, a (from English) khiu คิว; to line up in a queue khâo khiu (literally, 'enter'-'queue') เข้าคิว

quick, quickly rew เร็ว

quiet, to be ngîap เงียบ

quit/resign (to quit a job) laa àwk ลาออก; quit (as in 'stop' smoking or eating junk food) lôehk เลิก

quite (as in 'it's quite good') (COLLOQUIAL; 'it's quite pretty') tii diao ทีเดียว

quite, rather (e.g. 'it's quite/ rather good') khâwn khâang dii ค่อนข้างดี

R

rabbit, a krà-tàai กระต่าย

race (i.e. race of people – Caucasian, Asian, etc.) chúeah châat เชื้อชาติ

race, a (competition) kaan khaeng khăn การแข่งขัน

racism lát-thí yìat phĭu (literally, 'ism/doctrine'-'despise'-'skin') ลัทธิเหยียดผิว

radiation rang sĭi รังสี

radio wít-thá-yú วิทยุ

raft (also 'houseboat') phaeh แพ

rail: by rail/train dohy rótfai โดยรถไฟ

railroad, railway thaang rótfai ทางรถไฟ

rain n fŏn ฝน

rain, to fŏn tòk ฝนตก

raincoat sûea kan fŏn เสื้อกันฝน

raise, lift yók ยก

raise, to (children) líang เลี้ยง

rambutan ngá-w เงาะ

rancid, to be (foul smelling) mĕhn hŭehn เหม็นหืน

Rangoon (largest city in Burma) yâang kûng ย่างกุ้ง

rank (military, police) yót ยศ

rape v khòm khŭehn ข่มขืน

rapid (very quick) rûat rew รวดเร็ว

rare, to be (scarce) hăa yâak หายาก

rare (uncooked) dìp ดิบ

rarely, seldom, not often mâi bòi ไม่บ่อย

rash, a (skin complaint) phùen

114

ผื่น (NOTE: 'to have a rash' is
pen phùen เป็นผื่น)

rat/mouse, a นนู หนู

rate of exchange (for foreign
currency) àt-traa lâehk plìan
อัตราแลกเปลี่ยน

rather (i.e. 'rather big',
'rather expensive') khâwn
khâang.... ค่อนข้าง...

rational, to be (scientific;
reason as opposed to
superstition) mii hèht mii
phŏn มีเหตุมีผล, or simply
mii hèht phŏn มีเหตุผล

rattan (i.e. rattan furniture)
wăi หวาย

raw, uncooked dìp ดิบ

razor, a (for shaving) mîit
kohn มีดโกน (koon
pronounced like 'own' with a
'g' in front); a razor blade bai
mîit kohn ใบมีดโกน

reach/arrive, to thŭeng ถึง

react (to react to something)
mii pàtì-kì-rí-yaa มีปฏิกิริยา;
reaction, response pàtì-kì-rí-
yaa ปฏิกิริยา

read, to àan อ่าน

ready, to be phráwm พร้อม

ready, to get triam tua
เตรียมตัว

ready, to make tham hâi
phráwm ทำให้พร้อม

realize, be aware of rúu
tua รู้ตัว

real (to be genuine, not an
imitation) tháeh แท้; real (not
imaginary) khăwng jing
ของจริง

reality khwaam pen jing
ความเป็นจริง

really (in fact) thîi jing ที่จริง

really! (it's true) jing-jing
จริงๆ

really? (is that so?) jing rŭeh
จริงหรือ

rear (of the bus/plane/shop,
etc.) khâang lăng ข้างหลัง,
or dâan lăng ด้านหลัง

reason (as in a reason for
doing something) hèht phŏn
เหตุผล

reasonable/fair (price) phaw
sŏmkhuan พอสมควร

reasonable (appropriate)
má-w sŏm เหมาะสม

recall, to (an incident that
occurred/where some
missing object may be found)
núek àwk นึกออก

receipt, a bai sèt ใบเสร็จ

receive, to ráp รับ

recent, recently mûea rew-rew níi เมื่อเร็วๆ นี้

recipe sùut aà-hǎan สูตร อาหาร; recipe or cookbook tam-raa aà-hǎan ตำราอาหาร

recognize/remember, to jam dâi จำได้

recommend, to náenam แนะนำ

recover (to recover something) ao klàp kheun เอากลับคืน

recovered (to have (to be cured) hǎai láew (literally, 'disappear'-'already') หาย แล้ว

red sǐi daehng สีแดง

Red Cross, the (humanitarian organization) sà-phaa kaa-châat สภากาชาด

reduce, to (speed, weight, etc.) lót ลด

reflect, to (e.g. for light to reflect off the water) sà-tháwn สะท้อน

refreshment (i.e. a drink) khrûeang dùehm เครื่องดื่ม

refrigerator, a tûu yen (literally, 'cupboard'-'cold') ตู้เย็น

refugee, a phûu líi-phai ผู้ลี้ภัย

refuse/deny, to pàtì-sèht ปฏิเสธ; refusal kaan pàtì-sèht การปฏิเสธ

regarding/concerning kìao kàp เกี่ยวกับ

region (of a country – general geographic term) phuùmí-phâak ภูมิภาค (NOTE: Thailand has four major regions – the centre, the north, the north-east, and the south.) The word used to refer to 'region' is phâak ภาค, more commonly for the Central Region phâak klaang ภาคกลาง and the Northern Region phâak nǔea ภาคเหนือ. The Northeast Region is commonly referred to as ii-sǎan อีสาน, while Southern Thailand is pàk tâi (literally, 'part'-'south') ปักษ์ใต้.

register (a marriage etc.), to jòt thá-bian จดทะเบียน

registered post (i.e. registered letter) jòtmǎai long thá-bian จดหมายลงทะเบียน

regret, to (to feel sorry) sĭa jai เสียใจ, or sĭa daai เสียดาย

regrettably (what a pity!) nâa sĭa daai น่าเสียดาย

regular, normal pàkàtì ปกติ

relatives (family) yâat ญาติ

relax/rest, to phák phàwn พักผ่อน

release, to (let go/set free) plòi ปล่อย

reliable (trustworthy) wái waang-jai ไว้วางใจ

religion sàat-sà-nǎa ศาสนา

remainder, the (that which is left over) thîi lǔea ที่เหลือ

remedy wí-thii kaan rák-sǎa (literally, 'method'-'treat') วิธี การรักษา

remember, to jam (pronounce like 'jum' in 'jumble') จำ

remind, to tuean เตือน (also the word for 'to warn')

remove (take something out of...) aw àwk (literally, 'take'-'out') เอาออก

rent, to châo เช่า

rent out, to hâi châo ให้เช่า

repair, to (a car, etc.) sâwm ซ่อม

repeat, to tham sám (sám

pronounced similar to the English word 'sum') ทำซ้ำ; repeatedly sám-sám ซ้ำๆ

replace, to See 'instead'

reply/answer, to tàwp ตอบ

reply, to (in writing) khǐan tàwp เขียนตอบ

report, a/report, to N, v raai ngaan รายงาน

reporter See 'journalist'

request, to (in the sense of imploring someone to do something etc.) khǎw ráwng ขอร้อง

request, to (to ask for, as in 'can you....?') khǎw ขอ

require/want, to tâwng kaan ต้องการ

rescue/help, to chûai lǔea ช่วยเหลือ

research kaan wí-jai การวิจัย

research, to tham wí-jai ทำวิจัย

resemble, be similar to (COLLOQUIAL) duu khláai ดูคล้าย, also duu mǔean ดูเหมือน

reserve, to (a room in a hotel) jawng จอง

resident, inhabitant phûu aa-sǎi ผู้อาศัย

resign *See* 'quit'

resist, to tàw-tâan ต่อต้าน, or simply tâan ต้าน

resolve, to (a problem) kâeh panhăa แก้ปัญหา

respect N khwaam khao-róp ความเคารพ

respect, to (somebody) khao-róp เคารพ, or náp-thŭeh นับถือ

respond (FORMAL) tàwp sà-năwng ตอบสนอง

responsible, to be ráp phìt châwp รับผิดชอบ; responsibility N khwaam ráp phìt châwp ความรับผิดชอบ

rest (i.e. the remainder/what's left over) thîi lŭeah ที่เหลือ

rest/relax, to phák phàwn พักผ่อน

restaurant ráan aa-hăan ร้าน อาหาร

restless/agitated (COLLOQUIAL) yùu mâi sùk อยู่ไม่สุข

restrain, to dueng ao wái ดึงเอาไว้

restrict (limit availability/to be limited – time, etc.) jam-kàt จำกัด

restroom (bathroom) hâwng náam ห้องน้ำ

result (e.g. of a test, etc.) phŏn ผล

resulting from, as a result pen phŏn maa jàak… เป็น ผลมาจาก...

retail (price) *See* 'wholesale'

retarded (to be mentally retarded) panyaa àwn (literally, 'intellect'-'weak/soft') ปัญญาอ่อน

retired plòt kà-sĭan ปลด เกษียณ, or (MORE COLLOQUIALLY) kà-sĭan aa-yú เกษียณอายุ

return/go back, to klàp กลับ

return home, to klàp bâan กลับบ้าน

return ticket, a tŭa pai klàp (literally, 'ticket'-'go'-'return') ตั๋วไปกลับ

return, to give back khuehn คืน

reveal, to (make known/to be open – not keeping secrets) pòeht phŏei เปิดเผย

reverse, back up, to thŏi lăng ถอยหลัง, or simply thŏi ถอย

reversed, backwards, inside out klàp khâang กลับข้าง

118

revolt/rebellion/coup d'état, a pàtìwát ปฏิวัติ

revolting/disgusting, to be nâa rang-kìat น่ารังเกียจ, or khà-yà khà-yǎehng ขยะแขยง

reward/prize, a rang-wan รางวัล

rhythm See 'tempo'

rice (cooked) khâaw sǔai ข้าวสวย

rice (uncooked) khâaw sǎan ข้าวสาร

rice (food) khâaw ข้าว

rice fields (irrigated) naa นา

rich/wealthy, to be ruai รวย

rid: get rid of/eliminate (pests, termites etc.) kamjàt กำจัด

ride (in car) nâng rót นั่งรถ

ride, to (on a bicycle, an animal) khìi ขี่

ridiculous (meaningless) rái sǎará ไร้สาระ

right/correct, to be thùuk ถูก, or thùuk tâwng ถูกต้อง

right (right-hand side) khwǎa ขวา; to be right-handed thànàt mueh khwǎa ถนัดมือขวา

rights sìt-thí สิทธิ (often pronounced as simply sìt สิทธิ)

right now dǐao níi เดี๋ยวนี้

rind/peel (i.e. orange peel) plùek เปลือก, (also the general word for) 'bark' on a tree, e.g. plùek mái เปลือกไม้

ring (jewelry) wǎehn แหวน

ring (boxing ring), stage (for performances) weh-thii เวที

ring, to (to ring someone on the phone) thoh pai โทรไป

ring, to (doorbell) kòt krìng กดกริ่ง

rinse/wash (plates, hands, etc.) láang ล้าง: e.g. wash your face láang nâa ล้างหน้า

riot, a jà-laàjon จลาจล

rip/tear, to chìik ฉีก

ripe, to be (of fruit) sùk สุก

rise, ascend khûen ขึ้น

rise, increase, to phôehm khûen เพิ่มขึ้น

risk/risky sìang เสี่ยง

ritual/ceremony phí-thii พิธี

rival khûu khàeng คู่แข่ง

river mâeh náam (literally, 'mother'–'water') แม่น้ำ

road/street (major thoroughfare) thà-nǒn ถนน

roast, grill, BBQ yâang ย่าง

roasted, toasted pîng ปิ้ง

rob, to (a bank) plôn ปล้น; to rob (a person/to hold someone up) jîi จี้

robot, a hùn yon หุ่นยนต์

rock, a hǐn หิน

rocket, a jà-rùat จรวด

role (a role in a movie, the role of the press, etc.) bòt bàat บทบาท

roll (to roll over) klîng กลิ้ง

roll, a (as in a roll of toilet paper) múan ม้วน; to roll/make a cigarette muan bùrìi มวนบุหรี่

roof lǎng khaa หลังคา

room, a (in house/hotel, etc.) hâwng ห้อง

room (to have some free space/extra room) thîi wâang ที่ว่าง

root (of plant or a tooth) râak ราก

rope/string chûeak เชือก

rose (flower) kù-làap กุหลาบ

rotten, to be nâo เน่า

rough (as in a rough road/an unshaven face) khrù khrà ขรุขระ

roughly, approximately prà-maan ประมาณ

round (shape) klom กลม

round, around, surrounding râwp-râwp รอบๆ

routine ngaan prà-jam (literally, 'work'-'regular') งานประจำ

rub (also 'scrub') thǔu ถู

rubber yaang ยาง

rubber band (COLLOQUIAL) nǎng yaang หนังยาง

rubbish khà-yà ขยะ; rubbish bin thǎng khà-yà ถังขยะ

ruby tháp-thim ทับทิม (the word also means 'pomegranate'). NOTE: mét tháp-thim เม็ดทับทิม is slang for 'clitoris' (literally, 'seed'-'ruby')

rude/crude/coarse (speech/behaviour) yàap khaai หยาบคาย, also mâi sù-phâap ไม่สุภาพ

rules kòt กฎ

rumour khàaw lueh ข่าวลือ

run, to wîng วิ่ง

run away (i.e. to flee) wîng nǐi วิ่งหนี

rural (the countryside) chon-

nábòt ชนบท, (COLLOQUIAL)
bâan nâwk บ้านนอก
rust N sà-nǐm สนิม; to rust
sà-nǐm khûen สนิมขึ้น

S

sack (to dismiss an employee)
See 'fire'
sack (bag – e.g. sack of rice)
krà-sàwp กระสอบ
sacred/sacrosanct sàk-sìt
ศักดิ์สิทธิ์
sacrifice, to sǐa sàlà- เสีย
สละ; sacrifice kaan sǐa sàlà-
การเสียสละ
sad, to be sâo เศร้า
safe plàwt-phai ปลอดภัย;
safety khwaam plàwt-phai
ความปลอดภัย
safe, a (for keeping valuables
– from English) tûu sép ตู้เซฟ
sago (food) sǎ-khuu สาคู
sail, to (a yacht) lâen ruea
แล่นเรือ
salad (from English) sà-làt
สลัด; *also see* 'lettuce'
salary ngoen duean เงินเดือน
sale, for (also 'sell') khǎai ขาย
sale (reduced prices) lót raa-

khaa ลดราคา
sales assistant phá-nák-
ngaan khǎai พนักงานขาย
saliva (spittle) náam laai
น้ำลาย
salt kluea เกลือ
salt-water (sea water) náam
khem น้ำเค็ม
salty (taste) khem เค็ม
same, the mǔean เหมือน
sample/example tua yàang
ตัวอย่าง
sand saai ทราย
sandals rawng tháo tàe
รองเท้าแตะ
satay (grilled/BBQ meat/
chicken, etc. on a wooden
skewer) sà-téh สะเต๊ะ; satay
stick(s) mái sà-téh ไม้สะเต๊ะ
satisfied pen thîi phaw jai
เป็นที่พอใจ, or simply phaw
jai พอใจ; to satisfy someone
tham hâi phaw jai ทำให้
พอใจ
Saturday wan sǎo วันเสาร์
sauce (from English) sáwt ซอส
sauce (dipping sauce – spicy,
sweet/sour, etc.) nám jîm
น้ำจิ้ม
save, keep kèp เก็บ; to save

money **(to put in the bank)**
kèp ngoen เก็บเงิน

saw, a **(tool)** lûeai เลื่อย

say, to **(that...)** phûut wâa
พูดว่า

scales **N** taa châng ตาชั่ง

scandal, a rûeang êuh
chǎaw เรื่องอื้อฉาว

scanner, a **(from English)**
khrûeang sà-kaen เครื่อง
สแกน

scar, a phlǎeh pen แผลเป็น

scare, to **(to scare someone)**
tham hâi tòk-jai ทำให้ตกใจ

scarce mâi khôi mii ไม่
ค่อยมี, or hǎa yâak **(literally,
'find'-'difficult')** หายาก

scared/'to be scary' nâa
klua น่ากลัว

scarf, a phâa phan khaw
**(literally, 'cloth'-'wrap
around'-'neck')** ผ้าพันคอ

scenery, view **(from English)**
wiu วิว

schedule kam-nòt กำหนด

scholarship thun lâo rian
ทุนเล่าเรียน, or thun kaan
sèuk-sǎa ทุนการศึกษา

school, a rohng-rian
โรงเรียน

schoolchild, a dèk nák-rian
เด็กนักเรียน

science wít-thá-yaa-sàat
วิทยาศาสตร์

scissors kan-krai กรรไกร

scold/berate, to wâa ว่า

Scotland sà-káwt-laehn
สก็อตแลนด์

Scottish, Scots chaaw
sà-káwt ชาวสก็อต

scrap **(scrap of food, scrap of
paper, something left over,
etc.)** sèht เศษ: e.g. scrap of
food sèht aa-hǎan เศษอาหาร

scrape **(e.g. scrape paint off
something)** khùut ขูด

scratch **(scratch an itch)**
kao เกา, also **(aggressively
scratched – by someone with
long fingernails, a cat etc.)**
khùan ข่วน; a scratch **(e.g.
on a car)** roi khùut รอยขูด

scream, to ráwng kríit ร้อง
กรี๊ด

screen **(of computer or
television)** jaw **(pronounced
like the English word 'jaw')** จอ

screw **(COLLOQUIAL – used
with a screwdriver)** náwt
(pronounced very similar to

the word 'not') นอต

screwdriver khăi khuang ไขควง

scrub, to thŭu ถู; pân pân ปั่น ปั่น

sculpt, to pân ปั้น

sculpture rûup pân รูปปั้น

sea thá-leh ทะเล

seafood aa-hăan thá-leh อาหารทะเล

search for/look for/seek, to hăa หา; to ask 'what are you looking for?' khun hăa àrai (literally, 'you'-'look for'-'what') คุณหาอะไร

season rúe-duu ฤดู, or (MORE COLLOQUIALLY) nâa หน้า (NOTE: the same word as 'face', 'page of a book', etc.); summer/hot season nâa ráwn (literally, 'season'-'hot') หน้าร้อน (In Thailand the 'high season', in terms of tourist arrivals (Nov-Feb), is colloquially referred to as nâa hai หน้าไฮ)

seat, a thîi nâng ที่นั่ง

second (measure of time) wí-naa-thii วินาที

second (as in 2nd) thîi săwng ที่สอง

secondhand (e.g. a used car) mueh săwng มือสอง; a used car rót mueh săwng (literally, 'car/vehicle'-'hand'-'two') รถ มือสอง

secret, a khwaam láp ความ ลับ

secret, to keep a ráksăa khwaam láp รักษาความลับ

secretary lêh-khăa nú-kaan เลขานุการ, or (COLLOQUIALLY SIMPLY) leh-khăa เลขา

section/segment, a (of something) tawn ตอน

secure/stable, to be mân-khong มั่นคง

seduce, to lâw-jai ล่อใจ

see, to hĕn เห็น

seed, a má-lét เมล็ด (although commonly pronounced mét)

seek, to See 'search'

seem, to (it might rain) duu mŭean ดูเหมือน

see you later! phóp kan mài พบกันใหม่

seldom (or 'not often') mâi bòi ไม่บ่อย

select/choose, to lûeak เลือก

self ehng เอง, or tua ehng ตัวเอง

self-assured mân-jai tua ehng มั่นใจตัวเอง

selfish, to be hĕn kàe tua เห็นแก่ตัว

sell, to khăi ขาย

semen/sperm (medical term) náam à-sù-jì น้ำอสุจิ, also náam kaam น้ำกาม

send, to sòng ส่ง

sensible/reasonable, to be mii hèht phŏn มีเหตุผล

sensitive (tender feeling – physical) rúu-sùek wai รู้สึกไว

sentence (in written language) prà-yòhk ประโยค

separate, to yâehk แยก

September kan-yaa-yon กันยายน

sequence/order taam lam-dàp ตามลำดับ

serious, to be (i.e. not joking) ao jing เอาจริง

serious (severe) ráay raehng ร้ายแรง

servant khon chái คนใช้

serve, to (somebody) ráp chái รับใช้

service bawrí-kaan บริการ

sesame seeds ngaa งา; sesame oil náam-man ngaa

น้ำมันงา

set, a (a set of something – clothes, crockery, etc.) chút ชุด

seven jèt เจ็ด

seventeen sìp jèt สิบเจ็ด

seventy jèt sìp เจ็ดสิบ

several/many lăi หลาย

severe/violent run raehng รุนแรง

sew, to yép เย็บ

sex, gender phêht เพศ

sex, sexual activity (POLITE) rûam phêht ร่วมเพศ; (COLLOQUIAL) 'to have sex' ao kan เอากัน; 'sleep together' nawn dûai kan (literally, 'lie down'-'together') นอนด้วยกัน; (SLANG – vulgar and extremely rude) 'to fuck' yét เย็ด (NOTE: the English word 'sex' is widely known and pronounced sék เซ็กส์)

sexy See 'hot'

shack krà-thâwm กระท่อม

shade (the shade of a tree) rôm ร่ม

shadow, a ngao เงา

shake something, to khà-yào เขย่า

124

shake (e.g. for one's legs to shake) sàn sàn สั่น สั่น

shake (to shake hands with someone) jàp mueh kan จับมือกัน

shall, will (indicator of future tense/action) jà จะ: e.g. will/shall go jà pai จะไป

shallow (opposite of 'deep') tûehn ตื้น

shame N khwaam lá-aai jai ความละอายใจ

shame (as in 'what a shame!') nâa khăai nâa น่าขายหน้า

shampoo (hair shampoo) yaa sà phŏm ยาสระผม

shape (the shape of something) rûup รูป

shapely (i.e. to have a good figure) hùn dii หุ่นดี

shark plaa chà-lăam ปลาฉลาม, or simply chà-lăam ฉลาม

sharp, to be khom คม

sharp-tongued, to be (vitriolic) (COLLOQUIAL) pàak jàt ปากจัด

shave, to kohn โกน

she/her khăo เขา (NOTE: the same term is also used for

'he/him' and 'they')

sheep kàe แกะ

sheet (of paper) phàen krà-dàat แผ่นกระดาษ

sheet (for bed, i.e. bedsheet) phâa puu thîi nawn ผ้าปูที่นอน

shelf/shelves (for books) chán năng-sŭeh ชั้นหนังสือ

shell, a plùeak hŏi เปลือกหอย, (COLLOQUIAL SIMPLY) hŏi หอย

shift (as in a 'shift at work'/'night shift', etc.) wehn เวร: e.g. the 'night shift' wehn klaang kheun เวรกลางคืน, OR (MORE COLLOQUIALLY) 'a shift' (either day or night) kà กะ

shingles (medical condition) rôhk nguu sà-wàt โรคงูสวัด

shiny (skin/shoes, etc.) pen man เป็นมัน

ship, a ruea เรือ

shirt sûea chóeht (chóeht from English 'shirt') เสื้อเชิ้ต

shit See 'excrement'

shiver, to tua sàn ตัวสั่น

shock, to be in a 'state of shock') tòk tàleung ตกตะลึง, or aa-kaan cháwk (cháwk

125

from English 'shock') อาการ
ช็อก

shoe(s) rawng tháo รองเท้า

shoot, to (with a gun) ying ยิง

shop/store, a ráan ร้าน

shop, go shopping pai súeh
kháwng ไปซื้อของ – also
very common particularly
with reference to going to
a supermarket/department
store/mall (from English)
cháwp ช้อป, or cháwp-pîng
ชอปปิ้ง

shopkeeper jâo kháwng
ráan เจ้าของร้าน

short (dress/piece of writing,
etc.) sân สั้น

short (not tall) tîa เตี้ย

shortcut (get somewhere by
shortest route) thaang lát
ทางลัด

shorts (short trousers) kaang-
kehng kháa sân กางเกง
ขาสั้น

shorts (i.e. underpants/boxer
shorts) kaang-kehng nai
กางเกงใน

shoulder bàa บ่า

shout, to tà-kohn ตะโกน

show, to (e.g. one's feeling;

to perform in a film/play/live
performance etc.) sà-daehng
แสดง

show, a (live performance)
kaan sà-daehng sòt การ
แสดงสด

shower, a (in the bathroom)
fàk bua ฝักบัว

shower (or bath), to take
a àap náam อาบน้ำ

shrimp/prawn kûng กุ้ง

shrimp (prawn) paste kàpì
กะปิ

shrine, a sáan jâo ศาลเจ้า

shut/close, to; closed
pìt ปิด

shut up! (SLANG) hùp pàak
หุบปาก, or ngîap เงียบ

shy/bashful, to be aai; a
very shy person khon khîi
aai คนขี้อาย

sibling (older) phîi พี่ Also see
'older brother/sister'

sibling (younger) náwng น้อง

sick, ill pùai ป่วย, or simply
mâi sàbaai ไม่สบาย

side kháang ข้าง, also
(commonly used) dâan ด้าน

side effect(s) (of medicine/a
drug) phðn kháang khiang

126

ผลข้างเคียง

sightseeing, to go pai thát-sá-naa-jawn ไปทัศนาจร

sign/poster/placard, a (ranging from small to very large) pâai ป้าย

sign, to sen เซ็น; to sign your name sen chûeh เซ็นชื่อ

signal, a (radio signal, etc.) săn-yaan สัญญาณ

signature, a laai sen ลายเซ็น

significant/important săm-khan สำคัญ

silent, to be ngîap เงียบ

silk măi ไหม; silk cloth phâa măi ผ้าไหม

silly, to be (difficult to readily convey in Thai the sense this word is commonly used in English – arguably, the Thai for 'without reason/irrational' is acceptable, although somewhat formal; the word for 'stupid' would be simply too strong): rái hèht-phŏn ไร้เหตุผล

silver (metal) ngoen เงิน (NOTE: the same word as 'money'); silver (the colour) sĭi ngoen สีเงิน

similar, to be khláai คล้าย, or mŭean เหมือน

simple/easy, to be ngâai ง่าย

since tâng-tàeh ตั้งแต่

sincere jing-jai (literally, 'real/true'-'heart/mind') จริงใจ

sing, to ráwng phlehng (literally, 'sing'-'song') ร้องเพลง

singer, a nák ráwng นักร้อง

Singapore sĭngkhá-poh สิงคโปร์

single, to be (not married) sòht โสด

single (i.e. one person) khon diao คนเดียว; just the one/single (thing) yàang diao อย่างเดียว

singlet/undershirt See 'vest'

sink/sunk (also 'drown') jom จม

sink (for washing up), also 'bathtub' àang náam อ่างน้ำ

sir (a polite form of address to, or talking about a higher status person – 'you', 'he/she') thâan ท่าน

sister (older) phîi săaw พี่สาว

sister (younger) náwng săaw น้องสาว

127

sister-in-law (older) phîi sà-phái พี่สะใภ้

sister-in-law (younger) náwng sà-phái น้องสะใภ้

sit, to nâng นั่ง

sit down, to nâng long nâng ลง นั่งลง

situated, to be tâng yùu ตั้งอยู่

situation (e.g. political situation, etc.) sà-thăan-nákaan สถานการณ์

six hòk หก

sixteen sìp hòk สิบหก

sixty hòk sìp หกสิบ

size khà-nàat ขนาด (NOTE: the English word 'size' is also used in Thai: sái ไซส์)

skewer, a mái sìap ไม้เสียบ

ski (from English – noun/verb) sà-khii สกี; waterski sà-khii náam สกีน้ำ; jet ski jet sà-khii เจ็ตสกี

skilful mii tháksà มีทักษะ; (COLLOQUIAL) the word for 'clever/adept' – kèng เก่ง

skill (COLLOQUIAL) fíi mueh ฝีมือ

skin phǐu-năng ผิวหนัง, or simply phǐu ผิว

skirt krà-prohng กระโปรง

skull hǔa kà-lòhk หัวกะโหลก

sky fáa ฟ้า

slang phaa-săa tà-làat (literally, 'language'–'market') ภาษาตลาด (the English word 'slang' is also used sà-laeng สแลง)

sleep, to nawn làp นอนหลับ

sleepy, to be ngûang-nawn ง่วงนอน, or simply ngûang ง่วง

slender (but shapely) sà-òht sà-ong สะโอดสะอง

slice (slice/piece of cake, etc.) chín ชิ้น

slightly, a little bit nít nòi นิดหน่อย

slim/thin, to be phǎwm ผอม

slip, to; slippery (surface) lûehn ลื่น

slip (petticoat, underskirt – from English) sà-líp สลิป

slippers/flip flops/thongs rawng tháo tàe รองเท้าแตะ

slope lâat khǎo ลาดเขา

sloppy/slovenly (work) sà-phrâo สะเพร่า

slow, to be cháa ช้า; (to speak/drive) slowly cháa cháa ช้าๆ

slum, a chum-chon aeh-àt ชุมชนแออัด, (also from

English – pronounced similar to the English but with two syllables) sà-lam สลัม

small, to be (in size) lék เล็ก

smart chà-làat ฉลาด (NOTE: sometimes used, somewhat ironically, to refer to someone else's 'cleverness' to 'further their own interests')

smartphone See 'mobile/cell phone'

smell, to have a bad odor (also see 'stink') mii klìn มีกลิ่น

smell/sniff, to (something) dom ดม

smelling salts yaa dom (literally, 'medicine/drug'-'smell') ยาดม

smile, to yím ยิ้ม

smoke N khwan ควัน

smoke, to (tobacco) sùup สูบ (NOTE: the English work 'smoke' pronounced sà-móke สโม๊ก is sometimes used to refer to oral sex (i.e. fellatio))

smooth (to go smoothly) râap rûehn ราบรื่น

smooth, to (of surfaces) rîap เรียบ

SMS/sms (texting) (from English) es-em-es เอสเอ็มเอส

smuggle, to lák lâwp ลักลอบ

snail, a thâak ทาก

snake, a nguu งู

snatch See 'grab'

sneeze, to jaam จาม

sniff/snort (a substance) nát นัด

snore, to kron กรน

snow hì-má หิมะ

snow, to hì-má tòk หิมะตก

snowpeas thùa lan-tao ถั่วลันเตา

so, therefore dang nán ดังนั้น

soak, to jùm จุ่ม, or châeh แช่

soap sà-bùu สบู่

sober, to be mâi mao ไม่เมา

soccer (from English) fút bawn ฟุตบอล, (COLLOQUIAL) bawn บอล

society săng-khom สังคม; sociable châwp săng-khom ชอบสังคม

socket (electric)/powerpoint thîi sìap plák ที่เสียบปลั๊ก

socks thǔng tháo ถุงเท้า

sofa, couch (from English) soh-faa โซฟา

soft (to the touch): for skin nîm

129

นิ่ม; for cloth, etc. nûm นุ่ม

soft drink (a fizzy drink) náam àt lom น้ำอัดลม

sold khăai láew (literally, 'sell'-'already') ขายแล้ว

soldier thá-hǎan ทหาร

sold out khăai mòt láew ขายหมดแล้ว

sole (of the foot) fàa tháo ฝ่าเท้า (Note: palm (of hand) fàa mueh ฝ่ามือ)

solid khǎwng khǎeng ของแข็ง

solve/to (a problem) kâeh panhǎa แก้ปัญหา

some, partly bâang บ้าง

somebody, someone baang khon บางคน

something baang yàang บางอย่าง

sometimes baang thii บางที

somewhere/some place baang hàeng บางแห่ง

son lûuk chaai ลูกชาย

son-in-law lûuk khǒei ลูกเขย

song, a phlehng เพลง

soon nai mâi cháa ในไม่ช้า

sore/painful, to be jèp เจ็บ

sorrow/to be sad sâo เศร้า

sorry, to feel regretful sĭa jai เสียใจ

sorry! khǎw thôht ขอโทษ

sort, type chá-nít ชนิด

sort out, deal with, arrange jàt kaan จัดการ

sound/noise, a sĭang เสียง

soul/spirit win-yaan วิญญาณ

soup (from English) súp ซุป, (clear soup) náam súp น้ำซุป

sour (taste) prîao เปรี้ยว (As a slang, this word is also used to describe young women who dress and act with little trace of modesty)

source/cause/reason (e.g. of/for a problem) sǎahèht สาเหตุ

south (direction) tâi ใต้

south-east tà-wan àwk chǐang tâi ตะวันออกเฉียงใต้

Southeast Asia eh-sia aa-khá-neh เอเชียอาคเนย์

south-west tà-wan tòk chǐang tâi ตะวันตกเฉียงใต้

souvenir, a khǎwng thîi rálúek ของที่ระลึก

soybean(s) thùa lǔeang ถั่วเหลือง, or (more commonly – e.g. when referring to tofu) tâo hûu เต้าหู้; soyabean milk náam tâo hûu น้ำเต้าหู้

soy sauce **(salty)** sii-íu ซีอิ๊ว

soy sauce **(sweet)** sii-íu wǎan ซีอิ๊วหวาน

space, a **(a physical space or gap)** châwng wâang ช่องว่าง

space **(outer)** à-wá-kàat อวกาศ

spacious thîi kwâang ที่ว้าง

spade/shovel phlûa พลั่ว

sparrow **(ubiquitous small bird)** nók krà-jàwk นก กระจอก (NOTE: the word kràjàwk กระจอก which, by itself, means 'small/petty' is also used as a slang term to mean 'crappy/lousy/shitty' to describe something of very poor quality)

speak, to phûut พูด

special, to be phí-sèht พิเศษ

specific/in particular dohy chà phá-w โดยเฉพาะ

specimen/example tua yàang ตัวอย่าง

spectacles/glasses wâen taa แว่นตา

speech, a kham praa-sǎi คำ ปราศรัย

speed khwaam rew ความเร็ว

speedboat ruea rew เรือเร็ว,

(from English) sà-pìit bóht สปีดโบ๊ท

spell, to **(a word)** sà-kòt สะกด

spell, a **(magical incantation)** khaa-thǎa คาถา

spend, to **(as in 'spend money/time')** chái ใช้: e.g. spend money chái ngoen ใช้เงิน

sperm *See* 'semen'

spew *See* 'vomit'

spices khrûeang thêht เครื่อง เทศ

spicy phèt เผ็ด

spider maehng mum แมงมุม; spider web yai maehng mum ใยแมงมุม

spill, to **(to spill a glass of water)** tham hòk ทำหก

spin pàn ปั่น (e.g. used in making a 'milkshake', 'pedalling a bicycle' etc.) ปั่น; a milkshake/fruit shake/a 'smoothie' náam pàn น้ำปั่น, mǔn (more general term for 'spin'; also means 'dial' for old style telephones) หมุน

spinach phàk khǒhm ผักโขม

spine krà-dùuk sǎn lǎng กระดูกสันหลัง

spirit *See* 'soul'

spirit house **(found everywhere in Thailand – to propitiate the local spirits)** săan phrá-phuum ศาล พระภูมิ

spirits, hard liquor lâo เหล้า

spoiled **(of food)** sĭa เสีย

spokesman/spokeswoman/ spokesperson khoh-sòk โฆษก

sponge, a fawng náam ฟองน้ำ

spoon, a cháwn ช้อน

sport(s) kii-laa กีฬา

spot **(small mark)** jùt จุด

spotted **(pattern)** laai jùt ลายจุด

spouse **(husband or wife)** khûu sŏm-rót (literally, 'pair'- 'marriage') คู่สมรส

spray **(i.e. to spray something)** e.g. mosquito repellent: sà-preh สเปรย์, (from English) chìit sà-preh ฉีดสเปรย์

spring **(metal part) (from English)** sà-pring สปริง

square **(shape)** sìi lìam สี่เหลี่ยม

square **(as in Tiananmen Square)** jà-tùrát จัตุรัส

squid/calamari plaa mùek ปลาหมึก

squirrel, a krà-râwk กระรอก

stab, to thaeng แทง

stable/secure mân-khong มั่นคง

staff **(member in a store)** phá- nák-ngaan พนักงาน

stage **(for performances, also 'boxing ring')** weh-thii เวที

stagger **(e.g. stagger along drunk)** doehn soh-seh เดิน โซเซ

stain, a roi pûean รอยเปื้อน

stairs ban-dai บันได

stall **(of vendor)** phǎehng khǎai khǎwng แผงขายของ

stamp **(ink)** traa pám ตราปั๊ม

stamp **(postage – from English)** sà-taehm แสตมป์

stand, to yuehn ยืน

stand up, to lúk khûen ลุกขึ้น

standard **(i.e. commercial/ legal standard)** mâat-trà- thǎan มาตรฐาน

stapler **(for stapling pieces of paper) (COLLOQUIAL)** máek แม็ก

star, a **(in the heavens)** daaw ดาว (NOTE: also used in the

English sense of a famous
person or celebrity)

stare, to (to stare at someone)
mawng มอง, or jâwng จ้อง

start/begin, to rôehm เริ่ม

stationery khrûeang khǐan
เครื่องเขียน

statue rûup pân รูปปั้น

status (financial status) thǎa-
ná ฐานะ

stay, to (somewhere) yùu อยู่,
or phák yùu พักอยู่ (NOTE:
'Where are you staying?'
('you' understood) is phák
yùu thîi nǎi พักอยู่ที่ไหน)

stay/remain, to yùu kàp thîi
อยู่กับที่

stay overnight, to kháang
khuehn ค้างคืน

steal v khà-mohy ขโมย (NOTE:
the same word is also a noun
meaning 'a thief/thieves')

steam ai náam ไอน้ำ

steam, to; steamed (e.g.
rice) nûeng นึ่ง

steel lèk เหล็ก

steep, to be (e.g. a steep hill)
chan ชัน

steer, to mǔn phuang maa-
lai หมุนพวงมาลัย

steering wheel phuang
maa-lai พวงมาลัย

step, a (when walking) kâaw
ก้าว

step, to (on something) yìap
เหยียบ

steps, stairs bandai บันได

stepfather phâw líang พ่อ
เลี้ยง; stepmother mâeh
líang แม่เลี้ยง

sterile, to be (unable to have
children) pen mǎn เป็นหมัน

stick, branch of tree gìng
mái กิ่งไม้; a walking stick
mái tháo ไม้เท้า

stick out, to yûehn àwk maa
ยื่นออกมา

stick to, to tìt kàp ติดกับ

sticky, to be nǐao เหนียว

sticky rice khâaw nǐao ข้าว
เหนียว

stiff (as in 'hard'/opposite of
'flexible') khǎeng แข็ง

still, even now yang ยัง: e.g.
(he's) 'still in Thailand' yang
yùu mueang thai (literally,
'still'-'stay/be located'-
'Thailand') ยังอยู่เมืองไทย

sting, to (burning/stinging
sensation) sàep แสบ

stink, to měn เหม็น

stir, to (a liquid/when cooking etc.) khon คน, or kuan กวน

stock market tà-làat hûn (literally, 'market'-'share(s)') ตลาดหุ้น

stomach tháwng ท้อง (NOTE: also the word for 'pregnant')

stone (material) hĭn หิน; a stone/rock kâwn hĭn ก้อนหิน

stool See 'excrement'

stop (i.e. a bus stop) pâai rót-meh ป้ายรถเมล์

stop (to halt) yùt หยุด

stop, to (cease doing something) lôehk เลิก

stop by, pay a visit, pop in and see someone, to wáe แวะ

stop it! yùt ná หยุดนะ

store, to (to collect – e.g. collect stamps) sà-sŏm สะสม

storey (of a building) chán ชั้น

storm phaa-yú พายุ

story (tale) rûeang เรื่อง

stout (plump) oûan อ้วน, (COLLOQUIAL/PLAYFUL) pûm pûi ปุ้มปุ้ย

stove/charcoal cooker, a tao เตา

straight (not crooked) trong ตรง

straight ahead trong pai khâang nâa ตรงไปข้างหน้า

strait(s) (geographical feature, e.g. Straits of Hormuz) châwng khâehp ช่องแคบ

strange/unusual/weird plàehk แปลก

stranger, a khon plàehk nâa (literally, 'person'-'strange'-'face') คนแปลกหน้า

straw, a (for drinking) làwt หลอด

stream, a (water course) lam-thaan ลำธาร

street/road, a thà-nŏn ถนน

strength, power kamlang กำลัง

stress/stressful khwaam khrîat ความเครียด, or simply khrîat เครียด

stretch, to yûeht ยืด

strict, to be khrêng khrát เคร่งครัด

strike/protest prà-thúang ประท้วง

strike, hit tii ตี

string/rope chûeak เชือก

strip (take clothes off) kâeh phâa แก้ผ้า

striped mii laai มีลาย (more generally, this also means 'to have a pattern/design' on material/surface)

strong khǎeng raehng แข็งแรง

structure (e.g. the structure of a building/of society) khrohng sâang โครงสร้าง

stubborn, to be dûeh ดื้อ

stuck, to be (i.e. won't move) tìt ติด

student nák-rian นักเรียน

study/learn, to rian เรียน

stuffy (hot, airless atmosphere) òb âaw อบอ้าว

stupid ngôh โง่

style/design bàehp แบบ (the English word 'style' is also used in various ways – e.g. for clothing and behaviour etc. – but pronounced in the Thai way sàty/sàtai สไตล์)

stylish/fashionable/ modern, to be than sà-mǎi ทันสมัย

submarine N ruea dam náam เรือดำน้ำ

succeed, to sǎmrèt สำเร็จ

success khwaam sǎmrèt ความสำเร็จ

such as, for example... chên... เช่น...

suck, to dùut ดูด, also om อม (Note: this word is also a slang term used to describe female on male oral sex (i.e. fellatio))

sudden/suddenly than thii ทันที

sue, to (to sue someone; also to 'accuse') fáwng ฟ้อง

suffer, to thon thúk ทนทุกข์

suffering khwaam thúk ทุกข์

sufficient/enough phaw-phiang พอเพียง, or simply phaw พอ

sugar náam-taan น้ำตาล

sugarcane ôi อ้อย

suggest, to náehnam แนะนำ

suggestion kham náehnam คำแนะนำ

suicide (to commit suicide) khâa tua taai ฆ่าตัวตาย

suit (clothes) (from English) sùut สูท

suitable, fitting, appropriate mà-w-sǒm เหมาะสม

135

suitcase krà-pǎo sûea phâa
กระเป๋าเสื้อผ้า

summary/summarize
sà-rùp สรุป

summer nâa ráwn หน้าร้อน

summit (mountain peak)
yâwt ยอด

sun, the phrá aàthít
พระอาทิตย์

Sunday wan aa-thít วันอาทิตย์

sunglasses wâen kan dàeht
แว่นกันแดด

sunlight sǎehng dàeht
แสงแดด

sunny, to be dàeht àwk
แดดออก

sunrise phrá aa-thít khûen
พระอาทิตย์ขึ้น

sunset phrá aa-thít tòk din
พระอาทิตย์ตกดิน

superficial (not deep – used
figuratively) phǐu phǒen
ผิวเผิน

superior/better dii kwàa ดีกว่า

supermarket (from English)
suu-pôeh-maa-kèt
ซูเปอร์มาเก็ต

superstitious (believing
in ghosts, omens, etc.)
(COLLOQUIAL) thǔeh phǐi ถือผี

supervise/oversee/control
(work) khûap khum ควบคุม;
supervise/look over (e.g.
children) duu-laeh ดูแล

supply (goods/provisions,
etc.) v jàt hǎa จัดหา

support (to provide support)
sà-nàp sà-nǔn สนับสนุน,
also ùt-nǔn อุดหนุน

suppose, to sǒm-mút สมมุติ

suppress (illegal activity)
pràap praam ปราบปราม

supreme sǔung sùt สูงสุด

sure, to be nâeh jai แน่ใจ

surf, to (on a surfboard) lên
tôh khlûehn เล่นโต้คลื่น

surface phǐu phúehn ผิวพื้น

surface mail/ordinary mail
prai-sà-nii tham-má-daa
ไปรษณีย์ธรรมดา

surfboard, a krà-daan tôh
khlûehn กระดานโต้คลื่น

surgery (medical operation)
phàa tàt ผ่าตัด

surgery, a N hâwng phàa tàt
ห้องผ่าตัด

surname naam sà-hun
นามสกุล

surprised, to be plàehk jai
แปลกใจ

136

surprising nâa plàehk jai น่า
แปลกใจ
surroundings sìng wâeht
láwm สิ่งแวดล้อม (also the
word for the 'environment')
survey, to sǎm-rùat สำรวจ
survive, to râwt chii-wít รอด
ชีวิต, (COMMON IDIOM) 'to save
one's own skin' ao tua râwt
เอาตัวรอด
suspect, to sǒng-sǎi สงสัย
suspicion khwaam sǒngsǎi
ความสงสัย
swallow, to kluehn กลืน
swamp/waterhole bueng บึง
swear (as in 'I swear it wasn't
me') sǎa-baan สาบาน; to
swear at someone dàa ด่า
sweat ngûea เหงื่อ
sweat, to ngûea àwk เหงื่อออก
sweep, to kwàat กวาด; a
broom mái kwàat ไม้กวาด
sweet, to be wǎan หวาน
sweet/dessert a khǎwng
wǎan ของหวาน
sweet and sour prîao wǎan
เปรี้ยวหวาน
sweetheart/darling thîi
rák ที่รัก
sweets/candy khà-nǒm

ขนม; a sweet you suck on
lûuk om ลูกอม
swim, to wâai náam ว่ายน้ำ
swimming costume,
swimsuit chút wâai náam
ชุดว่ายน้ำ
swimming pool sà wâai
náam สระว่ายน้ำ
swing, to kwàeng แกว่ง
switch, a (from English)
sà-wít สวิทช์
switch, to (change) plìan
เปลี่ยน
switch on, turn on pòeht
เปิด
swoon See 'faint'
sword dàap ดาบ
symbol sǎnyálák สัญลักษณ์
sympathy/sympathetic hěn
òk hěn jai (literally, 'see'-
'chest'-'see'-'heart') เห็นอก
เห็นใจ
symptom, a aa-kaan อาการ
synthetic sǎng-khrá-w
สังเคราะห์
syringe khěm chìit yaa
(literally, 'needle'-'inject'-
'medicine/drug') เข็มฉีดยา
syrup (cordial/sweet
concentrate) náam chûeam

น้ำเชื่อม, also (from English) sai-ràp ไซรัป

system (e.g. of government/ of running a business etc.) rá-bòp ระบบ

T

table tó โต๊ะ (Note: at times this word is also used colloquially to refer to chairs)

tablecloth phâa puu tó ผ้าปูโต๊ะ

tablet(s) yaa mét ยาเม็ด

tablet PC (computer) (from English) tháep-lét phii sii แท็บเล็ทพีซี

tail (of an animal) hǎang หาง

take, to ao เอา (Note: used in conjunction with other words to express various distinct meanings – e.g. take the book away ao nǎngsǔeh pai เอาหนังสือไป; bring the book here ao nǎng-sǔeh maa เอาหนังสือมา

take care of, to duu laeh ดูแล

take off (clothes/shoes) thàwt ถอด

talk, to phûut พูด

talk about phûut rûeang… พูดเรื่อง…

tall sǔng สูง

tame, to be (of an animal) chûeang เชื่อง

tampon ('sanitary napkin') phâa à-naa-mai ผ้าอนามัย

tank thǎng ถัง (same word used for 'bucket'): e.g. petrol tank thǎng náam-man ถัง น้ำมัน

tank (military vehicle) rót thǎng รถถัง

tap (i.e. turn on the tap) kók náam ก๊อกน้ำ

tape, adhesive (from English) théhp เทป

target (used for shooting practice) pâo เป้า (Note: slang/colloquial – used to refer to the groin region of males)

taste (the taste) rót rs, or (more fully) rót châat รสชาติ

taste, to (e.g. sample food) chim ชิม

tasty àròi อร่อย, or mii rót châat (literally, 'have'-'taste') มีรสชาติ

tattoo, a sàk สัก

tax phaa-sǐi ภาษี (Note: 'to pay tax(es)' is sǐa phaa-sǐi เสีย ภาษี. Also see 'VAT')

taxi tháek-sîi แท็กซี่; motorcycle taxi (very common in most areas of Bangkok) maw-toeh-sai ráp jâang มอเตอร์ไซค์รับจ้าง (Note: a motorcycle taxi rank is known colloquially as a win วิน)

tea chaa ชา, or náam chaa น้ำชา (Note: some types of tea – usually very sweet – commonly sold in Thailand are as follows: hot tea chaa ráwn ชาร้อน; iced tea chaa yen ชาเย็น; iced black tea chaa dam yen ชาดำเย็น)

teach, to sǎwn สอน

teacher (from the Sanskrit derived term 'guru') khruu ครู

teak/teakwood mái sàk ไม้สัก

team (from English – pronounced very similar to the original) thiim ทีม; group kháná, คณะ

tear/rip, to chìik ฉีก

tears náam-taa (literally, 'water'-'eye{s}') น้ำตา

tease, to yâeh แหย่

teaspoon cháwn chaa (literally, 'spoon'-'tea') ช้อนชา

technician/tradesperson (general term) châang ช่าง

teenager(s) wai rûn วัยรุ่น

teeshirt/T-shirt sûea yûeht เสื้อยืด

teeth/tooth fan ฟัน

telephone thoh-rá-sàp โทรศัพท์ (also see 'mobile/ cell phone')

telephone number boeh thoh-rá-sàp เบอร์โทรศัพท์

television (COLLOQUIAL) thii wii ทีวี, also (more formally) thoh-rá-thát โทรทัศน์

tell, to (a story) lâo เล่า

tell (e.g. to tell someone) bàwk บอก

temperature ùn-hà-phuum อุณหภูมิ

temple (Buddhist) wát วัด; an ancient temple wát boh-raan วัดโบราณ

temple (Chinese) sǎn jâo ศาลเจ้า

tempo/rhythm jang-wà จังหวะ

temporary chûa khraaw
ชั่วคราว

ten sìp สิบ

tendon en เอ็น

tennis (from English) then-nít
(pronounced 'ten'-'nit')
เทนนิส

tens of, multiples of ten
lǎai sìp หลายสิบ

tense (as in a tense or strained
muscle) tueng ตึง

tent (from English) tén เต็นท์

ten thousand mùehn หมื่น

terrible, to be yâeh แย่

terrorist, a phûu kàw kaan
rái ผู้ก่อการร้าย

test trùat sàwp ตรวจสอบ

test, to (to test something)
thót lawng ทดลอง

testicles (medical term) lûuk
an-thá ลูกอัณฑะ, (COLLOQUIAL)
khài ไข่ (not particularly
vulgar, but better left unsaid
– the word used here means
'egg(s)', the equivalent of the
English 'balls/nuts')

Thai thai ไทย; Thai language
phaa-sǎa thai ภาษาไทย

Thailand mueang thai เมือง
ไทย, or (FORMAL) prà-thêet

thai ประเทศไทย

than kwàa กว่า: e.g. more
than... mâak kwàa...
มากกว่า; better than... dii
kwàa... ดีกว่า

thank, to/thank you khàwp
khun ขอบคุณ

that nán นั้น; those lào nán
เหล่านั้น

that, which, the one who
thîi... ที่...

theater (drama) rohng
lá-khawn โรงละคร

their/theirs khǎwng khǎo
ของเขา

then (used as a connecting
word when relating a series
of events – e.g. 'she went to
the beach and then over to
see her friends in town and
then....') láew แล้ว

there thîi nân ที่นั่น

therefore dang nán ดังนั้น

there is, there are (also 'to
have') mii มี

they, them khǎo เขา, or
(something like 'that group')
phûak khǎo พวกเขา

thick (of liquids) khôn ข้น

thick (of things) nǎa หนา

140

thief, a khà-mohy ขโมย (also see 'steal')

thigh khăa àwn ขาอ่อน

thin (of persons) phăwm ผอม

thin (of things) baang บาง

thing khăwng ของ, or sìng สิ่ง; things sìng khăwng สิ่งของ

think (something over), ponder, to trài trawng ไตร่ตรอง

think, to khít คิด, also commonly néuk นึก: e.g. 'I can't think of it' néuk mâi àwk นึกไม่ออก; or 'I've thought of it/I've got it' néuk àwk láew นึกออกแล้ว

third (⅓) sèht nùeng sùan săam เศษหนึ่งส่วนสาม

third... (the third brother, in third place, etc.) ...thîi săam ...ที่สาม

thirsty hĭu námm หิวน้ำ

thirteen sìp săam สิบสาม

thirty săam sìp สามสิบ

this níi นี้; these lào níi เหล่านี้

though, even though máeh wâa แม้ว่า

thought(s) khwaam khít ความคิด

thousand phan พัน

thread, a dâai ด้าย

threaten, to khùu ขู่

three săam สาม

thrill/thrilling/exciting tùen-tên ตื่นเต้น (Note: a word that means 'a thrill' (as in an adrenaline 'rush') is sĭao เสียว. This term is also used, for example, when hearing the sound of someone scratching their nails on a blackboard, or when getting a thrill from doing something dangerous (e.g. bungee jumping). In addition sĭao also refers to the pleasurable tingling sensation when sexually aroused)

throat lam khaw ลำคอ, or simply khaw คอ

through (pass through/pass by) phàan ผ่าน

throw, to khwâang ขว้าง

throw away, throw out khwâang thíng ขว้างทิ้ง, or simply thíng ทิ้ง

thunder fáa ráwng ฟ้าร้อง

Thursday (FULL FORM) wan phá-rúe-hàt sà-bae-dii วัน

141

พฤหัสบดี, (NORMAL COLLOQUIAL TERM) wan phá-rúe-hàt วัน พฤหัส

thus, so dang nán ดังนั้น

ticket, a (for transport/entertainment, etc.) tǔa ตั๋ว (NOTE: tickets for entertainment/ sport, etc. are also referred to as bàt บัตร – pronounced like the word 'but')

ticket (a fine) bai sàng ใบสั่ง

tickle, to jîi จี้ (NOTE: also slang, meaning 'to rob someone with a weapon')

ticklish, to be ják-kà jîi จั๊กจี้

tidy/neat/well behaved (in dress/speech/behaviour) rîap rói เรียบร้อย

tie, necktie (from English) nék-thai เน็คไท

tie, to phùuk ผูก

tiger, a sǔea เสือ

tight nâen แน่น (NOTE: the English word 'fit' is commonly used to refer to tight fitting clothing, fít ฟิต)

till/until jon kwàa จนกว่า, or kwàa jà กว่าจะ

timber/wood mái ไม้

time wehlaa เวลา; 'what's the

time?' weh-laa thâo rài เวลา เท่าไหร่, or (more commonly) kìi mohng láew (literally, 'how many'-'hour'-'already') กี่โมงแล้ว

times (i.e. 4 × 4 = 16) khuun คูณ

timetable taa-raang wehlaa ตารางเวลา

tin, a (e.g. a tin of beans) krà-pǎwng กระป๋อง

tiny lék mâak เล็กมาก

tip (the end of something, e.g. end of one's nose, etc.) plaai ปลาย

tip (to give someone a tip for their service) (from English) thíp ทิป

tire/tyre (on a car) yaang rót ยางรถ (NOTE: a flat tire/tyre is yang baehn ยางแบน)

tired (sleepy) ngûang ง่วง

tired (worn out) nùeai เหนื่อย

tissue (paper) (from English) krà-dàat thít-chûu กระดาษ ทิชชู

title (to a piece of land) chànòht thîi din โนนดที่ดิน

to, toward(s) (a place) pai yang… ไปยัง…

142

tobacco yaa sùup ยาสูบ, or
yaa sên ยาเส้น

today wan níi วันนี้

toe níu tháo นิ้วเท้า; toe nail
lép tháo เล็บเท้า

tofu/soyabean tâo hûu เต้าหู้

together dûai kan ด้วยกัน

toilet (i.e. bathroom) hâwng
náam ห้องน้ำ

toilet paper krà-dàat cham-
rá กระดาษชำระ, (COLLOQUIAL)
krà-dàat chét kôn (literally,
'paper'-'wipe'-'bottom')
กระดาษเช็ดก้น

tomato ma-khǔea thêht
มะเขือเทศ

tomorrow phrûng níi พรุ่งนี้

tongue, the lín ลิ้น

tonight khuehn níi คืนนี้

too (also) dûai ด้วย

too (excessive) koehn pai
เกินไป; e.g. 'too expensive'
phaehng koehn pai แพงเกิน
ไป, (MORE COLLOQUIAL) phaehng
pai แพงไป

too much mâak koehn pai
มากเกินไป

tool, utensil, instrument
khrûeang mueh เครื่องมือ

tooth fan ฟัน (fan pronounced

like the English word 'fun')

toothbrush praehng sǐi fan
แปรงสีฟัน

toothpaste yaa sǐi fan ยาสีฟัน

toothpick mái jîm fan
ไม้จิ้มฟัน

top (on top) khâang bon
ข้างบน; top/peak (of hill,
mountain) yâwt ยอด

topic (in essay, etc.) hǔa
khâw หัวข้อ

top secret khwaam láp sùt
yâwt ความลับสุดยอด

torch, flashlight fai chǎai
ไฟฉาย

torn/ripped (e.g. torn jeans
– also refers to worn out
clothes etc.) khàat ขาด

total (the whole lot) tháng mòt
ทั้งหมด

touch, to tàe แตะ

tough, to be (chewy – a
tough piece of meat) nǐao
เหนียว

tough (as in strong physically)
khǎeng raehng แข็งแรง;
tough (as in mentally tough)
jai khǎeng ใจแข็ง

tourism kaan thâwng thîao
การท่องเที่ยว

tourist nák thâwng thîao
นักท่องเที่ยว

tow, to (i.e. to tow a caravan)
lâak ลาก

towel phâa chét tua ผ้าเช็ดตัว,
also (MORE COLLOQUIALLY) phâa
khŏn nûn ผ้าขนหนู

tower hăw khoi หอคอย

town mueang เมือง (also
used in certain cases to refer
to a country e.g. Thailand
mueang thai เมืองไทย,
China mueang jiin เมืองจีน)

toxic, to be (poisonous) pen
phít เป็นพิษ

toy khăwng lên ของเล่น

trade N kaan kháa การค้า

trade, to exchange lâehk
plìan แลกเปลี่ยน

traditional dâng doehm ดั้งเดิม

traffic kaan jà-raa-jawn การ
จราจร

traffic jam rót tìt รถติด

train, to (someone) fùek ฝึก

train, a rót fai รถไฟ

train station sà-thăa-nii rót
fai สถานีรถไฟ

translate, to plaeh แปล (Note
the following useful expression:
'what does it/that mean?'

plaeh wâa àrai แปลว่าอะไร

transparent, to be (used
both in the usual sense of
'clear' and referring to the
operations of a company/
government etc. – 'trans-
parency') pròhng sái โปร่งใส

transport, to v khŏn sòng
ขนส่ง (NOTE: this term is used
colloquially to refer to a bus
station serving inter-province
travel)

transvestite (ladyboy)
kà-thoei กะเทย

travel, to doehn thaang เดิน
ทาง

travel agency (COLLOQUIAL)
baw-rí-isàt thâwng thîao
บริษัทท่องเที่ยว

traveler, a nák doehn thaang
นักเดินทาง, or khon doehn
thaang คนเดินทาง

tray, a thàat ถาด

tread (walk on) yìap เหยียบ

treasure/wealth sàp sŏmbàt
ทรัพย์สมบัติ

treat, to (someone to dinner)
líang เลี้ยง

treat, to (behave towards)
tham tàw ทำต่อ

treat, to (medically) rák-săa รักษา

tree tôn mái ต้นไม้

tremble/shake (with fear) sàn สั่น, or tua sàn ตัวสั่น

trendy (i.e. the latest something) than sá-măi ทันสมัย (NOTE: than pronounced similar to the English word 'ton'; the English word 'trend' has also found its way into Thai – tren เทรนด์)

trespass (on someone's property) rúk lám รุกล้ำ

trespass (on someone's person, i.e. inappropriate touching) lûang koen ล่วงเกิน

triangle săam lìam สามเหลี่ยม (NOTE: the tri-border area [Thailand, Burma, Laos] the 'Golden Triangle' – săam lìam thawng kham สามเหลี่ยมทองคำ)

tribe phào เผ่า; hill-tribe chaaw khăo ชาวเขา

tricky, to be (as in a tricky person trying to pull the wool over someone's eyes) mii lêh lìam มีเล่ห์เหลี่ยม

trip/journey, a kaan doehn thaang การเดินทาง

tripe/offal (COLLOQUIAL) phâa khîi ríu ผ้าขี้ริ้ว (NOTE: this term phâa khîi ríu also means 'rag' (for wiping things up))

troops, the army kawng tháp กองทัพ

trouble (as in 'hardship') khwaam lam-bàak ความลำบาก

troublemaker khon kàw kuan คนก่อกวน

troublesome (e.g. for life to be troublesome/difficult) lam-bàak ลำบาก

trousers/pants kaang-kehng กางเกง

truck rót ban-thúk รถบรรทุก

true, to be jing จริง

truly jing-jing จริงๆ

trust, to wái jai ไว้ใจ

truth, the khwaam jing ความจริง; to speak the truth phûut khwaam jing พูดความจริง

try, to phá-yaa-yaam พยายาม

try on (clothes) lawng sài ลองใส่

try out (to try something out) lawng ลอง

145

Tuesday wan ang-khaan วัน
อังคาร

tuktuk taxi rót túk túk รถตุ๊ก
ตุ๊ก, or simply túk túk ตุ๊กตุ๊ก

tunnel, a ù-mohng อุโมงค์

turkey, a (fowl) kài nguang
ไก่งวง

turn, make a turn in a car
líao เลี้ยว

turn around, to líao klàp
เลี้ยวกลับ

turn off, to pìt ปิด

turn on, to pòeht เปิด

turtle/tortoise tào เต่า

tutor N khruu phí-sèht
(literally, 'teacher'-'special')
ครูพิเศษ

TV (from English) thii wii ทีวี

tweezers khiim nìip คีมหนีบ

twelve sìp sǎwng สิบสอง

twenty yîi sìp ยี่สิบ

twice (as in 'twice a day')
sǎwng khráng สองครั้ง

twin (as in 'twin bed') pen
khûu เป็นคู่

twins (children/people) fǎa
fàet ฝาแฝด (often just the
word fàet แฝด is used)

twist (e.g. as in a 'twisted leg')
bìt บิด

two sǎwng สอง

type, sort chá-nít ชนิด

type/print, to phim พิมพ์

typhoon tâi-fûn ได้ฝุ่น

typical pen tham-má-daa
เป็นธรรมดา

tyre See 'tire'

U

ugly (physically ugly) nâa klìat
น่าเกลียด (NOTE: in Thai this
is commonly expressed as
'not pretty/beautiful' – mâi
sǔai ไม่สวย. Furthermore,
it should be noted that the
term nâa klìat น่าเกลียด is
also commonly used to refer
to 'unsightly/inappropriate
behaviour')

umbrella rôm ร่ม (NOTE: this
word also means 'shade')

unable (not capable of doing
something/do not have ability
to do something) mâi
sǎa-mâat ไม่สามารถ; (MORE
COLLOQUIAL) cannot do (something) tham mâi dâi (literally,
'do'-'no'-'can') ทำไม่ได้

unaware, to be mâi rúu tua
ไม่รู้ตัว

146

unbearable (to be intolerable – as in 'I can't handle it') thon mâi dâi ทนไม่ได้, or thon mâi wǎi ทนไม่ไหว

uncertainty ʀ khwaam mâi nâeh nawn ความไม่แน่นอน

uncle (general term – also see 'aunt') lung ลุง (NOTE: this word is pronounced with a very short 'u' – and it does not sound like the English word 'lung'. It is a word that is often used to an unrelated elder male meaning 'you/he')

uncomfortable (e.g. an uncomfortable place) mâi sà-dùak sà-baai ไม่สะดวกสบาย; uncomfortable (in the sense of feeling uncomfortable about something) mâi sà-baai jai ไม่สบายใจ

unconscious, to be mâi dâi sà-tì ไม่ได้สติ

uncover/reveal (e.g. the truth) pòeht phǒei เปิดเผย

under tâi ใต้

undergo/experience, to prà-sòp ประสบ

underpants kaang-kehng nai กางเกงใน

undershirt sûea chán nai เสื้อชั้นใน

understand, to khâo jai เข้าใจ; to misunderstand khâo jai phìt เข้าใจผิด

underwear chút chán nai ชุดชั้นใน

undress/to get undressed kâeh phâa แก้ผ้า

unemployed, to be wâang ngaan ว่างงาน

unequal mâi thâokan ไม่เท่ากัน

unfaithful (in matters of the heart) nôwk jai (literally, 'outside'-'heart') นอกใจ; for a married person to have a lover mii chúu มีชู้

unfortunate/unfortunately chôhk ráai โชคร้าย

unhappy mâi mii khwaam sùk (literally, 'no'-'have'-'happiness') ไม่มีความสุข

uniform (clothing – police/ military uniform etc.) khrûeang bàehp เครื่องแบบ

uninteresting *See* 'boring'

United Kingdom (FORMAL TERM) sà-hà râat-chá aa-naa-jàk สหราชอาณาจักร, or simply (UK) yuu kheh ยูเค

147

United States (FORMAL TERM)
sà-hà-rát à-meh-rí-kaa
สหรัฐอเมริกา, or simply
à-meh-rí-kaa อเมริกา, or
sà-hà-rát สหรัฐ

universal (i.e. occidental – of
the 'modern' Western world)
săa-kon สากล; in general
thûa pai ทั่วไป

university má-hăwít-
thá-yaa-lai มหาวิทยาลัย,
(COLLOQUIAL) má-hăalai มหาลัย

unless nâwk jàak...
นอกจาก...

unlimited, to be mâi jam-kàt
ไม่จำกัด

unlucky chôhk ráai โชคร้าย

unnecessary mâi jam-pen
ไม่จำเป็น

unripe mâi sùk ไม่สุก

unsatisfactory mâi phaw
jai ไม่พอใจ, or mâi dii phaw
ไม่ดีพอ, or (not as good as it
should be) mâi dii thâo thîi
khuan ไม่ดีเท่าที่ควร

until jon krà-thâng จนกระทั่ง,
also **(MORE COLLOQUIALLY)** jon
kwàa...จนกว่า..., or simply
kwàa กว่า

unwrap kâeh àwk แก้ออก

up, upward khûen ขึ้น

update (from English, with
essentially the same meaning
and pronunciation) àp deht
อัพเดท

upset, unhappy mâi sà-baai
jai ไม่สบายใจ

upside down, to be (e.g. a
car on its roof) ngăai tháwng
หงายท้อง

upstairs khâang bon ข้างบน

urban nai mueang ในเมือง

urge, to push for (e.g. equal
rights) rîak ráwng เรียกร้อง

urgent rêng dùan เร่งด่วน, or
simply dùan ด่วน

urinate, to (medical/formal
term) pàt-săa-wá ปัสสาวะ,
(COLLOQUIAL – whereas in
English one might say 'piss'
– in Thai this is not a vulgar
word) chìi ฉี่, or (mildly vulgar)
yîao เยี่ยว

use, to chái ใช้

used to (to be used to) chin
ชิน; to be accustomed to...
khún khoei kàp... คุ้นเคย
กับ...

used to do something
khoei เคย (NOTE: for fuller

148

description of how the word
khoei เคย is used – see
'have')

useful, to be mii prà-yòht มี
ประโยชน์

useless mâi mii prà-yòht
ไม่มีประโยชน์, (COLLOQUIAL –
as in a 'useless person') mâi
dâi rûeang ไม่ได้เรื่อง

usual pà-kà-tì ปกติ

usually taam pà-kà-tì
ตามปกติ, or (MORE SIMPLY
COLLOQUIAL) pà-kà-tì ปกติ

uterus/womb mót lûuk มดลูก

V

vacant wâang ว่าง: e.g. (at
a hotel) 'do you have any
vacant rooms?' mii hâwng
wâang măi (literally, 'have'-
'room'-'vacant'-'question
marker') มีห้องว่างไหม

vacation/holiday wan yùt
phák phàwn (literally, 'day'-
'stop'-'rest') วันหยุดพักผ่อน

vaccination chìit wák-siin
ฉีดวัคซีน

vacuum, a sŭn-yaa-kàat
สุญญากาศ

vagabond/vagrant/
homeless person (FORMAL)
khon phá-neh-jawn คน
พเนจร, or (COLLOQUIAL) khon
rêh-rôn คนเร่ร่อน

vagina (colloquial – not too
vulgar) jǐm จิ๋ม, also (VERY
COLLOQUIAL) pǐi ปี๋, (colloquial
and extremely vulgar, the
equivalent of the English
word 'cunt') hǐi หี

vague, to be khlum khruea
คลุมเครือ

vain (self-important) thŭeh tua
ถือตัว, or yìng หยิ่ง

valid/usable chái dâi ใช้ได้

valley hùp khăo หุบเขา

valuable, to be mii khun
khâa มีคุณค่า

value, the (cost/price) raa-
khaa ราคา

value, to (to estimate a price)
tii khâa ตีค่า

van (vehicle) rót tûu รถตู้

vanish hăi pai หายไป

vase jaeh-kan แจกัน

VAT (value added tax –
Thailand does have one)
phaa-sǐi mun-lá-khâa
pôehm ภาษีมูลค่าเพิ่ม

**venereal disease/VD
(general term for STDs)**
kaam-má-rôhk กามโรค

vegetable(s) phàk ผัก

vegetarian mang-sà-wí-rát
มังสวิรัติ

vegetarian, to be kin jeh
กินเจ

**vehicle (general term for
wheeled vehicles)** rót รถ

vein (in the body) sên lûeat
เส้นเลือด

verandah See 'porch'

**vernacular/colloquial/
spoken language** phaa-
săa phûut ภาษาพูด

very, extremely mâak มาก

vest, waistcoat sûea kák
เสื้อกั๊ก

vet (animial doctor) sàt-tà-wá-
phâet สัตวแพทย์

via phàan ผ่าน

vibrant/lively/full of life mii
chii-wít chii-waa มีชีวิตชีวา,
or râa roehng ร่าเริง

**Vientiane (the capital of
Laos)** wiang-jan เวียงจันทน์
(pronounced something like
wiang-jahn)

Vietnam wîat-naam เวียดนาม

Vietnamese (people) chaaw
wîatnaam ชาวเวียดนาม

**view, panorama (from
English)** wiu วิว

view, to look at chom wiu
ชมวิว

village mùu bâan หมู่บ้าน

**villager (also more generally
'ordinary folk' – both in the
country and the city)** chaaw
bâan ชาวบ้าน

vinegar nám sôm น้ำส้ม (Thai
vinegar is not quite the same
as 'western vinegar'. It is
something which one adds to
such things as noodle soup,
etc. to enhance the flavour)

violent, to be run raehng
รุนแรง; **violence** khwaam
run raehng ความรุนแรง

virus (from English) chúea
wai-rát เชื้อไวรัส, or simply
wai-rát ไวรัส

visa (from English) wii-sâa
วีซ่า

visit, to yîam เยี่ยม

visit, to go and pay a pai
yîam ไปเยี่ยม

visitor (guest in one's home)
khàek แขก

150

vitamin(s) (from English)
wí-taa-min วิตามิน

vocabulary (words) sàp sàpt
(pronounced very similar to
the English word 'sup' – from
'supper')

voice/sound sĭang เสียง (also
the colloquial word for 'a
vote' in an election)

voicemail (from English)
wois-mehl วอยซ์เมล์

volcano phuu khăo fai ภูเขาไฟ

volume (quantity) pà-rí-maan
ปริมาณ; volume (sound level)
rá-dàp sĭang ระดับเสียง

vomit, to (POLITE) aa-jian
อาเจียน, (colloquial – though
less polite) spew/chuck/throw
up ûak อ้วก

voodoo, black magic săi-
yá-sàat ไสยศาสตร์

vote, to (from English) wòht
โหวต, also àwk sĭang ออก
เสียง, or long khá-naehn ลง
คะแนน

vulgar/crude/coarse yàap
khaai หยาบคาย

W

wages khâa jâang ค่าจ้าง *Also
see* 'salary'

waist (of the body) eh-o เอว

wait for, to raw รอ

waiter/waitress, a (COLLOQUIAL)
dèk sòehp เด็กเสิร์ฟ

wake someone up, to plùk
ปลุก

wake up, to tùehn ตื่น

walk, to doehn เดิน

walking distance (within)
doehn pai dâi เดินไปได้

wall (i.e. a stone/solid wall)
kam-phaehng กำแพง; wall
(internal wall of a house) phà-
năng ผนัง

wallet krà-pǎo sà-taang
กระเป๋าสตางค์, or (MORE
COLLOQUIALLY) krà-pǎo tang
กระเป๋าตังค์

want to (FORMAL) with the
sense of 'need' tâwng kaan
ต้องการ, or (COLLOQUIAL) more
like the sense of 'wanting'
something yàak อยาก

war sŏng-khraam สงคราม

war, to make tham sŏngkhraam ทำสงคราม

warm, to v ùn อุ่น (also for something (e.g. food) to be warm)

warmth (the feeling of 'warmth') òp ùn อบอุ่น

warn, to tuean เตือน

warning kham tuean คำเตือน

wash, to (objects – e.g. car, windows, etc. but also to wash the face, hands, feet) láang ล้าง

wash the dishes láang jaan ล้างจาน; wash clothes sák phâa ซักผ้า; to wash hair sà phǒm สระผม

wart, a hùut หูด

watch (wristwatch; also 'clock') naa-lí-kaa นาฬิกา

watch, to (show, movie) duu ดู

watch/stare, to mawng มอง

watch over, guard fâo เฝ้า

water náam น้ำ

water buffalo khwaai ควาย

waterfall náam tòk น้ำตก

watermelon taehng moh แตงโม

waterproof, to be kan náam กันน้ำ

water-ski sà-kii náam สกีน้ำ

wave (in the sea) khlûehn คลื่น

wave, to (hand) bòhk mueh โบกมือ

wax khîi phûeng ขี้ผึ้ง; ear wax khîi hǔu ขี้หู

way (i.e. the way to get somewhere) thaang ทาง; 'which way do you go?' pai thaang nǎi (literally, 'go'-'way'-'which') ไปทางไหน

way/method (of doing something) wí-thii วิธี

way: by way of (e.g. bus/ train etc.) dohy โดย

way in, the thaang khâo ทางเข้า

way out/exit, the thaang àwk ทางออก

we, us rao เรา

weak, to be (of a person) àwn aeh อ่อนแอ

wealthy mâng khâng มั่งคั่ง, or simply 'rich' ruai รวย

weapon aa-wút อาวุธ

wear, to sài ใส่

weary nùeai เหนื่อย

weather aa-kàat อากาศ

weave, to (cloth etc.) thaw (pronounced 'tore') ทอ

weaving kaan thaw การทอ

website (from English) wép sái เว็บไซต์

wedding ngaan tàeng-ngaan งานแต่งงาน

Wednesday wan phút วันพุธ

weed (i.e. a weed in the garden) wát-chá-phûet วัชพืช

week (FORMAL) sàp-daa สัปดาห์, (more commonly) aa-thít อาทิตย์

weekend, the wan sùt sàp-daa วันสุดสัปดาห์, (COLLOQUIAL) sǎo aa-thít เสาร์อาทิตย์

weekly thúk aa-thít ทุก อาทิตย์

weep/cry, to ráwng hâi ร้องไห้

weigh, to châng ชั่ง; to weigh yourself/for someone to weigh themselves châng náam-nàk ชั่งน้ำหนัก

weight náam-nàk น้ำหนัก

weight, to gain náam-nàk khûen น้ำหนักขึ้น, (COLLOQUIAL) ûan khûen (literally, 'fat'-'increase/go up') อ้วนขึ้น

weight, to lose lót náam-nàk ลดน้ำหนัก

welcome! yin-dii tâwn ráp ยินดีต้อนรับ

welcome, to (to welcome someone) tâwn ráp ต้อนรับ

well (as in 'do something well') dii ดี

well (for water) bàw náam baa-daan บ่อน้ำบาดาล, or simply bàw náam บ่อน้ำ

well-behaved, to be tham tua dii ทำตัวดี

well-cooked/well-done, to be sùk สุก

well done! dii mâak ดีมาก

well-mannered maa-rá-yâat dii มารยาทดี

well off/wealthy, to be ruai รวย

west (direction) tà-wan tòk ตะวันตก

Westerner chaaw tàwan tòk ชาวตะวันตก

wet, to be pìak เปียก

whale plaa waan ปลาวาฬ

what? (or which?) àrai อะไร (NOTE: unlike English, 'what?' in Thai comes at the end of a sentence. For example – 'what's your name' khun chûeh àrai (literally, 'you'-

153

'name'-'what?') คุณชื่ออะไร

'what colour is it? สีนี้ อะไร
(literally, 'colour'-'what?')
สีอะไร, or 'what's your
telephone number?' thoh-
rá-sàp boeh arai (literally,
'telephone'-'number'-'what?')
โทรศัพท์เบอร์อะไร

what for? phûea arai เพื่ออะไร

what kind of? chá-nít năi
ชนิดไหน, **(MORE COLLOQUIAL)**
bàehp năi แบบไหน

what time is it? kìi mohng
láew กี่โมงแล้ว

wheel, a láw ล้อ

when? mûea-rài เมื่อไหร่
(usually used at the end of a
sentence): e.g. 'when are you
going?' khun jà pai mûearrai
(literally, 'you'-'will'-'go'-
'when') คุณจะไปเมื่อไหร่

whenever (as in the
expression: 'whenever you
like' or, 'any time at all')
mûea-rài kâw dâi เมื่อไหร่ก็ได้

where? thîi năi ที่ไหน
(usually used at the end of
a sentence): e.g. 'where is
she?' khăo yùu thîi năi เขา
อยู่ที่ไหน

where to? pai thîi năi ไปที่ไหน

which? năi ไหน (usually used
at the end of a sentence): e.g.
'which person?' khon năi
คนไหน

while/during nai khà-nà
thîi… ในขณะที่…

whisper, to krà-síp กระซิบ

whistle, to phîu pàak ผิวปาก

white sǐi khăaw สีขาว

who? khrai ใคร

whole, all of tháng mòt
ทั้งหมด

whole (e.g. a set to be whole/
complete) khróp ครบ

wholesale (price) khăai sòng
ขายส่ง (NOTE: retail price is
khăai plìik ขายปลีก)

why? tham-mai ทำไม
(generally used, in contrast
to English, at the end of a
sentence)

wicked/evil, to be rái ร้าย

wide kwâang กว้าง

width khwaam kwâang ความ
กว้าง

widow mâeh mâai แม่ม่าย

widowed, to be pen mâai
เป็นม่าย

widower phâw mâai พ่อม่าย

wife **(FORMAL/POLITE)** phan-
rá-yaa ภรรยา, **(COMMON
COLLOQUIAL)** mia เมีย

Wifi/wifi (from English) wai-
fai วายฟาย

wig, a (from English) wík วิก

wild (of animals) pàa ป่า: e.g.
wildcat maew pàa แมวป่า

will/shall (common marker of
future tense) jà จะ

win, to v chá-ná ชนะ; (a/the)
winner N phûu chá-ná ผู้ชนะ

wind (a breeze and stronger)
lom ลม

window (in house) nâa tàang
หน้าต่าง

wine (from English) waai ไวน์

wing (of a bird) pìik ปีก

wink, to kà-príp taa กะพริบ
ตา

winter (in Thailand the 'cool
season' – Nov-Jan) nâaw
nǎow หน้าหนาว

wipe, to chét เช็ด

wire lûat ลวด; an electrical
wire sǎi fai สายไฟ

wise chà-làat ฉลาด

wish/hope, to wǎng หวัง;
to wish or hope for... wǎng
wâa... หวังว่า...

witch, a mâeh mót แม่มด

with kàp กับ

withdraw/take out (money
from a bank/a tooth etc.)
thǎwn ถอน

with pleasure dûai khwaam
yin-dii ด้วยความยินดี

within reason/limits
phaai nai khâw jamkàt
(pronounced 'jum-gut')
ภายในข้อจำกัด

without pràat-sà-jàak
ปราศจาก, or dohy mâi mii
โดยไม่มี

witness, a phá-yaan พยาน;
to witness hěn pen phá-yaan
เห็นเป็นพยาน

wobble, to (as in 'to walk with
a wobble') sohy seh โซเซ

woman, a phûu yǐng ผู้หญิง

womanizer (philanderer,
cassanova) jâo chúu เจ้าชู้

wonderful nâa prà-làat jai
น่าประหลาดใจ

wood/timber mái ไม้

wooden (i.e. made from wood)
tham dûai mái ทำด้วยไม้, or
tham jàak mái ทำจากไม้

wool (from a sheep) khǒn kàe
ขนแกะ

155

word, a kham คำ

work/occupation aa-chîip อาชีพ, (MORE COLLOQUIAL) ngaan งาน

work, to tham ngaan ทำงาน

work (e.g. for a piece of machinery, etc. to function) tham ngaan ทำงาน (NOTE: the English word 'work' is also commonly used in this sense but with a slightly 'Thai-ified' pronunciation)

world lôhk โลก

worm (general term for 'worm-like' creatures) nǎwn หนอน; earthworm sâi duean ไส้เดือน

worn out, tired nùeai เหนื่อย, (COLLOQUIAL) to have 'no more energy' mòt raehng หมดแรง

worn out/torn (clothes etc.) khàat ขาด (NOTE: this term is also used to refer to something that is 'lacking' or 'missing' – from a dish of food/a part from a machine, etc.)

worn out/broken/unrepairable (machine) phang (similar in sound to 'pung' with the 'ung' sound pro-

nounced as in 'bungle') พัง

worry, to (about someone) pen hùang เป็นห่วง; to feel worried, be anxious kang-won กังวล

worse, to get (e.g. a medical condition) yâeh long แย่ลง

worship, to buu-chaa บูชา

worst, the yâeh thîi sùt แย่ ที่สุด

worth, to have mii khâa มีค่า

worthless, to be rái khâa ไร้ค่า

worthwhile/to be worth it (i.e. value for money) khúm khâa คุ้มค่า, or simply khúm คุ้ม

wound, a bàat phláeh บาดแผล, or simply phláeh แผล

wrap, to hàw ห่อ

wreck, to See 'destroy'

wrist khâw mueh ข้อมือ

write, to khǐan เขียน

writer nák khǐan นักเขียน

wrong (incorrect) phìt ผิด

wrong (mistaken) khâojai phìt เข้าใจผิด

wrong (morally) tham phìt ทำผิด

X

x-ray (from English) ék-sà-reh
เอกซเรย์

Y

yatch/sailboat ruea bai
เรือใบ
yank/pull violently/snatch
(as in to have your bag
'snatched') krà-châak
กระชาก
yard (open space) laan ลาน
yawn, to hǎaw หาว
yeah (English colloquial
form of 'yes') châi ใช่, (MORE
COLLOQUIAL) jâ จ๊ะ
year pii ปี
years old (e.g. 16 years old)
pii ปี
yell/shout, to tà-kohn ตะโกน
yellow sǐi lǔeang สีเหลือง
yes châi ใช่ (NOTE: there are
a number of other ways to
say 'yes' in Thai depending
on the form of the question
asked. But this is the general
form used to respond to

many simple questions in
the affirmative. The opposite
to châi ใช่ is mâi châi ไม่ใช่
which means 'no' – again,
this being dependent on the
form of the question asked.
Also see 'no', 'not')
yesterday mûea waan níi
เมื่อวานนี้
yet (as in 'not yet') yang ยัง
(NOTE: the word yang is part
of the question form 'have
you/he/they (verb)?' rúe
yang หรือยัง: e.g. 'have you
eaten yet?' khun kin khâaw
rúe yang คุณกินข้าวหรือ
ยัง. If you haven't eaten yet
you would normally answer
yang (not yet). If, on the other
hand, you had eaten you
could answer – kin láew 'I've
eaten' กินแล้ว. For another
important meaning of yang
see 'still')
you (general polite term) khun
คุณ; you (INTIMATE) thoeh เธอ
(NOTE: the corresponding
'intimate' Thai word for 'I'
that thoeh is paired with is
chǎn ฉัน. These terms for

'I' and 'you' are found in the vast majority of Thai popular songs. Try listening for them)

you're welcome! mâi pen rai ไม่เป็นไร

young (in years) aa-yú nói อายุน้อย

younger brother or sister (or more generally meaning 'you' when addressing a junior person in a store/restaurant etc.) náwng น้อง

youth (plural – young people) yao-wá-chon เยาวชน

youths nùm săaw (literally,

'young men'-'young women') หนุ่มสาว

Z

zebra, a máa laai (literally, 'horse'-'stripe/striped') ม้าลาย

zero sŭun ศูนย์

zip/zipper, a (from English) síp ซิป

zone/area khèht เขต

zoo sŭan sàt (literally, 'garden/park'-'animal') สวนสัตว์

Thai–English

A

aa N อา aunt or uncle (i.e. a younger sister or brother of one's father)

aa-chíip N อาชีพ occupation, profession, career

aa-hăan N อาหาร food

aa-hăan cháo N อาหารเช้า breakfast, morning meal

aa-hăan jeh (pronounced similar to 'jay') อาหารเจ Chinese vegetarian food, vegan food

aa-hăan klaang wan N อาหารกลางวัน/อาหารเที่ยง lunch, midday meal

aa-hăan tháleh N อาหารทะเล seafood

aa-hăan wâang N อาหาร ว่าง an entrée/starter/hors d'oeuvres

aa-hăan yen N อาหารเย็น dinner, evening meal

aai (long vowel) ADJ อาย to be shy, embarrassed

aa-jaan N อาจารย์ teacher (usually with degree), university lecturer

aa-jian N อาเจียน (POLITE) to vomit; (COLLOQUIAL) ûak อ้วก throw up/puke/spew

aa-kaan N อาการ (physical) condition/symptom

aa-kàat N อากาศ weather, air

àan V อ่าน to read

àan lên อ่านเล่น to read for pleasure

àan mâi àwk ADJ อ่านไม่ออก illegible

àang àap náam N อ่างอาบน้ำ a bath(tub)

àang láang nâa N อ่างล้างหน้า wash basin

ao N อ่าว a bay, gulf (as in the 'Gulf of Thailand' **ăo thai** อ่าวไทย)

âo อ้าว (COLLOQUIAL) an exclamation meaning something like 'Oh!', 'huh!', 'eh!'

àap náam V อาบน้ำ bathe, take

a bath, take a shower, to have a wash

àap náam fàk bua v อาบน้ำ ฝักบัว to have a shower

aarom N อารมณ์ emotion, mood, temper

àat AUX v อาจ may, might

àat jà AUX v อาจจะ could, might, may; perhaps, maybe, possibly

àat (jà) pen pai dâi อาจ(จะ) เป็นไปได้ (that) could well be possible

aa-thít N อาทิตย์ a week

aa-thít thîi-láew N อาทิตย์ที่ แล้ว last week

àat-yaa-kawn N อาชญากร (FORMAL) criminal, (COLLOQUIAL) **phûu ráai** ผู้ร้าย 'evil doer'/ 'baddie'

aa-wút N อาวุธ a weapon (general term), arms

aa-yú N อายุ age

aa-yú mâak/sŭung aa-yú ADJ อายุมาก/สูงอายุ aged, to be (very) old

aa-yú nói ADJ อายุน้อย young (in age)

aa-yú thâo rài อายุเท่าไหร่ how old (are you/is she/it)?

(NOTE: the pronoun – 'you/ she/he' etc. – comes before the question tag)

à-dìit ADJ อดีต (the) past, former (e.g. prime minister/ husband)

aeh N (pronounced like 'air') แอร์ air (conditioning)

àep v แอบ to hide

áeppôen N (from English) แอปเปิล apple

ai (short vowel) v ไอ to cough

ai náam N ไอน้ำ steam

ai-sà-kriim N (commonly pronounced something like 'ai-tim' – from English) ไอศกรีม ice cream

à-kà-tanyuu N อกตัญญู to be ungrateful, thankless

à-khá-ti N อคติ bias, prejudice

àk-săwn N อักษร letter (in alphabet)

àk-sèp VT อักเสบ become inflamed; a response of body tissues to infection

à-lài N อะไหล่ spare part (of machine), replacement part(s)

à-mátà ADJ อมตะ to be immortal (NOTE: also commonly used in the sense of something being 'classic' – as in a 'classic song' etc.)

à-meh-rí-kaa N เมริกา America

à-meh-rí-kan N เมริกัน an American/from America

amnâat N อำนาจ authority/to have power

amphoeh N (pronounced similar to 'am-pur') อำเภอ an administrative district (often written in English as 'amphoe')

an N (pronounced like 'un') อัน universal classifier (i.e. counting word) for things when the specific classifier for the item is unknown – e.g. may be used in the case of such things as hamburgers, spectacles, etc.

à-naa-jaan ADJ อนาจาร lewd/ immoral act or conduct

à-na-khót N อนาคต the future

ang-krìt N อังกฤษ England, English

à-ngùn N องุ่น grapes

an-tàraai ADJ อันตราย danger; to be dangerous; peril, harm; dangerous

à-númát V (FORMAL) อนุมัติ to approve/consent, e.g. of a building, or a tender (for a project) etc.

à-núrák V อนุรักษ์ to preserve/ conserve, e.g. an old building/historical site etc.

ànú-sáa-wárii N อนุสาวรีย์ a monument

à-nú-sá-wárii chai N อนุสาวรีย์ชัยฯ (COLLOQUIAL – slightly shortened version of the formal full name) the Victory monument in Bangkok, commemorating the Thai armed forces and temporary gains of territory in WW II

à-nú-sá-wárii prà-chaa-thíp-pàtai N อนุสาวรีย์ประชา ธิปไตย the Democracy Monument in Bangkok commemorating the establishment of a representative form of politics after the overthrow of the Absolute Monarchy in 1932

à-nú-yâat V อนุญาต to let, allow, permit

ao V เอา to take, receive or

accept (something from someone)

ao àwk v เอาออก to take out, remove

ao cháná เอาชนะ to defeat/ beat (someone/something)

ao iik láew (COLLOQUIAL) เอาอีก แล้ว Not again!/Here we go again/(they're) at it again

ao jai v เอาใจ to please someone, make (someone) happy, to go along with (someone)

ao jai sài v เอาใจใส่ to pay attention (to), take an interest (in), be conscientious, put one's mind to something

ao jing (COLLOQUIAL) เอาจริง serious (i.e. to do something seriously/not kidding around)

ao kan (COLLOQUIAL/SLANG) เอา กัน to have sex/to mate/to screw

ao lá (COLLOQUIAL) เอาละ OK then, now then

ao loei (COLLOQUIAL) เอาเลย go for it!

ao maa v เอามา to bring

ao mǎi v (colloquial question

form used for offering something to someone) เอา ไหม Do you want it?

ao pai v เอาไป to take (away)

ao priap v เอาเปรียบ to take advantage of (someone else), to exploit (someone)

ao tàeh jai tua ehng เอาแต่ ใจตัวเอง to be self-centered/ self-indulgent/think of one's own interests rather than anyone else's

ao tua râwt (COLLOQUIAL/IDIOM) เอาตัวรอด to save one's own skin, to get out of a predicament

à-páatmehn N (from English) อะพาร์ตเมนต์ apartment

à-phai v ภัย to pardon/forgive (When used in speech as in to 'forgive' someone you say **hâi à-phai** ให้อภัย)

àrai อะไร (question word generally used at the end of a sentence) what?

àrai iik อะไรอีก (is there) anything else?

àrai kan (COLLOQUIAL) อะไรกัน 'what's going on?', 'what's up?'

162

àrai kâw dâi (COLLOQUIAL) อะไร
ก็ได้ anything at all/anything
is OK, e.g. in response to the
question 'what would you
like to eat? – 'anything at all/
anything would be OK'

àrai ná (COLLOQUIAL) อะไรนะ
pardon me? what did you
say?

àròi ADJ อร่อย to be delicious,
tasty

àt v อัด to compress, pack
tight, press

àt-chàriya N อัจฉริยะ a genius,
prodigy, master (of some art
or skill)

àt dii wii dii v อัดดีวีดี to
record a DVD

àt siang v อัดเสียง to record
(music/a voice/a sound)

àthi-baai v อธิบาย to explain

àt-traa lâeh plian N อัตราแลก
เปลี่ยน rate of exchange for
foreign currency

à-wá-kâat N อวกาศ space (i.e.
outer space)

àwk ออก out

àwk jàak ออกจาก to leave,
depart

àwk kamlang kaai v (pro-

nounced something like
'ork gum-lung guy')
ออกกำลังกาย to exercise

àwk pai v ออกไป go out,
leave, exit; also used when
someone (in a room/house)
is angry and orders/
commands another person
to 'get out!'

àwk siang v ออกเสียง to
pronounce (a word), also –
to vote (in an election)

âwm v อ้อม to go around, to
make a detour

àwn ADJ อ่อน soft, tender, mild
(not strong), weak, feeble

àwn aeh ADJ อ่อนแอ to be
weak/to feel weak

âwn wawn v อ้อนวอน to
plead/to beg

àwn yohn ADJ อ่อนโยน to be
gentle (behaviour)/graceful/
gracefully

awp-fít N (from English)
ออฟฟิศ office

áwt-sà-treh-lia N ออสเตรเลีย
Australia

B

bàa N บ่า shoulder

bâa ADJ บ้า to be insane, crazy; (COLLOQUIAL) **âi bâa** ไอ้บ้า 'You must be mad/out of your mind', 'You jerk/dickhead'

baa N (from English) บาร์ a bar (serving drinks)

bài N บ่าย afternoon, from midday until 4 p.m. – generally referred to as *tawn bài* ตอนบ่าย

bài biang V บ่ายเบี่ยง to be evasive, equivocate, dodge (e.g. answering a question)

bâan N บ้าน home, house: (COLLOQUIAL) **klàp bâan** กลับ บ้าน to go home/return home; **phûean bâan** (literally, 'friend'-'house') เพื่อนบ้าน neighbour

bâan nâwk N (COLLOQUIAL) บ้านนอก the country, rural, up-country, the sticks

bâang บ้าง some, partly, somewhat: **phǒm khǎw bâang** ผมขอบ้าง can I (male speaking) have some?

baang บาง some: e.g. **baang khon** บางคน some people; **baang khráng** บางครั้ง some time(s); **baang hàeng** บาง แห่ง some places; **baang yàang** บางอย่าง some things

baang ADJ บาง to be thin (of objects)

bàap N บาป sin, moral wrongdoing

bàat N บาท Baht (Thai currency) (IDIOM/COLLOQUIAL) **mâi tem bàat** ไม่เต็มบาท to be mad/not the full quid (Baht) / a few screws loose

bàat V บาด to cut/slice/ wound; **bàat jèp** บาดเจ็บ to be injured/wounded; **bàat jai** บาดใจ to be hurt, for one's feelings to be hurt; **bàat phlǎeh** บาดแผล a wound/ cut/laceration (NOTE: a very loud or deafening noise, e.g. deafening music is **bàat hǔu** บาดหู; also to be intolerable/ offensive to the eyes/ dazzling **bàat taa** บาดตา)

bàat N บาตร the alms or begging bowl of a Buddhist monk (NOTE: to make an offering of food to a monk by placing food in his bowl is to **tàk bàat** ตักบาตร)

bàat lǔang N บาทหลวง a priest (from any one of the Christian denominations)

baehn ADJ แบน to be flat (e.g. a flat tyre)

baehn V, N (from English) แบน to ban/a ban

bàehp N แบบ design/style/ kind/pattern (for tailoring) (NOTE: a female model is **nang bàehp** นางแบบ while a male model is **naai bàehp** นายแบบ)

bàehp fawm N (from English 'form') แบบฟอร์ม a form (a document with blanks for filling in with information)

bàehp nii ADV แบบนี้ (COLLOQUIAL) (do it) like this (NOTE: to elicit the response 'like this' – you could ask the following question 'how do you do it?' **bàehp nǎi** แบบไหน)

bàeng V แบ่ง to divide/share/ separate

bàet-toeh-rîi N (from English) แบตเตอรี่ battery (NOTE:

in colloquial speech this is commonly just **bàet** แบต)

bai N (from English) ใบ bisexual

bai à-nú-yâat N ใบอนุญาต a permit/a form giving approval (e.g. to build a house)/a licence

bai khàp khìi N ใบขับขี่ a driver's licence (for a car, truck, or motorbike)

bai mái N ใบไม้ a leaf/leaves

bai sàng N ใบสั่ง order (placed for food, goods); a ticket (fine)/police summons

bai sàng yaa N ใบสั่งยา a prescription

bai sèt N ใบเสร็จ a receipt

bam-bàt V (pronounced 'bum-but') บำบัด to treat/cure/ alleviate (a condition) (NOTE: physiotherapy is **kaai-yá-phâap bam-bàt** กายภาพบำบัด)

bà-mìi N บะหมี่ egg noodles

bam-naan N (pronounced 'bum-narn') บำนาญ a pension

banchii N บัญชี an account (e.g. a bank account) (NOTE:

to open a bank account is
pòeht banchii (เปิดบัญชี)

bandai N บันได steps, stairs,
a ladder

bandai lûean N บันไดเลื่อน an
escalator

bâng fai N บั้งไฟ skyrocket
(commonly fired during
certain festivals in NE
Thailand)

bang-kà-loh N (from English)
บังกะโล lodge, bungalow
(guest house)

bangkháp V บังคับ to force,
compel

bang-oehn ADV บังเอิญ accidentally, by accident, by
chance, unexpectedly (e.g. to
meet someone by accident)

banjù V บรรจุ to load (up),
pack (a suitcase)

banphá-burùt N บรรพบุรุษ
ancestor(s)

banthúek N, V บันทึก a note/
memorandum; to note, to
record (e.g. minutes of a
meeting, etc.)

**banthúek khàaw prajam
wan** N บันทึกข่าวประจำวัน
diary, journal

banyaai V บรรยาย to lecture,
describe

ban-yaa-kàat N บรรยากาศ
climate, atmosphere,
ambience

bao ADJ เบา to be light
(not heavy) (NOTE: to do
something gently/softly –
e.g. a massage/to speak – is
bao-bao เบาๆ)

bao wǎen N เบาหวาน
diabetes

bàt N (pronounced like the
word 'but') บัตร a card/
ticket/coupon (NOTE: an
identity card – held by all
adult Thai citizens – is **bàt
prà-chaachon** บัตรประชาชน;
also widely used in Thailand
– name card/business card
naam bàt นามบัตร)

ba-w N เบาะ cushion/padded
seat (in car etc.)

bàw náam baa-daan N บ่อน้ำ
บาดาล a well (for water)

bàwk V บอก to tell; let
someone know

bàwk khàwp khun บอก
ขอบคุณ to say thank you

bàwk láew V (COLLOQUIAL) บอก

166

แล้ว (I) told you already, (I) told you so

bàwk mâi thùuk (COLLOQUIAL) บอกไม่ถูก (I) can't say, (I) can't put my finger on it

bàwk sĭa jai บอกเสียใจ to say sorry

bawm N (from English) บอมบ์ bomb (also commonly used following the troubles in the three southernmost provinces on Thailand's east coast: **khaa bawm** คาร์บอมบ์ car bomb)

bawn N (from English) บอล a ball, (COLLOQUIAL) the game of football (soccer)

bàwn N บ่อน place for gambling (the full expression for 'a gambling den' is **bàwn kaan phá-nan** บ่อนการพนัน)

bâwng kanchaa N บ้องกัญชา a bong (water pipe) for smoking marihuana

bawri-jàak v บริจาค to donate, give to charity

bawri-kaan N, V บริการ service/to give service

bawri-sàt N บริษัท company, firm

bawri-sùt ADJ บริสุทธิ์ to be pure, innocent – also used to refer to a virgin

bawri-wehn N บริเวณ vicinity, area

bàwt ADJ บอด to be blind; **khon taa bàwt** (literally 'person'-'eye[s]'-'blind') คน ตาบอด a blind person

bàwt sĭi ADJ บอดสี to be colour blind (literally, 'blind'- 'colour')

bèt N เบ็ด a fish hook

beung N บึง a swamp/marsh

bia N (from English) เบียร์ beer

bi-daa N บิดา (formal term for) father

bin N (from English) บิล (the) bill

bin v บิน to fly

bláek-meh v (from English) แบล็กเมล์ blackmail

boeh N (from the English word 'number' and pronounced 'ber') เบอร์ (most commonly used to refer to telephone numbers and sometimes numbers of lottery tickets; also used when selecting a particular young woman in a massage parlor or a dancer in a go-go bar – these women generally wear 'numbers' when working)

bòehk v เบิก to withdraw (money), to requisition (funds)

bòhk mueh v โบกมือ to wave a hand/hands

boh-nút N (from English) โบนัส a bonus

bohraan ADJ โบราณ ancient, antique, old-fashioned

bòht N โบสถ์ a temple but of a non-Buddhist variety: e.g. a Christian church **bòht faràng** โบสถ์ฝรั่ง; a synagogue **bòht yiu** โบสถ์ยิว

bòi ADV บ่อย often, frequent

bon PREP บน on, at

bòn v บ่น to complain

bòt bàat N บทบาท a role (i.e. a role in a movie/in real life)

bòt khwaam N บทความ an article (e.g. in a newspaper)

bòt rian N บทเรียน a lesson (i.e. in a classroom/in real life)

bòt sònthá-naa N (FORMAL) บท

สนทนา conversation

bòt sùat mon N บทสวดมนต์ a prayer

bráwkkhohlîi N (from English) บรอกโคลี broccoli

brèhk N, v (from English) เบรก a brake (in a car); to brake (while driving) (NOTE: the same word is also used for the English word 'break' as in to 'have a break' [while working])

bua N บัว lotus (flower), water lily

bùak PREP บวก plus, to add

buam ADJ บวม to be swollen

bûan v บ้วน to spit out; **náam yaa bûan pàak** น้ำยาบ้วนปาก mouthwash (e.g. Listerine)

bùat v บวช to be ordained, to enter the (Buddhist) monkhood (the full expression being **bùat phrá** บวชพระ)

bùea v เบื่อ to be bored, to be tired of, fed up (with), cannot stand (someone or something)

bûeang tôn ADJ เบื้องต้น introductory/ elementary/primary (e.g. level of learning);

168

initially/at the outset

bùkkhá-lík ɴ บุคลิก character/
personality

bun ɴ บุญ Buddhist concept of
merit (for the afterlife)

bun khun ɴ บุญคุณ a favour,
kindness, sense of indebted-
ness to someone else for
their kindness or support.
A very significant aspect of
Thai culture.

burii ɴ บุหรี่ cigarette

bùt ɴ บุตร (pronounced similar
to 'put' but with a 'b' rather
than a 'p', and a low tone)
child/children/offspring
(Note: an adopted child is
bùt bun-tham บุตรบุญธรรม)

buu-chaa v บูชา to worship/
revere/venerate

bùut adj บูด to be rancid/sour/
spoiled (of food) (Note: to
be sullen looking/sour-faced
is nâa bùut หน้าบูด)

CH

Note: all the entries here begin
with 'ch' – this being a sound
found both in English and
Thai. As for the single English
letter 'c' (pronounced as 'see')
– this is represented by other
letters and in other ways with
the system of romanization
used in this dictionary

chaa ɴ ชา tea; also to be
numb, without sensation

cháa adj ช้า to be slow; cháa-
cháa ช้าๆ (e.g. drive/speak)
slowly

chăai v ฉาย to shine a light
(Note: chăai năng v ฉายหนัง
is to screen/show a movie/
film)

chaai ɴ ชาย male, masculine
(general term and only for
humans)

chaai daehn ɴ ชายแดน
border (between countries)

chaai hàat ɴ ชายหาด beach

chaam ɴ ชาม a bowl

cháang ɴ ช้าง an elephant

châang N ช่าง a tradesperson, skilled person (a few examples are included in the following entries)

châang fai-fáa N ช่างไฟฟ้า an electrician (NOTE: the word **fai-fáa** ไฟฟ้า means 'electricity/electrical')

châang mái N ช่างไม้ carpenter (NOTE: the word **mái** ไม้ means 'wood')

cháang náam N ช้างน้ำ hippopotamus (nowadays the abbreviated English form 'hippo' is commonly used in Thailand: **híppo** ฮิปโป)

châang tàt phŏm N ช่าง ตัดผม barber

châat N ชาติ nation, country

chaaw bâan N ชาวบ้าน villager(s) (also general term for 'common people' whether in cities, towns, or villages)

chaaw indohnii-sia N ชาว อินโดนีเซีย Indonesian person/people

chaaw khàmĕhn N ชาวเขมร Cambodian person/people

chaaw khăo ชาวเขา hill tribe(s)

chaaw maa-lehsia N ชาว มาเลเซีย Malaysian person/people

chaaw naa N ชาวนา a farmer, someone who works the land (rice growers etc.)

chaaw phà-mâa N ชาวพม่า Burmese person/people

chaaw phúehn mueang N ชาวพื้นเมือง indigenous people(s)

chaaw phút N ชาวพุทธ Buddhist(s)

chaaw tàang prathêht N ชาวต่างประเทศ a foreigner/foreigners

chaaw tà-wan tòk N ชาว ตะวันตก a westerner

chaaw wîat-naam N ชาว เวียดนาม Vietnamese person/people

chaaw yîipùn N ชาวญี่ปุ่น Japanese person/people

chà-bàp ฉบับ classifier for counting newspapers, letters, and documents

châeh V แฉ to reveal, disclose, expose

châeh khăeng V แช่แข็ง to freeze; to be frozen

chái ใช้ to use, utilize

châi ใช่ yes (Note: one of numerous ways 'yes' is expressed in Thai)

chái dâi (COLLOQUIAL) ใช้ได้ It's usable/it works; also valid

chái mâi dâi (COLLOQUIAL) ใช้ ไม่ได้ no good, unusable, out of order

chái nîi v ใช้หนี้ pay off a debt, repay

chai yoh ไชโย hooray, cheers!

chák v ชัก to have convulsions, to pull, jerk

chák chuan v ชักชวน to invite, persuade, induce (someone to do something)

chák wâaw v ชักว่าว to fly a kite; (SLANG) to masturbate, jerk off

chà-lǎam N ฉลาม shark

chà-làat ADJ ฉลาด astute, bright, smart, intelligent

chà-lǎwng v ฉลอง to celebrate (e.g. on passing an exam)

chà-lìa v เฉลี่ย to average (numbers), divide equally

chà-lǒem v เฉลิม to celebrate (e.g. the King's birthday)

chám ADJ ช้ำ to be bruised

chamnaan v ชำนาญ to be highly skilled at something, have expertise

chamrút ADJ ชำรุด to be damaged

chan ADJ ชัน to be steep (e.g. a hill)

chán N ชั้น a layer, level, storey (of a building); class, category

chǎn PRON (INFORMAL/INTIMATE) ฉัน I, me

chá-ná v ชนะ to win, to beat, defeat, be victorious

chang v ชัง to hate, detest

châng v ชั่ง to weigh (something)

châng man (COLLOQUIAL) ช่างมัน 'Who cares!', 'Forget it!', 'To hell with it!'

chá-nít N ชนิด type, sort

chánít nǎi (or more commonly) bàehp nǎi แบบ ไหน what kind of?

chà-nòht N โฉนด land titles, property

châo v เช่า to hire, rent

cháo N เช้า morning

cháo mûehd N เช้ามืด dusk

171

cháo trùu N เช้าตรู่ dawn, very early in the morning

chà-phá-w ADV เฉพาะ only, exclusively for

chát ADJ, ADV ชัด clear, clearly (e.g. the image on a television screen; to speak clearly or fluently)

chát jehn ADJ ชัดเจน to be distinct (a view, the meaning of what is said, the way someone speaks), very clear

cháwk-khoh-láet N (from English) ช็อกโกแลต chocolate

cháwn N ช้อน spoon

cháwn chaa N ช้อนชา teaspoon

châwng N ช่อง hole, aperture, slot, space, gap (also used when referring to a television channel – e.g. Channel 7 is **châwng jèt** ช่องเจ็ด)

châwng khâehp N ช่องแคบ strait (i.e. Straits of Gibraltar), narrow channel

châwng khlâwt N (polite medical term) ช่องคลอด vagina

châwng tháwng N ช่องท้อง abdomen

châwng wâang N ช่องว่าง a gap, a vacant space

châwp V ชอบ to be fond of; like, be pleased by

châwp mâak kwàa ชอบ มากกว่า to prefer

chék N, V เช็ค a (bank/ travellers') cheque/check (also used in the English sense of 'to check something to see if it is OK/functioning' etc.)

chên เช่น... for example ..., such as

chên khoei เช่นเคย as usual, as before (e.g. he's doing it again, as usual)

chên nán เช่นนั้น like that, in that way/manner

chét V เช็ด to wipe

chia V เชียร์ (from English) to cheer

chīao chaan ADJ เชี่ยวชาญ to be skilled, experienced, expert

chíi V ชี้ to point (at, to)

chìi V (COLLOQUIAL) ฉี่ to urinate, to pee

chíi níu V ชี้นิ้ว to give orders (i.e. point the finger ordering

172

someone to do this, that and
the other)

chiik v ฉีก to tear, rip

chiit v ฉีด to inject: **chiit yaa**
ฉีดยา to give an injection of
liquid medicine

chiit sà-preh v ฉีดสเปรย์ to
spray

chiit wák-siin v ฉีดวัคซีน
to vaccinate, to perform a
vaccination

chii-wit N ชีวิต life

chii-wit chii-waa ADJ
(COLLOQUIAL) ชีวิตชีวา to be
lively, vigorous, full of life

chim v ชิม to taste or sample
something

chin ADJ ชิน to be accustomed
(to), used to, familiar (with)

chín N ชิ้น piece, section,
morsel, slice

choehn v (pronounced like
'churn') เชิญ to invite
(formally); please (go ahead)

chóeht N (from English) เชิ้ต
shirt with collar

choei ADJ (COLLOQUIAL) เชย to
be outdated, old fashioned,
not with it,

chöei ADJ เฉย to be impartial,

indifferent, uninterested in
(commonly reduplicated
when spoken: **chöei–chöei**
เฉยๆ)

chôhk N โชค luck

chôhk dii โชคดี good luck! to
be lucky

chôhk dii thîi... ADV โชคดีที่...
fortunately

chôhk ráai ADV โชคร้าย
unluck(il)y, unfortunately

chók v ชก to punch, strike

chók muai ชกมวย boxing
(Western style), fighting

chom v ชม to admire,
compliment, praise

chom wiu ชมวิว to view,
look at

chomphuu N ชมพู pink
(colour) (for a list of the
most common colours see
the entry under **sǐi** สี which
means 'colour')

chomphûu N ชมพู่ rose apple
(fruit)

chon v ชน to collide with/
bump into, to crash into

chon klùm nói N ชนกลุ่มน้อย
ethnic group, minority group

chong v ชง to infuse, steep

173

chong chaa v ชงชา to make (a cup/pot of) tea

chonná-bòt N (FORMAL) ชนบท (COLLOQUIAL) **bâan nâwk** N บ้านนอก countryside, rural area

chót choei v ชดเชย to compensate (for damage to property, etc.), indemnify

chûa khànà N ชั่วขณะ a moment, an instant

chûa khrao ADJ ชั่วคราว to be temporary

chûa mohng N ชั่วโมง an hour; classifier for counting hours

chûai v ช่วย to assist, help; please (request for help: e.g. 'can you please give me that glass')

chûai dûai ช่วยด้วย help! (there's a fire/there's been an accident)

chûai lŭea v ช่วยเหลือ to rescue

chuan v ชวน to invite (ask along)

chûea v เชื่อ to believe

chûea fang v เชื่อฟัง to obey

chúea raa N เชื้อรา fungus, mould/mold

chúea rôhk N เชื้อโรค germs,

infection (often simply **chúea** เชื้อ)

chûeak N เชือก rope, string, cord

chûeang ADJ เชื่อง to be tame (of an animal)

chûeh N ชื่อ name

chûeh lên N ชื่อเล่น nickname

chûeh tua N ชื่อตัว first name, personal name

chúehn ADJ ชื้น damp, humid

chúi ADJ (COLLOQUIAL) ฉุย crappy, lousy; to be done in a careless, slipshod way

chùk chŏehn N ฉุกเฉิน emergency

chŭn ADJ ฉุน to be pungent (odour); to be angry

chúp v ชุบ to soak; to plate (metal)

chút N ชุด set (of clothes, furniture, etc.)

chút chán nai N ชุดชั้นใน underwear (more typically used to refer to female underwear)

chút nawn N ชุดนอน nightclothes, pajamas

chút wâai náam N ชุดว่ายน้ำ swimming costume, swimsuit

D

dàa v ด่า to curse, to scold or berate; to tell someone off; to swear at

dâai N ด้าย thread (e.g. cotton thread)

dâan N ด้าน side (e.g. the back side of a house, the other side of an object, etc.), direction

dâan ADJ ด้าน to be hard/calloused, rough to the touch; also matte finish, dull, not shiny (NOTE: **nâa dâan** หน้าด้าน is thick skinned, shameless, brazen)

dâan khwǎa N ด้านขวา on the right side

dâan nâa N ด้านหน้า front, in the front

dâan nâwk N ด้านนอก outside

dâan sáai N ด้านซ้าย on the left side

daa-raa N ดารา movie/TV star

daaw N ดาว star

daehng N แดง red (for a list of the most common colours see the entry under **sǐi** สี which means 'colour')

dàeht แดด sunlight, sunshine (NOTE: **àab dàeht** v อาบแดด is to sunbake, sunbathe)

dàeht àwk ADJ แดดออก to be sunny

dâi v ได้ to obtain, get, be able to, can; get to, gain (An important 'function' word in Thai. For example, 'can you?' (**dâi mǎi** ได้ไหม) questions are formed in this way: 'name of activity' + 'can you?' – **ao rót maa dâi mǎi** เอารถมาได้ไหม 'Can you bring the car?' To simply answer yes is **dâi** ได้; to answer no is **mâi dâi** ไม่ได้.)

dâi dii v ได้ดี to make good, do well

dâi phǒn ได้ผล to be effective, to get results

dâi ráp v ได้รับ to get, receive

dâi ráp à-nú-yâat v ได้รับอนุญาต to be allowed to, to be given permission

dâi ráp bàat jèp v ได้รับบาดเจ็บ to be injured

dâi thîi v ได้ที่ get the upper hand, not excessive or extreme

dâi yin v ได้ยิน to hear

dam N ดำ black, a dark hue (for a list of the most common colours see the entry under **sǐi** สี which means 'colour')

dan v (pronounced like 'dun') ดัน to push, shove

dang ADJ (pronounced like 'dung') ดัง to be loud (sound); also to be famous

dâng doehm ADJ ดั้งเดิม traditional, original

dang nán ADV (FORMAL) ดังนั้น so, therefore

dao v เดา to guess, speculate

dàp v ดับ go out (fire, candle), to extinguish; (also slang meaning) to die/be killed

dàt v (pronounced like 'dut') ดัด to bend; to shape; to straighten out

dàt phǒm v ดัดผม to perm hair

dàwk bîa N ดอกเบี้ย interest (money)

dàwk bua N ดอกบัว lotus, water lily

dàwk kà-làm N ดอกกะหล่ำ cauliflower

dàwk mái N ดอกไม้ flower

dáwktoeh N (from English) ด็อกเตอร์ Doctor (PhD)

dawn N (pronounced like 'don') (COLLOQUIAL) ดอล dollar

dawng ADJ (pronounced like 'dong') ดอง pickled, preserved (fruit, vegetables)

dèk N เด็ก child (young person; also commonly used to refer to adults who are in very junior, or lowly, positions in an organization)

dèk àwn N เด็กอ่อน infant, baby, small child

dèk chaai N เด็กชาย boy

dèk kamphráa N เด็กกำพร้า an orphan

dèk nák-rian N เด็กนักเรียน schoolchild(ren)

dèk phûu-yǐng N เด็กผู้หญิง girl

dèk wát v, N เด็กวัด temple boy

dèt ADJ เด็ด decisive, resolute, bold ADV really, quite

dèt khàat ADV เด็ดขาด absolutely, strictly, definitely

dǐao ADV เดี๋ยว for a moment, just a moment

diao ADJ เดียว single, one, only (NOTE: **khon diao** N คน เดียว is 'alone', 'by oneself'; 'single person')

diao kan เดียวกัน the same – as in **khon diao kan** คน เดียวกัน 'the same person'

diao nii เดี๋ยวนี้ right now, now

diao nii ehng เดี๋ยวนี้เอง just now

dichǎn PRON (FORMAL) ดิฉัน I (female speakers)

dii N (COLLOQUIAL) ตี้ (feminine) lesbian (from the English word 'lady')

dii ADJ ดี fine (okay), good, nice, well

dii jai ADJ ดีใจ glad, happy

dii khûen V ดีขึ้น to improve, get better

dii kwàa ADV, ADJ ดีกว่า better, better than

dii mâak ADJ ดีมาก well done! very good

dii thîi sùt ADJ ดีที่สุด (the) best

dii wii dii N (from English) ดีวีดี DVD

dík N (COLLOQUIAL – from English 'dictionary') ดิค dictionary

din N ดิน earth, soil, ground

din-sǎw N ดินสอ pencil

dip ADJ ดิบ raw, uncooked, unripe, rare (as with a steak)

doehm ADJ เดิม former, previous, old, original

doehn V เดิน to walk

doehn lên V เดินเล่น to go for a stroll; a walk for leisure

doehn maa V เดินมา on foot (coming); **doehn pai** V เดินไป on foot (going)

doehn pai dâi เดินไปได้ (within) walking distance

doehn ruea V เดินเรือ to operate/sail a vessel/ship/ boat

doehn thaang V เดินทาง to travel, take a trip

doehn thaang dohy plàwt phai ná (POLITE EXPRESSION) เดินทางโดยปลอดภัยนะ Have a safe trip

dohn V (pronounced as in 'Methad*one*') โดน passive form, e.g. **dohn rót chon** โดน รถชน to be hit by a car, to be punished, to get it in the neck (NOTE: **dohn dii** V (COLLOQUIAL) โดนดี to cop it, to get what one is asking for)

dohy PREP โดย by (author, artist); by way of, by means of

dohy bang-oehn ADV โดย บังเอิญ accidentally, by chance

dohy chà-phá-w ADV โดย เฉพาะ particularly, especially

dohy mâi mii ADV โดยไม่มี without

dohy mâi tâng-jai โดยไม่ตั้งใจ by chance, not intentionally

dohy pà-kà-tì ADV โดยปกติ normally, usually

dohy rótfai โดยรถไฟ (to go/ be transported) by rail, by train

dohy sîn choehng ADV โดยสิ้นเชิง completely (thoroughly)

dohy thûa pai ADV โดยทั่วไป in general, generally

dohy trong ADV โดยตรง directly

dòk ADJ ดก abundant, plentiful

dom V ดม to smell, inhale, sniff

dontrii N ดนตรี music

dù ADJ ดุ fierce, vicious (e.g. a vicious dog); V to blame, to find fault with, to censure

dù ráai ADJ ดุร้าย ferocious, pugnacious, wild

dûai ด้วย as well, with, by, too, also

dûai kan ADV ด้วยกัน together

dûai khwaam praat-thànăa dii (FORMAL) ด้วยความ ปรารถนาดี best wishes

duai khwaam sĭa jai (FORMAL) ด้วยความเสียใจ with regret(s), regrettably

dûai khwaam wăng (FORMAL) ด้วยความหวัง hopefully

dûai khwaam yindii (FORMAL) ด้วยความยินดี with pleasure

dûai mueh V ด้วยมือ by hand

dûai wí-thii (FORMAL) ด้วยวิธี... by means of, using the method of

dùan ADJ ด่วน to be urgent, pressing, express (e.g. as in express bus)

duang jan N ดวงจันทร์ (the) moon

duean N เดือน month

duean nâa N เดือนหน้า next month

duean níi N เดือนนี้ this month

178

dùeat v, ADJ เดือด to reach the boiling point, to rage at

dùeat ráwn ADJ เดือดว้าน to be in trouble, in a fix, distressed

dûeh ADJ ดื้อ stubborn, obstinate, headstrong

dùehm v ดื่ม to drink

dùek ADV ดึก late at night

dueng v ดึง to pull

dueng ao wái v ดึงเอาไว้ (pull up) to restrain; to tighten (a rope etc.) up

duu v ดู to look at, to see, to watch (TV, movie)

duu àwk v ดูออก to be able to see through (someone or something), to understand, to be able to tell

duu duang v ดูดวง to look at one's horoscope; N fortune telling

duu laeh v ดูแล to take care of, look after

duu lên v ดูเล่น to look at something for fun (to pass time)

duu mǎw v (COLLOQUIAL) (**mǎw** is pronounced 'more' with a rising tone) ดูหมอ to have your fortune told/read, see a

fortune teller

duu mǔean ดูเหมือน to seem (e.g. as if something was going to happen), look as if

duu mǔeankan ดูเหมือนกัน to look the same

duu sí (COLLOQUIAL) ดูซิ look!

duu thùuk v ดูถูก to look down on someone, insult, disparage

dùut ดูด to suck, to absorb, soak up

E

eh-ds N เอดส์ AIDS (the fuller form is **rôhk eh-ds** (literally, 'disease' + 'AIDS') โรคเอดส์)

èhk-kàchon N เอกชน private (company/sector)

èhk-kà-phâap N เอกภาพ unity, solidarity

èhk-kà-râat N เอกราช (of a state, nation) independent, free sovereign

èhk-kà-sǎan N เอกสาร document(s), printed material, records

ehng N เอง self (NOTE: **tua ehng** ตัวเอง is 'myself')

eh-o N เอว waist

eh-sia N เอเชีย Asia

en N เอ็น tendon

F

fǎa N ฝา lid, cover, (internal) wall

fàa v ฝ่า to go against/undergo, violate, disobey

fàa N ฝ่า palm (of the hand), sole (of the foot)

fǎa ADJ ฝ้า clouded (like a cloudy film of the surface of something); scum, blemish; **pen fǎa เป็นฝ้า** to have freckles

fáa N ฟ้า sky, light blue colour (for a list of the most common colours see the entry under **sǐi สี** which means 'colour')

fáa phàa N ฟ้าผ่า lightning

fǎa phànǎng N ฝาผนัง wall (of a room or building)

fáa ráwng N ฟ้าร้อง thunder

fâai N ฝ้าย cotton

fàai N ฝ่าย side, group, party

fàai diao N ฝ่ายเดียว one (party, side)

fàai trong khâam N ฝ่ายตรงข้าม opponent(s), (the) opposition (in politics etc.)

fàak v ฝาก leave behind for safekeeping, deposit, entrust to someone, leave with

faam N (from English 'farm', pronounced similar to the English) ฟาร์ม farm

faeh-chân N (from English) แฟชั่น fashion (i.e. the latest fashion, etc.)

faehn N แฟน boy/girlfriend, fan (admirer) (NOTE: also commonly used to refer to a husband or wife)

fáek N (from English) แฟกซ์ fax (message or machine)

fàet ADJ แฝด twin, double, coupled, paired (NOTE: **fǎa fàet ฝาแฝด** is 'twins')

fǎi N ไฝ mole, beauty spot

fai N ไฟ fire; light (lamp)

fai chǎai N ไฟฉาย flashlight, torch

fai cháek N ไฟแช็ค cigarette lighter

fai fáa N ไฟฟ้า electric, electricity

fai mâi v ไฟไหม้ to be on fire

fák thawng N (pronounced 'fuck tong') ฟักทอง pumpkin

fan N (pronounced like 'fun') ฟัน tooth, teeth

fǎn V, N (pronounced like 'fun' with a rising tone) ฝัน to dream; a dream

fǎn klaang wan N ฝันกลางวัน to daydream

fǎn ráai N ฝันร้าย a nightmare

fǎn thǔeng V ฝันถึง to dream about (somebody)

fang V ฟัง to listen, to hear

fǎng V ฝัง to bury, implant

fàng N ฝั่ง bank (river), shore

fang yùu V ฟังอยู่ (to be) listening (the use of **yùu** อยู่ after a verb indicates the present continuous tense – '…ing')

fâo V เฝ้า watch over, tend, take care of, keep watch

fâo duu V เฝ้าดู keep an eye on, keep watch (over, on)

fâo rá-wang V เฝ้าระวัง to guard against, be on the alert/lookout (for)

fàràng N ฝรั่ง caucasian, westerner; guava (fruit)

fàràngsèht N ฝรั่งเศส France, French

fawng N ฟอง foam, bubbles, froth, lather; a classifier for eggs

fáwng V ฟ้อง to sue, file legal proceedings, accuse, complain to someone about somebody else

fawng náam N ฟองน้ำ a sponge

fǐi N ฝี boil, pustule, abscess (NOTE: **plùuk fǐi** ปลูกฝี is 'to vaccinate')

fǐi mueh ADJ ฝีมือ workmanship, craftsmanship, handiwork, skill; **fǐi pàak** ADJ ฝีปาก verbal skill/gift of the gab

filippin N ฟิลิปปินส์ Philippines

fim N ฟิล์ม film (for camera; or the tinted film on a car windscreen)

fìn N ฝิ่น opium

fíu N (from English) ฟิวส์ fuse

fláet N (from English) แฟลต flat, apartment

foeh-ní-jôeh N (from English – pronounced like 'fer-ni-jer') เฟอร์นิเจอร์ furniture

fǒn N ฝน rain (NOTE: **nâa fǒn** หน้าฝน is the 'rainy season')

– generally from late May/
early June to the end of
October)

fŏn tòk v ฝนตก to rain,
raining, it is raining

fùeak N เฟือก cast or split (e.g.
for a broken arm/leg)

fúehn N ฟื้น to recover, to
regain consciousness, come
to (after fainting)

fŭehn v ฝืน to disobey,
contrary to, do something
against (the law, one's will,
etc.)

fùek v ฝึก to practise, to drill/
train

fùek hàt v ฝึกหัด to train

fûm-fueh-ai ADJ ฟุ่มเฟือย
luxury, luxurious, extra-
vagant, unnecessary

fùn N ฝุ่น dust

fút N ฟุต foot (length)

fút bawn N ฟุตบอล (COLLOQUIAL)
bawn บอล soccer/football

fŭung ADJ ฝูง a crowd, group,
herd, flock, pack

fŭung nók N ฝูงนก a flock
of birds

fŭung plaa N ฝูงปลา a school
of fish

H

hâa ห้า five

hàa N ห่า cholera demon/spirit
held responsible for plagues;
(SLANG – rude) **âi hàa** ไอ้ห่า
shit, damn, bastard

hăa v หา to look for, look up
(find in book), search for

hăa kin v (COLLOQUIAL) หากิน to
make a living

hăa maa dâi v หามาได้ to
earn

hăa mâi joeh v (COLLOQUIAL)
หาไม่เจอ cannot find
(something)

hăa ngoen v (COLLOQUIAL)
หาเงิน to make (some)
money, to make a living

hăa rûeang v (COLLOQUIAL) หา
เรื่อง to look for trouble; be
abrasive, provocative

hâa sip ห้าสิบ fifty

hăa wâa v หาว่า to accuse
(someone of doing something)

hăa yâak ADJ หายาก rare
(scarce)

háad dis N (from English)
ฮาร์ดดิสก์ hard disk

hăai v หาย lost, disappear; ADJ to be missing

hăai jai v หายใจ to breathe; hăai jai àwk v หายใจออก to breathe out; hăai jai khâo v หายใจเข้า to breathe in

hăai pai v หายไป to disappear, vanish

hăai wai wai หายไวๆ get well soon!

hâam v ห้าม to forbid, to be forbidden

hàan N ห่าน goose

hăan v หาร to divide

hăan dûai v หารด้วย divided by, e.g. 4 hăan dûai 4 = 2 (4 ÷ 4 = 2)

hăang N หาง tail

hàang ADJ ห่าง to be apart/ distant from

hâang sàp-phá-sĭnkháa N ห้างสรรพสินค้า (COLLOQUIAL) hâang ห้าง department store

hàat N หาด beach

hăaw v หาว to yawn

haehm N (from English) แฮม ham

hâehng ADJ แห้ง to be dry

hâehng láehng ADJ แห้งแล้ง dry (weather), drought

hàeng N แห่ง of; classifier for places

hâi v ให้ to give; to, for; to allow, have something done (A very important 'functional' word in Thai. Here are a couple of examples [space limitations make it impossible to go into greater detail about the broad range of uses of hâi ให้]: To have something done: hâi kháo ao rót maa ให้เขาเอา รถมา – 'have him/get him to bring the car (along)'; To do something for somebody: kháo súeh yean hâi faehn เขา ซื้อยีนให้แฟน 'he brought a pair of jeans for his girl-friend'. In the first example the meaning of hâi ให้ is rendered by the word 'have'; in the second example it is the equivalent of the English word 'for'.)

hâi aa-hăan v ให้อาหาร to feed (the dog)

hâi àphai v ให้อภัย to forgive

hâi châo v ให้เช่า to rent out

hâi kaan v ให้การ to plead (in court)

183

hâi khuehn v ให้คืน, (or simply) **khuehn** v คืน to return, give back

hâi yuehm v ให้ยืม to lend

hàk ADJ หัก to break/fracture (e.g. of bones); also to deduct (money owed etc.)

hàk lăng v (COLLOQUIAL) หักหลัง to double-cross, betray

hăm N (SLANG; Isaan dialect) หำ balls (gonads)

hàn v หั่น to cut up, slice

hăn v หัน to turn

hăn klàp v หันกลับ to turn back

hăn nâa v หันหน้า to face, turn one's head, to turn the face toward a direction

hăn phuang-maa-lai v หัน พวงมาลัย to steer (to turn the steering wheel – 'steering wheel' is **phuang-maa-lai** พวงมาลัย)

hanlŏh (from the English greeting) ฮัลโหล hello! (used on the phone)

hào v เห่า to bark

hàt N (pronounced 'hut' with a low tone) หัด measles, German measles; **hàt yur-man** หัด เยอรมัน v to drill, to practise

hàw v (pronounced 'hor') ห่อ to wrap (up a parcel, etc.)

hàw khăwng N ห่อของ package

hăw khoi N หอคอย tower

hăw phák N หอพัก dormitory, hostel

hăwm ADJ หอม to be sweet-smelling, fragrant, aromatic

hăwm v หอม to kiss (the old Thai way of kissing is more like nuzzling or sniffing of one another's cheeks, i.e. face cheeks)

hăwm yài N หอมใหญ่ onion (or **hŭa hăwm** หัวหอม)

hâwng v, N ห้อง room (in house, hotel)

hâwng khrua N ห้องครัว kitchen

hâwng kong N ฮ่องกง Hong Kong

hâwng náam N ห้องน้ำ toilet (bathroom), lavatory

hâwng nâng lên N ห้องนั่งเล่น sitting room, living room, lounge (room)

hâwng nawn N ห้องนอน bedroom

hâwng sà-mùt N ห้องสมุด library

184

hâwng thŏhng N ห้องโถง hall (as in 'assembly hall')

hâwp V หอบ to pant, breathe heavily

hèht-kaan N เหตุการณ์ happening, incident, event

hèht phŏn N เหตุผล reason

hěn V เห็น to see, regard, to think (used to give opinion in reporting speech, e.g. 'I think that'); **hěn dûai** V เห็นด้วย to agree

hěn jai ADJ เห็นใจ to be sympathetic, to understand someone else's position

hěn kàeh tua ADJ เห็นแก่ตัว to be selfish

hěn pen phá-yaan V เห็นเป็นพยาน to witness (something)

hèt N เห็ด mushroom(s)

hĭi N (COLLOQUIAL, EXTREMELY RUDE) หี vagina (or, more accurately, 'cunt')

hiip N หีบ chest (box)

himá N หิมะ snow

himá tòk V หิมะตก to snow, snowing

hĭn N หิน rock, stone

hĭn pà-kaa-rang N หินปะการัง coral (commonly simply

pà-kaa-rang ปะการัง)

hĭu V หิว to be hungry

hĭu V หิ้ว to carry

hĭu náam V หิวน้ำ to be thirsty

hŏi N หอย mollusc/oyster/clam

hôi V ห้อย to hang, be suspended

hŏi naang rom N หอยนางรม a type of large, fleshy oyster

hŏi thâak N หอยทาก snail (or simply **thâak** ทาก)

hòk หก six

hòk V หก to spill (liquid)

hòk lóm V หกล้ม to fall over, take a tumble, (or, more simply, **lóm** ล้ม)

hòk sip หกสิบ sixty

hŏng N หงส์ a swan

hòt V หด to shrink

hŭa N หัว head, top

hŭa boh-raan ADJ หัวโบราณ to be old fashioned, conservative

hŭa jai N หัวใจ heart

hŭa jai waai V, N หัวใจวาย a heart attack

hŭa khăeng ADJ หัวแข็ง obstinate, stubborn, headstrong

hŭa khào N หัวเข่า knee

185

hŭa khâw n หัวข้อ subject, topic, heading

hŭa láan adj หัวล้าน bald

hŭa nâa n หัวหน้า chief, leader, head, boss

hŭa nom n หัวนม nipple(s)

hŭa săi adj (COLLOQUIAL) หัวใส bright, shrewd

hùai adj (COLLOQUIAL/SLANG) ห่วย lousy, crappy, crummy, suck (slang)

hŭai n หวย underground lottery

hŭan v, adj, adv ห้วน to be brusque, curt, uncouth (talk or speech)

hŭan v หวน to turn back

hŭang v หวง to be jealous (of), possessive (of things), unwilling to part with something

hùang adj ห่วง to be anxious, concerned/worried (about)

hŭa rá-w v หัวเราะ to laugh

hŭa rá-w yá-w v หัวเราะเยาะ to laugh at

hŭeng v หึง jealous (commonly of a sexual nature)

hùn n หุ่น dummy, mannequin, also the shape/appearance

of someone's figure (NOTE: 'robot' is **hùn yon** หุ่นยนต์)

hûn n หุ้น share, stock (as traded on the stock market)

hûn sùan n หุ้นส่วน partner (in business)

hŭng v หุง to cook (rice)

hùp khăo n หุบเขา valley

hùp pàak v หุบปาก close the mouth, (COLLOQUIAL) shut up!

hŭu n หู ear(s)

hŭu nùak adj หูหนวก (to be) deaf

I

iik adv ... อีก again

iik adv อีก... another (different); else, more

iik an nùeng อีกอันหนึ่ง (Can I have) another one

iik khon nùeng (COLLOQUIAL) อีกคนหนึ่ง another person, one more person

iik khráng nùeng (COLLOQUIAL) อีกครั้งหนึ่ง again/one more time

iik mâi naan (COLLOQUIAL) อีกไม่ นาน soon

iik sàk nòi (COLLOQUIAL) อีกสัก

หน่อย (Could I have) a little more

iik yàang nùeng (IDIOM) อีก อย่างหนึ่ง by the way, another thing

ii-meh N (from English) อีเมล์ email (message)

ii-sǎan N อีสาน the north-eastern region of Thailand – commonly written in English as Isaan, Isarn

i-lék-thrawnìk ADJ (from English) อิเล็กทรอนิก electronic

im V อิ่ม to be full, eaten one's fill, had enough

india N อินเดีย India

indohniisia N อินโดนีเซีย Indonesia (colloquially Indonesia is often referred to as **in-doh** อินโด)

ing V อิง to lean on/against

inthoehnét N (from English) อินเทอร์เน็ต Internet (or simply **nèt** เน็ต)

ìt N อิฐ brick, a brick

i-taa-lìi N อิตาลี Italy, Italian

ìtchǎa V อิจฉา envy, be jealous of

it-sà-laam N (alternative pronunciation 'islaam') อิสลาม Islam

it-sà-rà ADJ อิสระ to be free, independent

it-sà-rà-phâap N อิสรภาพ freedom

it-thí-phon N อิทธิพล influence

J

jà AUX V จะ shall, will; future indicator

jâa ADJ จ้า bright (light), intense, glaring

jàai V จ่าย to pay; **jàai láew** จ่ายแล้ว (for a bill that has been) paid

jàak PREP จาก of, from

jàak kan V จากกัน to separate (from one another)

jàak pai V จากไป depart, go away from a place

jaam V จาม to sneeze

jaan N จาน a plate/dish

jâang V จ้าง to hire

jàehk V แจก to hand out, distribute

jaeh-kan N แจกัน a vase (for flowers)

187

jâehng v แจ้ง to inform, to notify; **jâehng khwaam** แจ้งความ to report (to the police)

jáekkèt N (from English) แจ็คเก็ต a jacket, coat

jai N ใจ heart, mind

jai dii ADJ ใจดี to be kind, good (of people)

jai kwâang ADJ ใจกว้าง to be generous, broad-minded, magnanimous

jam v (pronounced like 'jum' in 'jump') จำ to remember, to retain

jam dâi v จำได้ to remember/recognize

jam-nuan N จำนวน amount

jam-pen ADJ จำเป็น to be necessary; v to need

jà-mùuk N จมูก nose

jang ADV (COLLOQUIAL) จัง very (used as an intensifier, e.g. 'very beautiful' **sǔai jang** สวยจัง)

jang-wàt N (pronounced something like 'jung-what') จังหวัด a province (regional administrative unit)

jâo bàaw N เจ้าบ่าว bridegroom/groom

jâo nâa thîi N เจ้าหน้าที่ official, bureaucrat, public servant, authority (person in charge)

jâo phâap N เจ้าภาพ host (of a party, wedding, etc.)

jâo sǎaw N เจ้าสาว bride

jàp v จับ to capture, arrest, catch, grab

jà-raa-jawn N จราจร traffic

jàt v (pronounced like the English word 'jut' as in 'to jut out') จัด to arrange (e.g. furniture); also used as an intensifier: e.g. extreme, intense – **ráwn jàt** ร้อนจัด intense/extreme heat

jàt hâi rîap rói v จัดให้เรียบร้อย to tidy up

jàt-kaan v จัดการ to manage, organize, sort out, deal with

jàt tó v จัดโต๊ะ to lay or set a table

jaw N (pronounced like the English word 'jaw') จอ screen, monitor (of television/computer)

jawng v จอง to reserve, to book (seats, tickets)

jàwt rót v จอดรถ to park a vehicle

jeh N (pronounced similar to 'jay') เจ vegetarian; **kin jeh** v กินเจ to eat vegetarian food

jéng ADJ (COLLOQUIAL) เจ๋ง (of an object – e.g. a mobile phone) to be broken, worn out, kaput; (for a business) to go broke/bankrupt

jěng (COLLOQUIAL) เจ๋ง 'that's cool, great, awesome'

jèp ADJ เจ็บ to be sore, hurt (injured)

jèp mâak ADJ, ADV เจ็บมาก to be very painful

jèt เจ็ด seven

jèt sìp เจ็ดสิบ seventy

jiin N (pronounced like the English word 'jean(s)') จีน China, Chinese

jiin klaang จีนกลาง Mainland China; also used to refer to Mandarin Chinese (language)

jiip v (pronounced like 'jeep' with a low tone) จีบ to flirt with someone, to court, to try to chat up someone

jing ADJ, ADV จริง to be true, real

jing-jing ADV จริงๆ really, truly, indeed!

jing-jôh N จิงโจ้ kangaroo

jing-jòk N จิ้งจก house lizard

jing-rìit N จิ้งหรีด cricket (insect)

jing rŭeh INTERJ จริงหรือ Really? Is that so? (used to express surprise)

joeh v (pronounced like 'jer' in 'jerk') เจอ to meet, find

johm tii v โจมตี to attack (in a war)

jom v จม to sink or drown

jom náam v จมน้ำ to drown

jon ADJ จน to be poor

jon krà-thâng CONJ จนกระทั่ง until

jòp v จบ to end (finish)

jòt-mǎai N จดหมาย letter; mail

jòt-mǎai-long thàbian จดหมายลงทะเบียน registered letter/mail

jòt nóht v จดโน้ต to take notes

juan ADV จวน almost

juea jaang ADJ เจือจาง thin (of liquids)

jùeht ADJ จืด bland, tasteless

jueng CONJ จึง (FORMAL – more written than spoken language) consequently, therefore

189

jùt N จุด point, dot

jùt fai V จุดไฟ to light a fire

jùt-jùt ADJ จุดๆ spotted (pattern)

jùt-măai plaai thaang N จุด
หมายปลายทาง destination

jùt mûng măai N จุดมุ่งหมาย
purpose

jùt rôehm tôn N จุดเริ่มต้น
origin, starting point

jùup V, N จูบ kiss

K

NOTE: this letter should not
be confused with the English
'k' sound. In this case 'k' is
pronounced like 'g' in 'gun', or
like the 'k' in the word 'skin'

kà V กะ to estimate (the price),
guess; N a shift – as in a shift
at work (i.e. the night shift)

kaa-faeh N (pronounced 'gar-
fey') กาแฟ coffee

kaam-má-thêhp N กามเทพ
Cupid, Eros

kaan N การ... the action/task/
business of...

kaan bàat jèp N การบาดเจ็บ
injury

kaan bin N การบิน flying,
aviation

kaan doehn thaang N การ
เดินทาง trip, journey

kaan hâi àphai N การให้อภัย
forgiveness, mercy

kaan kàw sâang N การก่อสร้าง
building, construction

kaan khàeng khăn N การ
แข่งขัน competition, a race
of game

kaan lûeak tâng N การเลือก
ตั้ง election

kaan mueang N การเมือง
politics

kaan ngoen N การเงิน finance

kaan pàtìbàt ngaan N การ
ปฏิบัติงาน performance (of
work)

kaan pàtìsèht N การปฏิเสธ
refusal

kaan phát-thá-naa N การ
พัฒนา development

kaan sà-daehng N การ
แสดง a display, a show, a
performance

kaan sĭa sàlà N การเสียสละ
sacrifice

kaan sùek-săa N การศึกษา
education

kaan tàwp sànǎwng N การ
ตอบสนอง reaction, response

kaan thák thaai N การทักทาย
greetings

kaan tham aa-hǎan N การทำ
อาหาร cooking, cuisine

kaan thòk panhǎa N การถก
ปัญหา discussion (of issues)

kaan thót sàwp N การทดสอบ
test, examination

kâang N ก้าง fishbone

kaang-kehng N กางเกง
trousers, pants

kaang-kehng khǎa sân N
กางเกงขาสั้น shorts (short
trousers)

kaangkehng nai N กางเกงใน
underpants, panties

kaa-tuun N (from English)
การ์ตูน cartoon

kaaw N กาว glue

kâaw V ก้าว step

kâaw nâa V ก้าวหน้า to
advance, go forward

kàe N แกะ sheep

kàe sàlàk V แกะสลัก to carve

kaeh PRON (COLLOQUIAL, INFORMAL)
แก you, he, she, they

kàeh ADJ แก่ old (of persons),
strong (coffee)

kâeh V แก้ to fix (repair); to
loosen, untie; to amend,
revise, correct

kàeh dàet ADJ (COLLOQUIAL)
แก่แดด to be cheeky, a
whipper snapper, smart
arse kid

kâeh hâi thùuk V แก้ให้ถูก
to correct

kwàa ADJ แก่กว่า to be
older, elder

kâeh panhǎa V แก้ปัญหา to
solve (a problem)

kâeh phâa V แก้ผ้า to get
undressed, take off clothing,
to be naked

kàeh tua V แก่ตัว to get old,
grow old

kâeh tua V แก้ตัว to make
excuses, find an excuse/make
up for one's losses/failures

kâehm N แก้ม cheek(s)

kaehng N แกง curry

káet N (from English) แก๊ส
(e.g. cooking gas)

kâew N แก้ว glass (for drinking)

kài N (pronounced similar to
'guy') ไก่ chicken

kái N (from English) ไกด์ a
guide

191

kài yâang N ไก่ย่าง BBQ or grilled chicken

kà-làm dàwk N กะหล่ำดอก cauliflower

kà-làm plii N กะหล่ำปลี cabbage

kam N (pronounced like 'gum') กรรม karma

kam mueh V กำมือ clench the fist

kamjàt V (pronounced 'gum-jut') กำจัด to rid, get rid of

kamlang AUX (pronounced 'gum-lung') กำลัง to be presently doing; N strength, power, (armed force)

kamlang doehn thaang V กำลังเดินทาง on the way, in the process of travelling

kam-má-phan ADJ (pronounced 'gummàpun') กรรม พันธุ์ hereditary, congenital, genetic

kamnan N (pronounced 'gum none') กำนัน sub-district headman, chief of sub-district (tambon)

kamnòt N กำหนด schedule, program

kam-phaehng N กำแพง

(stone or brick) wall (of a yard or town)

kamrai N กำไร profit

kan ADV กัน together, mutually; to prevent

kan thòe กันเถอะ let's (e.g. go) (used at the end of a sentence to urge the other party to do something)

kan-chaa N (pronounced 'gun jar') กัญชา marihuana, hemp, grass, dope, pot, weed

kankrai N กรรไกร scissors

kan-yaa-yon N กันยายน September

kao V เกา to scratch lightly

kào ADJ เก่า old (of things)

kâo เก้า nine

kâo îi เก้าอี้ chair

kâo sìp เก้าสิบ ninety

kaolǐi nǔea เกาหลีเหนือ North Korea

kaolǐi tâi เกาหลีใต้ South Korea

kàp CONJ กับ with, and

kàp khâaw N (COLLOQUIAL) กับข้าว the food eaten with rice (e.g. curry/vegetables/soup, etc.)

kàp klâem N กับแกล้ม hors

d'oeuvres, entrée, a light meal

kà-phrao N กะเพรา sweet basil

kàpi N กะปิ fish paste

kà-rá kà-daa-khom N กรกฎาคม July

kàru-naa กรุณา please ... (a very polite, formal means of asking for something); kindness, mercy

kà-sèht-trà-kam N เกษตรกรรม agriculture

kàt V (pronounced like 'gut' with a low tone) กัด to bite

kàt kan V (COLLOQUIAL) กัดกัน to be at odds with another person, to snipe at

kà-thí N กะทิ coconut cream/ milk

kà-thoei N กะเทย a transvestite, also referred to by the English term 'ladyboy'

ka-w N เกาะ island

kâw ADV (pronounced 'gor') ก็ also, too, either (used to add an agreeing thought); **kâw loei** CONJ ก็เลย then, so

kàw tâng V ก่อตั้ง to establish, set up

káwf N (from English) กอล์ฟ golf

kàwn ADV ก่อน first, earlier, before

kâwn N ก้อน lump; classifier for lump-like objects, cube (e.g. cube of sugar)

kàwn níi ADV ก่อนนี้ earlier, before this, previously

kawng tháp N กองทัพ troops, the military, the army (in particular)

kaw-rá-nii N กรณี a case (e.g. a legal case), a particular instance (NOTE: (COLLOQUIAL) **khûu kaw-rá-nii** คู่กรณี the other party in an accident/ incident)

kàwt V กอด to embrace, hug

ké N เก๊ะ a drawer (in a table etc.)

kéh ADJ เก๊ fake

kèh ADJ เก๋ to be with it, stylish, chic

keh N (pronounced 'gay') (from English) เกย์ gay, homosexual

kehm N (from English) เกม match, game

kèng ADJ เก่ง clever, smart,

good at something (also used colloquially to mean 'a lot'; e.g. **kin kèng** กินเก่ง 'to eat a lot'; **nawn kèng** นอนเก่ง 'to sleep a lot')

kèp v เก็บ to save, collect, accumulate, keep, pick up

kèp khǎwng v เก็บของ gather things together, to pack (luggage)

kèp kòt v (COLLOQUIAL) เก็บกด to suppress (one's true feelings)

kèp tó v เก็บโต๊ะ to clear the table (e.g. after dinner)

kèp tua v เก็บตัว to avoid others, to keep to oneself, to shun society)

kiao N เกี๊ยว small Chinese dumpling or wonton

kiao v เกี่ยว to pertain (to), be related (to) (often used in a negative sense/statement, e.g. 'It's got nothing to do with it/He's got nothing to do with it', etc. **mâi kiao** ไม่ เกี่ยว)

kiao kàp PREP เกี่ยวกับ about, regarding, concerning

kiao khâwng v เกี่ยวข้อง to involve, in connection with

kiao náam N เกี๊ยวน้ำ wonton soup

kiat N เกียรติ honour, dignity

kii ... กี่... how many...?: **kii chûa mohng** กี่ชั่วโมง how many hours (e.g. will it take to clean the house?)

kii-laa N กีฬา sport(s)

kii mohng láew (EXPRESSION) กี่โมงแล้ว what's the time?

kiit khwǎang v กีดขวาง to hinder, obstruct

kiitâa N (from English) กีตาร์ guitar

ki-loh(kram) N (COLLOQUIAL – **kiloh**) กิโล(กรัม) kilogram

ki-loh(méht) N (COLLOQUIAL – **kiloh**) กิโล(เมตร) kilometer

kin v กิน to eat; (SLANG) to be corrupt, take bribes

kin aa-hǎan cháo v กินอาหาร เช้า eat breakfast

kin jeh v กินเจ to be vegetarian

kin jù v กินจุ to eat a lot (until you're stuffed)

kin khâaw v กินข้าว to eat (breakfast, lunch, dinner, a meal; the expression itself means literally, 'eat'-'rice')

194

kin mueh v กินมือ to eat with the hands

king mái N (pronounced 'ging' [low tone]-'mai' [high tone]) กิ่งไม้ the branch of a tree

kit-jà-kam N กิจกรรม activity

klâa hăan ADJ กล้าหาญ to be brave, daring

klaai pen v กลายเป็น to become (e.g. friends)

klâam núea N กล้ามเนื้อ muscle(s)

klaang N กลาง in the middle, center

klaang khuehn N กลางคืน night

klaang mueang N กลางเมือง city/town center

klaang wan N กลางวัน day/ daytime

klàaw hăa v กล่าวหา to accuse

klàaw kham praa-săi v (FORMAL) กล่าวคำปราศรัย to make (give) a speech

klàaw thǔeng v (FORMAL) กล่าว ถึง to mention

klâehng v แกล้ง to pretend, to tease someone (maliciously), to annoy (deliberately, intentionally)

klâi ADJ ใกล้ near, nearby, close to

klai ADJ (with a mid tone and a longer sounding vowel than the word for 'near' than **klâi** ใกล้) ไกล to be far away, distant, a long way

klâi wehlaa ใกล้เวลา almost time (e.g. to go), to approach (in time)

klàp v กลับ to return (e.g. home), to turn over (e.g. a steak on a BBQ pit)

klàp bâan v กลับบ้าน to return home, go back home

klàp jai v กลับใจ to have a change of heart, to turn over a new leaf, be reformed

klàp khâang ADJ กลับข้าง to be inside out, to be on back to front

klàp maa v กลับมา to come back to (from where you began)

klàp pai v กลับไป to return (to from where you began)

klawng N กลอง a drum

klâwng N กล้อง a camera; also pipe

klàwng N กล่อง box

klàwng krà-dàat N กล่อง
กระดาษ cardboard box

kliat v เกลียด to hate

klin N กลิ่น odour, a smell

klom ADJ กลม round (shape)

klua v กลัว to be afraid, fear

klua phǐi v กลัวผี to be afraid
of ghosts

klua taai v กลัวตาย to be
afraid of death/dying

klûai N กล้วย banana

klûai mái N กล้วยไม้ orchid(s)

klueah N เกลือ salt

kluehn v กลืน to swallow

klùm N กลุ่ม group

klûm jai ADJ กลุ้มใจ to be
depressed, glum

koehn ADV เกิน to exceed,
surpass

koehn pai v ...เกินไป too...
(e.g. expensive, small, big,
etc.), excessive

kòeht v (pronounced like
'gurt/girt') เกิด to be born

kòeht àrai khûen (COLLOQUIAL)
เกิดอะไรขึ้น what happened?

kòeht khuen v เกิดขึ้น to
happen, occur, come about

koh-hòk v (pronounced 'go
hok') โกหก to lie

kohn v โกน to shave

kohng v โกง to cheat

kôi N ก้อย the little finger, pinky

kôm v ก้ม to bend down,
stoop, bow

kôn N ก้น bottom, buttocks

kongsǔn N กงสุล consul,
consular

kòp N กบ a frog

kòt N กฎ rule, regulation, law

kòt v กด to press

kòt kring v กดกริ่ง to ring (a
door bell)

kòtmǎai N กฎหมาย laws,
legislation

kraam N กราม jaw

kràap v กราบ to postrate
oneself (as a sign of respect),
(in some contexts this could
be) to grovel

krà-buai N กระบวย ladle, dipper

krà-buan kaan N กระบวนการ
a movement (e.g. for human
rights), a process

krà-daan N กระดาน board,
plank

krà-daan prà-kàat N กระดาน
ประกาศ signboard, bulletin
board

krà-dàat N กระดาษ paper

kra-dàat khǎeng N กระดาษ แข็ง cardboard (literally 'paper'-'hard/stiff')

kràdai N กระได stairs, stairway, ladder

kra-dòht V กระโดด to jump

kra-dùuk N กระดูก bone(s)

kra-dùuk sǎn lǎng N กระดูก สันหลัง the spine/backbone

kra-jaai sǐang V กระจายเสียง to broadcast

kra-jàwk ADJ (SLANG) กระจอก piddling, petty, of no significance, crap

kra-jòk N กระจก glass (material), the windshield of a car, a mirror

kra-pǎo N กระเป๋า a bag, a pocket in a garment

kra-pǎo doehn thaang N กระเป๋าเดินทาง (or kra-pǎo sûea phâa N กระเป๋าเสื้อผ้า) a suitcase

kra-pǎo ngoen N กระเป๋าเงิน, (or MORE COLLOQUIAL kra-pǎo tang กระเป๋าตังค์) a purse/wallet

kra-pǎo tham ngaan N กระเป๋าทำงาน briefcase

kra-pǎwng N กระป๋อง a can, tin

kra-phǒm PRON (FORMAL) กระผม I, me (males only)

kra-prohng N กระโปรง a skirt

kra-pùk N กระปุก (a smallish) receptacle or box (e.g. for ointment, jewelry, etc.)

kra-sǎeh N กระแส current, flow, stream (of a river, the sea); a trend/vogue

kra-sip V กระซิบ to whisper

kra-suang N กระทรวง (government) ministry

kra-sǔn N กระสุน a bullet

kra-tàai N กระต่าย rabbit

kra-thá N กระทะ a wok/ Chinese-style frying pan for making stir-fried dishes

kra-thâwm N กระท่อม hut, shack, cottage

kra-thiam N กระเทียม garlic

kra-thong N กระทง basket, small banana leaf receptacle, an integral part of the Loi/ Loy (which means 'float') Krathong ลอยกระทง Festival that marks the end of the rainy season

kràwk (baehp) fawm V กรอก(แบบ)ฟอร์ม to fill out a form

197

krawng v กรอง to filter, strain

kràwp ADJ กรอบ crisp, brittle

kràwp N กรอบ a frame, (within the) confines/limitations (of); **kràwp rûup** กรอบรูป a (picture) frame

krehng-jai N, v เกรงใจ a key Thai concept which means something like a fear of imposing on someone else; to be thought of, in Thai culture, as considerate

kreng v เกร็ง tense, stiffened; to flex a muscle

kròht v โกรธ to be upset, cross, angry

krom N กรม (a government) department, e.g. **krom tam-rùat** กรมตำรวจ the police department

kron v กรน to snore

krong N กรง cage

kròt N กรด acid (not LSD)

kruai kliao N กรวยเกลียว spiral

krung N กรุง city

krung-thêhp N กรุงเทพฯ Bangkok (literally 'City of Angels')

kŭai tĭao N ก๋วยเตี๋ยว noodles

kŭai tĭao náam N ก๋วยเตี๋ยวน้ำ noodle soup

kuan v กวน to bother, annoy, disturb (someone)

kuan jai ADJ กวนใจ to bother, disturb, be irritating

kùeap ADV เกือบ almost, nearly

kùlaap N กุหลาบ a rose (bush/flower)

kum-phaàphan N กุมภาพันธ์ February

kûng N กุ้ง shrimp, prawn: **kûng mangkawn** (literally, 'prawn'-'dragon') กุ้งมังกร lobster

kun-jaeh N กุญแจ key (to room)

kunjaeh mueh N กุญแจมือ handcuffs

kûu v กู้ to borrow (money), take a loan

kwàa ADJ กว่า over, more, more than (NOTE: this word is used to make comparisons in Thai – **dii kwàa** ดีกว่า better; **yài kwàa** ใหญ่กว่า bigger; **phaehng kwàa** แพงกว่า more expensive (than…))

kwâang ADJ กว้าง broad, spacious, wide

kwàat v กวาด to sweep

198

kwàeng v แกว่ง to swing

KH

NOTE: like the English sound 'k'

khâ ค่ะ female polite particle (when answering a question or making a statement)

khá คะ female polite particle (when asking a question)

khàa n ข่า galangal (spice used in Thai cooking)

khǎa n ขา leg(s)

khâa n ค่า value (cost)

khâa v ฆ่า kill, murder

khǎa àwn n ขาอ่อน thigh

khâa chái jàai n ค่าใช้จ่าย expenses

khâa dohy-sǎan n ค่าโดยสาร fare (for a bus, plane trip)

khâa jâang n ค่าจ้าง wage(s)

khǎa prà-jam n ขาประจำ a regular customer

khâa pràp n ค่าปรับ a fine (for an infringement)

khâa râat-chákaan n ข้า ราชการ government official(s), bureaucrat(s), public servant(s)

khâa tham-niam n ค่า ธรรมเนียม fee (for official service)

khǎai v ขาย for sale, to sell

khǎai láew v ขายแล้ว sold

khǎai mòt láew v ขายหมดแล้ว sold out, to have sold the lot

khâam v ข้าม across, cross, go over

khâam thà-nǒn v ข้ามถนน to cross the road

kháan v ค้าน to oppose, be opposed to

khâang n ข้าง side

khâang bon n, adj ข้างบน upstairs

khaang n คาง chin

khâang-khâang prep ข้างๆ next to, beside

khâang khuehn v ค้างคืน to stay overnight

khâang lâang n, adj ข้างล่าง below, downstairs

khâang lǎng prep ข้างหลัง in the rear of, behind

khâang nâa n, adj ข้างหน้า front, in the front

khâang nai n, adj ข้างใน inside

khâang nâwk n, adj ข้างนอก outside

199

khâang tâi PREP, N, ADJ ข้าง
ใต้ at the bottom (base),
underneath

khàat v ขาด to lack; to break
(e.g. a rope); N lack of; ADJ to
be lacking, to be insufficient,
to be torn

khàat mòt ADJ ขาดหมด
(completely) worn out (e.g.
of clothes)

khàat pai ADJ ขาดไป to be
missing (absent)

khàat thun v ขาดทุน to lose
money (on an investment),
take a loss

khàat wâa... v คาดว่า... to
expect that.. (e.g. he'll arrive
tomorrow)

khàaw N ข่าว news, report

khàaw N ข่าว news

khăaw ADJ ขาว white (for a
list of the most common
colours see the entry under
sǐi สี which means 'colour')

khâaw N ข้าว rice; **khâaw
klâwng** ข้าวกล้อง brown rice/
unpolished rice; **khâaw phàt**
ข้าวผัด fried rice; **khâaw nǐao**
ข้าวเหนียว sticky rice

khâaw kaehng N ข้าวแกง

rice and curry, (COLLOQUIAL)
(Thai) food

khâaw klâwng N ข้าวกล้อง
brown rice, unpolished rice

khâaw lǎam N ข้าวหลาม a
Thai sweetmeat – glutinous
rice with coconut milk
roasted in a section of
bamboo

khâaw lueh N ข้าวลือ a
rumour

khâaw nǐao N ข้าวเหนียว
sticky or glutinous rice

khâaw phôht N ข้าวโพด corn

khâaw sǎa-lii N ข้าวสาลี
wheat

khâaw sǎan N ข้าวสาร rice
(uncooked)

khâaw sǔai N ข้าวสวย rice
(cooked)

khâaw yài N ข่าวใหญ่ a big/
significant news story

khà-buan N ขบวน a
procession

khâe ADV แค่ just, only, merely,
e.g. (COLLOQUIAL) **khâe níi** แค่
นี้ 'just this much'; **khâe nǎi**
แค่ไหน 'to what degree' or
'how much' (e.g. do you
love her?)

200

khàehk N แขก guest, a person of swarthy complexion – in Thailand commonly used to refer to people from the Indian subcontinent and the Middle East

khàehk phûu mii kìat N แขกผู้มีเกียรติ guest of honour

khâehn N แขน arm(s)

khaeh-na-daa N แคนาดา Canada

khàehp ADJ แคบ narrow

khaeh-ráwt N (from English) แครอต carrot

khàeng V แข่ง to compete in a race

khàeng raehng ADJ แข็งแรง to be strong

kháep suun N (from English) แคปซูล capsule (medicine/vitamins)

khài N ไข่ egg

khâi N ไข้ fever

khài daehng N ไข่แดง egg yolk

khài dao N ไข่ดาว a fried egg

khài jiao N ไข่เจียว an omelette

khài khon N ไข่คน scrambled eggs

khài lùak N ไข่ลวก soft boiled egg

khài lûeat àwk N ไข้เลือดออก dengue fever

khài man N ไขมัน fat (body fat), grease

khài múk N ไข่มุก pearl(s)

khài múk thiam ไข่มุกเทียม cultured pearl(s)

khài tôm N ไข่ต้ม hard boiled egg(s)

khâi wàt yài N ไข้หวัดใหญ่ flu, influenza

khâm ADJ (pronounced like 'come' with a rising tone) ขำ to be funny, amusing,

kham N คำ word(s)

kham choehn N คำเชิญ an invitation

kham dàa N คำด่า abuse, blame; a swear word

kham mueang N คำเมือง the name of the dialect spoken in the northern part of Thailand

kham náe-nam N คำแนะนำ advice, suggestion

kham praa-săi N คำปราศรัย a speech

kham ráwng thúk N คำร้องทุกข์ a complaint

kham sàng N คำสั่ง order, command

kham sàp N คำศัพท์ vocabulary

kham tàwp N คำตอบ answer, response

kham thǎam N คำถาม question

kham tuean N คำเตือน warning

kham yók yâwng N คำยกย่อง (words of) praise

khàmêhn N เขมร Cambodia

khamnuan V คำนวณ to calculate

khà-mohy V ขโมย to steal; N a thief, thieves

khà-mùat khíu V ขมวดคิ้ว to frown

khà-mùk khà-mǔa ADJ ขมุกขมัว overcast (weather)

khan ADJ คัน to be itchy; N classifier for counting vehicles, umbrellas, spoons and forks

khân N ขั้น stage, grade, step, rank

khân N ขัน dipping bowl (used when bathing in the old style Thai manner)

khà-nà níi ADV ขณะนี้ at present, at this moment

khà-nàat N ขนาด size

khànǒm N ขนม sweets, dessert, snacks

khànǒm khéhk N ขนมเค้ก cake

khànǒm-pang N (**pang** pronounced like 'pung') ขนมปัง bread

khànǒm-pang kràwp N ขนมปังกรอบ a cracker (biscuit)

khà-nǒm wǎan N ขนมหวาน confectionery, dessert

khà-nǔn N ขนุน jackfruit

khǎo N เขา mountain

khǎo PRON เขา she, her, he, him, they, them

khào N เข่า knee

khâo V เข้า to enter, go in

khâo hǎa V เข้าหา to approach

khâo kan (COLLOQUIAL) เข้ากัน to get on well together, get on (with)

khâo khâang V (COLLOQUIAL) เข้าข้าง to take sides (with someone)

khâo khiu V เข้าคิว to queue, line up (**khiu** คิว from English)

khâo maa V เข้ามา come in

khâo rûam V เข้าร่วม to join in, attend, participate

202

khâo-jai v เข้าใจ understand

khâo-jai phit v เข้าใจผิด to misunderstand

kháp ADJ คับ to be tight (fitting)

khàp v ขับ to drive a vehicle

khát kháan v คัดค้าน to protest, object

khàt ngao v ขัดเงา to polish

kháw v เคาะ to knock

khǎw v ขอ to ask for, request (informally), apply for permission, please

khǎw N (pronounced like 'khor' with a falling tone) ข้อ joint (in the body), articulation; also clause, section, provision, question/point(s) (as in 'there are a number of questions/points to be addressed')

khaw N คอ neck

khǎw bòk-phrâwng N ข้อ บกพร่อง defect

khaw hǒi N คอหอย throat

khâw khwaam N ข้อความ message

khâw mueh N ข้อมือ wrist

khâw muun N ข้อมูล information, data

khǎw ráwng v ขอร้อง to request (formally)

khǎw sà-daehng khwaam yin-dii dûai (FORMULAIC EXPRESSION) ขอแสดงความยินดี ด้วย congratulations!

khâw sà-nŏeh N ข้อเสนอ a (formal) proposal

khaw sǎw ABBREV ค.ศ. anno domini – the Christian Era

khâw sàwk N ข้อศอก elbow

khǎw thaang nòi ขอทาง หน่อย excuse me! (can I get past)

khâw tháo N ข้อเท้า ankle

khâw thét jing N ข้อเท็จ จริง fact

khǎw thôht v ขอโทษ to apologize; sorry!, excuse me!

khâw tòk-long N ข้อตกลง an agreement

khǎw yuehm v ขอยืม to borrow

khawm-phiu-tôeh N คอมพิวเตอร์, (COLLOQUIAL) khawm คอม computer

kháwn N ค้อน hammer

khâwn khâang ADV ค่อนข้าง rather, fairly

khǎwng N ของ thing(s), belongings

khǎwng V ของ to belong to, indicates the possessive – "of"

khǎwng chán PRON ของฉัน my, mine

khǎwng hǎai N ของหาย lost property

khǎwng kào N ของเก่า antiques

khǎwng khǎo PRON ของเขา his, hers, their, theirs

khǎwng khwǎn N ของขวัญ a present (gift)

khǎwng kin N ของกิน edibles, things to eat

khǎwng lên N ของเล่น toy(s)

khǎwng plawm N ของ ปลอม a copy, a fake, pirated merchandise

khǎwng rao PRON ของเรา our, ours

khǎwng sùan tua N ของ ส่วนตัว one's own personal possession(s)

khǎwng thiam ADJ ของเทียม synthetic, artificial

khǎwng thîi ra-lúek N ของที่ ระลึก souvenir

khǎwng wǎan N (COLLOQUIAL) ของหวาน a sweet, dessert

khàwp N ขอบ border, edge

khàwp khun ขอบคุณ to thank, thank you

khà-yà N ขยะ garbage, rubbish

khà-yǎn ADJ ขยัน to be hardworking, diligent

khà-yào V เขย่า to shake (something)

khem ADJ เค็ม salty (to the taste)

khêm ADJ เข้ม intense, strong, concentrated

khěm N เข็ม a needle

khěm khǎeng ADJ เข้มแข็ง strong, unyielding; industrious, assiduous

khěm khàt N เข็มขัด belt

khêm khôn ADJ เข้มข้น concentrated (liquid), sharp taste, flavourful

khèt N เขต boundary, frontier, zone, district

khèt V เข็ด (COLLOQUIAL) to have learned one's lesson, chastened, dare not do something again

khǐan V เขียน to write, to draw

204

khîan v เฆี่ยน to whip

khĭan jòt-mǎai v เขียน
จดหมาย to correspond
(write letters)

khĭan tàwp v เขียนตอบ to
reply (in writing)

khĭang N เขียง a chopping
board

khĭao ADJ เขียว green (for
a list of the most common
colours see the entry under
sǐi สี which means 'colour')

khíao v เคี้ยว to chew

khìi v ขี่ to ride (a motorbike/
horse)

khîi N ขี้ faeces, excrement
(shit – although the Thai
word is in no way rude or
coarse as is the English term)

khîi aai ADJ ขี้อาย given to shy-
ness (actually 'extremely shy')

khíi-bawt N คีย์บอร์ด (from English)
keyboard (of
computer)

khîi kiat ADJ ขี้เกียจ to be lazy

khîi mao N, ADJ ขี้เมา a
drunkard

khîi nǐao ADJ ขี้เหนียว to be
stingy

khîi phûeng N ขี้ผึ้ง wax

khîi yaa N ขี้ยา a junkie, drug
addict

khiim N คีม pliers

khǐng N ขิง ginger

khít v คิด to think, to have an
opinion

khít dàwk bîa v คิดดอกเบี้ย
to charge interest (on a loan
etc.), or simply **khít dàwk**
คิดดอก

khít mâak ADJ (COLLOQUIAL)
คิดมาก to be anxious/
overly sensitive/to worry
incessantly

khít mâi thǔeng ADJ คิดไม่
ถึง (to be) unexpected; to
assume something wouldn't
happen

khít tang v (COLLOQUIAL) คิด
ตังค์ to ask for the bill in a
downmarket restaurant or
eatery on the street

khít thǔeng v คิดถึง to miss
(e.g. a loved one)

khíu N (from English –
although in practice the
concept generally has little
meaning in Thailand) คิว
queue, line

khíu N คิ้ว eyebrow

khláai ADJ คล้าย to be similar, analogous

khláwng ADJ คล่อง to be fluent (in a language), to do something physical well

khlawng N (often written in English as 'klong') คลอง canal, watercourse, channel

khláwt lûuk V คลอดลูก to give birth (to a child)

khlohn N โคลน mud, slush

khlûean thîi V เคลื่อนที่ to move

khlûehn N คลื่น a wave (in the sea)

khlùi N ขลุ่ย flute

khlum V คลุม to cover

khlum khruea ADJ คลุมเครือ to be vague, ambiguous

khoei ADV เคย ever – used to ask questions in the form 'have you ever…?' To respond 'yes (I have)' the answer can simply be **khoei** เคย. As for a negative response ('I have never…') the answer is simply **mâi khoei** ไม่เคย

khŏei N เขย male in-law (son-in-law, brother-in-law)

khoei pai V เคยไป to have

been to somewhere before

khoei tham V เคยทำ to have done something before

khoei tua V (COLLOQUIAL) เคยตัว to be habitual; used to doing something (e.g. going to bed very late etc.)

khohm fai N โคมไฟ lamp

khóhng ADJ โค้ง curved, convex

khóhng N โค้ง a curve, a bend in the road

khoi V คอย to wait for

khôi ADV ค่อย gradually, little by little

khôi yang chûa V ค่อยยังชั่ว to get better from an illness, to be on the mend

khŏm ADJ ขม bitter (taste)

khom ADJ คม to be sharp (of knives, razors, etc.)

khŏn N ขน body hair

khôn ADJ ข้น thick (of liquids), to be condensed (e.g. condensed milk)

khon N คน person, people; classifier for people

khon à-meh-rí-kan N คน อเมริกัน an American (person)

khon àwt-sà-treh-lia N คน

206

ออสเตรเลีย Australian (person)

khon bâa N คนบ้า a lunatic, mad person

khon chái N คนใช้ a servant

khon diao ADJ คนเดียว on one's own, alone; single (only one), sole

khon fâo ráan N คนเฝ้าร้าน shopkeeper

khon jiin N (pronounced 'jean') คนจีน Chinese (person)

khon jon N คนจน a poor person, someone who is poor

khon kao-lii N คนเกาหลี a Korean (person)

khon khâi N คนไข้ a patient, a sick person

khon kháp N คนขับ driver

khon khîi kohng N คนขี้โกง a cheat, a dishonest/crooked person

khon lao N คนลาว a Laotian person

khón phóp v ค้นพบ to discover, find out; **khon plàehk nâa** N คนแปลกหน้า a stranger

khôn sàt N ขนสัตว์ wool

khon sòehp N คนเสิร์ฟ waiter, waitress

207

khon thîi... คนที่... the one/ person who...

khong ADV คง probably, possibly

khóp v คบ to associate (with), to socialize

khòp khăn ADJ ขบขัน to be humorous

khrai PRON ใคร who? whom

khrai kâw dâi ใครก็ได้ anybody at all, anyone, e.g. in response to a question such as: 'who can go into the park?' (answer) **khrai kâw dâi** ใครก็ได้ anybody at all/ anyone

khráng N ครั้ง time; classifier for times, occasions – e.g. to say 'five times' is the number 5 (**hâa**) followed by **khráng** ครั้ง

khráng kàwn ADV ครั้งก่อน (**kàwn** pronounced 'gorn' with a low tone) previously, before; the last time

khráng khraaw ADV ครั้งคราว occasionally, from time to time

khráng râek ADV ครั้งแรก the first time

khrao N (often pronounced by Thais very similar to the English word 'cow') เครา beard

khráp ครับ (often pronounced like 'cup' with a high tone) male polite particle

khrá-w ráai N เคราะห์ร้าย misfortune

khrâwp khrawng V ครอบ ครอง to occupy, to rule over, to possess

khrâwp krua N ครอบครัว family

khrêng khrát ADJ เคร่งครัด strict, observant (of rules, regulations, religious teachings)

khriim N (from English) ครีม cream

khrístian N คริสเตียน Christian; **chaaw khrít** N ชาว คริสต์ a Christian

khrohng kaan N โครงการ project, scheme, program (e.g. as in some form of development project etc.)

khrohng sâang N โครงสร้าง structure (of a building, of society)

khrók N (pronounced 'crock') ครก mortar (for pulversing and grinding spices/ ingredients for a meal)

khróp ADJ, ADV ครบ to be com- plete/full (e.g. set of items)

khróp thûan ADJ ครบถ้วน in full

khrù khrà ADJ ขรุขระ rough, uneven, bumpy (surfaces – e.g. a road)

khrua N ครัว kitchen

khruea khàai N เครือข่าย network

khrûeang N เครื่อง machine

khrûeang bin N เครื่องบิน an aeroplane/airplane

khrûeang dùehm N เครื่องดื่ม drink(s), refreshment(s)

khrûeang fai fáa N เครื่อง ไฟฟ้า electrical appliance(s), electrical goods

khrûeang jàk N เครื่องจักร machine(ry)

khrûeang khǐan N เครื่อง เขียน stationery

khrûeang khít lêhk N เครื่อง คิดเลข calculator

khrûeang mueh N เครื่องมือ tool, utensil, instrument

208

khrûeang nawn N เครื่องนอน bedding, bedclothes

khrûeang phét phloi N เครื่องเพชรพลอย jewellery

khrûeang prà-dàp kaai N เครื่องประดับกาย bodily ornaments, accessories in fashion contexts

khrûeang ráp thoh-rá-sàp N เครื่องรับโทรศัพท์ an answering machine

khrûeang thêht N เครื่องเทศ spice(s)

khrûeang yon N เครื่องยนต์ an engine, a machine

khrûeng ADJ ครึ่ง half

khruu N ครู teacher

khruu yài N ครูใหญ่ headmaster

khuai N ควย (SLANG/EXTREMELY RUDE) penis (or, more accurately – dick/prick/cock)

khuan AUX V ควร should, ought to

khùan V ข่วน to scratch (as in a cat scratching something with its paws), scrape

khùap N ขวบ year – when used to refer to child's age, used for up to approximately

khùat N ขวด bottle

khùean N เขื่อน a dam

khuehn V คืน to give back, return; N night

khuehn níi คืนนี้ tonight

khûen V ขึ้น to rise, ascend, go up; to increase; to board/get on (e.g. a bus/plane)

khûen chàai N ขึ้นฉ่าย Chinese celery

khûen yùu kàp ขึ้นอยู่กับ (COLLOQUIAL) it depends on...

khui V คุย to chat

khúk N คุก jail, prison, the slammer

khúkkîi N (from English) คุกกี้ cookie, sweet biscuit

khun PRON คุณ you (respectful form of address)

khún khoei คุ้นเคย to be used to, accustomed to (also the more colloquial term **chin** ชิน)

khún khoei kàp... คุ้นเคย กับ... to be acquainted/ familiar with...

khun naai คุณนาย (term of address – NOTE: this would only ever be used by

209

a Thai person as it is integral to the very hierarchial nature of Thai society. For a non-Thai to address someone like this would be very odd)

khun-ná-sŏmbàt N คุณสมบัติ (educational) qualification, characteristic

khun pâa PRON คุณป้า aunt (respectful address to an older lady)

khùu V ขู่ to threaten

khûu N คู่ a pair

khûu khàeng N คู่แข่ง rival, competitor

khûu mân N คู่หมั้น fiancé, fiancée

khûu mueh N คู่มือ manual, handbook (e.g. instruction booklet for appliance etc.)

khûu nawn N คู่นอน lover, sexual partner (or, to use that dreadful expression 'fuck buddy')

khûu sŏmrót N (FORMAL) คู่สมรส partner, spouse

khuun V คูณ to multiply

khwăa ADJ ขวา right (i.e. on the right)

khwăa mueh ADJ ขวามือ right-hand side

khwaam N ความ the sense, the substance, the gist (of a matter, an account), also **khwaam...** ความ... ...ness, commonly used by being placed in front of adjectives/verbs to form abstract nouns expressing a state or quality: e.g. '...ness' as in **khwaam dii** ความดี goodness, virtue (see other examples in the following entries)

khwaam chûai lŭea N ความช่วยเหลือ help, assistance

khwaam chûea N ความเชื่อ belief, faith

khwaam hĕn N ความเห็น opinion

khwaam itchăa N ความอิจฉา jealousy

khwaam jam-pen N ความจำเป็น need, necessity

khwaam jàroen N ความเจริญ progress

khwaam jèp pùai N ความเจ็บป่วย illness

khwaam jing N ความจริง truth, the truth

khwaam khao-róp N ความ

210

เคารพ respect

khwaam khít ɴ ความคิด idea, thoughts

khwaam khlûean wǎi ɴ ความเคลื่อนไหว movement, motion

khwaam khrîat ɴ ความเครียด tension, stress; (COLLOQUIAL) khrîat เครียด 'to be stressed out'

khwaam kliat ɴ ความเกลียด hatred

khwaam klua ɴ ความกลัว fear

khwaam kòt dan ɴ ความ กดดัน pressure

khwaam krôht ɴ ความโกรธ anger

khwaam kwâang ɴ ความ กว้าง width

khwaam lambàak ɴ ความ ลำบาก hardship

khwaam láp ɴ ความลับ secret, confidentiality

khwaam lóm lěhw ɴ ความ ล้มเหลว failure, bankruptcy

khwaam mǎai ɴ ความหมาย meaning (i.e. the 'meaning' of something)

khwaam mâi sà-ngòp ɴ ความไม่สงบ a disturbance, turmoil, absence of peace

khwaam mân-khong ɴ ความ มั่นคง security

khwaam mân-jai ɴ ความ มั่นใจ confidence

khwaam òp-ùn ɴ ความอบอุ่น warmth

khwaam phá-yaa-yaam ɴ ความพยายาม attempt, effort

khwaam phìt ɴ ความผิด fault, mistake, error

khwaam plàwt phai ɴ ความ ปลอดภัย safety

khwaam rák ɴ ความรัก love, affection

khwaam ráp phit châwp ɴ ความรับผิดชอบ responsibility

khwaam ráp rúu ɴ ความรับรู้ awareness

khwaam rew ɴ ความเร็ว speed

khwaam rúu ɴ ความรู้ knowledge

khwaam rúu-sùek ɴ ความ รู้สึก feeling, emotion

khwaam sà-àat ɴ ความ สะอาด cleanliness

khwaam sǎa-mâat ɴ ความ สามารถ ability, capacity (to fulfill a task)

khwaam sǎmkhan N ความ
สำคัญ importance

khwaam sǎmrèt N ความ
สำเร็จ success

khwaam song jam N (**jam**
pronounced 'jum' as in
'jumble') ความทรงจำ
memory (i.e. one's memory)

khwaam sǒngsǎi N ความ
สงสัย suspicion, curiosity

khwaam sǒn-jai N ความสนใจ
interest (in something)

khwaam sǔung N ความสูง
height

khwaam taai N ความตาย
death

khwaam tàehk tàang N
ความแตกต่าง difference
(between this and that)

khwaam tâng-jai N ความ
ตั้งใจ intention

khwaam tâo thiam N ความ
เท่าเทียม equality

khwaam yâak jon N ความ
ยากจน poverty

khwaam yaaw N ความยาว
length

khwaan N ควาญ mahout/
elephant keeper/driver

khwâang V ขว้าง to throw, hurl

khwǎang V ขวาง to impede,
obstruct, thwart

khwǎang thaang V ขวางทาง
to bar/block the way

khwâang thíng V ขว้างทิ้ง
throw away, throw out

khwǎehn V แขวน to hang
(e.g. a picture on the wall)

khwai N ควาย a water buffalo

khwan N ควัน smoke (e.g.
from a fire)

L

lá ละ per, each one: e.g. **pii lá
khráng** ปีละครั้ง once a year

lâ ล่ะ a particle used at the end
of an utterance to ask the
following sort of question:
'and what about...?'

lá-aai V ละอาย to feel ashamed

laa àwk V ลาออก to resign,
quit (a job)

lâa cháa V ล่าช้า late/tardy

laa kàwn V ลาก่อน goodbye,
farewell

laa-mók ADJ ลามก obscene,
lewd, smutty

laa phák V ลาพัก to take leave
(from work)

laa pùai v ลาป่วย to take sick leave

lâa sùt ADV ล่าสุด the latest; also – at the latest

lǎai ADJ หลาย many, various, several

laai N, ADJ ลาย design/pattern (e.g. on a T-shirt/piece of material); patterned, striped

laai sen N ลายเซ็น signature

lǎai sìp N หลายสิบ tens of, multiples of ten, many

lâam N ล่าม (an) interpreter

láan ล้าน million

lǎan N หลาน grandchild, niece, nephew

laan N ลาน open space, ground

lǎan chaai N หลานชาย grandson, nephew

laan jàwt rót N ลานจอดรถ a parking lot

lǎan sǎaw N หลานสาว granddaughter, niece

laang N ลาง omen, portent, sign

lâang ADV ล่าง below, beneath

láang ADV ล้าง to wash/rinse/cleanse (e.g. dishes, a car, one's face, etc., not clothes)

laang dii N ลางดี good omen, favourable sign

láang jaan v ล้างจาน to wash the dishes

laang ráai N ลางร้าย bad/evil omen

laaw N ลาว Laos (the country), Lao (people/language)

láe CONJ (pronounced something like **léh**!) และ and

lâehk chék v แลกเช็ค to cash a check/cheque

lâehk ngoen v (COLLOQUIAL) แลกเงิน to change money

lâehk plìan v แลกเปลี่ยน to trade, exchange

lǎehm ADJ แหลม pointed, jagged; sharp (as in bright/clever)

lên ruea v แล่นเรือ to sail a boat

láew CONJ แล้ว already – a word which indicates completion/past tense: go already = gone **pai láew** ไปแล้ว; **láew** แล้ว is also used in conversation to 'connect' statements, meaning, for example, either 'then (so and so happened)', or 'and then (that happened)'

láew jà thammai (COLLOQUIAL)

213

แล้วจะทำไม So what!

láew tàeh IDIOMS (COLLOQUIAL) แล้วแต่ it depends, as you like, (that's) up to (so and so)

lǎi v ไหล to flow

lá-iat ADJ ละเอียด fine, delicate, to be pulverized (into powder/small pieces), meticulous/careful (craftsmanship)

lâi àwk v ไล่ออก to fire someone

lâi pai v ไล่ไป to chase away, chase out

lâi taam v ไล่ตาม to chase after

lák lâwp v ลักลอบ to smuggle (e.g. drugs, etc.)

lák mueang N หลักเมือง Lak Muang, the city pillar

lá-khawn N (pronounced 'làcorn') ละคร play, theatrical production; **lá-khawn thii wii** N ละครทีวี television soap opera

láksànà N ลักษณะ characteristic(s), (the) nature or appearance (of something)

làk-thǎan N หลักฐาน evidence

lambaa ADJ (**lam** pronounced like 'lum' in 'lumber',

bàak like 'bark') ลำบาก troublesome, tough (life)

lam-yai N ลำไย longan (fruit)

lǎng N, ADV หลัง back (part of body), back, rear

lǎng jàak CONJ หลังจาก after

lǎng jàak nán ADV หลังจากนั้น afterwards, then

lǎng-khaa N หลังคา roof

lang mái N ลังไม้ wooden box, crate

lâo N เหล้า spirits, liquor, alcohol

lâo v เล่า to tell a story, relate

làp v หลับ to sleep, nap; **làp taa** v หลับตา to close/shut one's eyes

látthí N ลัทธิ sect, doctrine, creed

látthí hǐnná-yaan N ลัทธิ หินยาน Lesser vehicle of Buddhism, Hinayana

látthí khaa-thawlìk N ลัทธิคาทอลิก Roman Catholicism

látthí khǒng júeh N ลัทธิขงจื๊อ Confucianism

látthí má-hǎa-yaan N ลัทธิ มหายาน Greater vehicle of Buddhism, Mahayana

làw ADJ (pronounced 'lor' with a low tone) หล่อ to be handsome

láw N (pronounced 'lor' with a high tone) ล้อ wheel; **săam láw** สามล้อ a trishaw (and common word for 'tuk-tuk' – a motorized 'trishaw')

láwk V (from English – and pronounced much like the English word) ล็อก to lock

láwk láew ADJ ล็อกแล้ว to be locked

láwk luang V (**làwk** pronounced like 'lork') หลอกลวง to deceive (in colloquial speech commonly just **làwk** หลอก)

lawng V ลอง to try, to try out, attempt (to do something), experiment (in the sense of trying something)

lawng sài V ลองใส่ try on (clothes)

làwt N หลอด tube, (drinking) straw

làwt-toeh-rîi N (from English) ล็อตเตอรี่ lottery

lêhk N เลข number, numeral

lêhk khîi N เลขคี่ (an) odd number; **lêhk khûu** N เลขคู่ (an) even number

lêhkhăa N เลขา secretary

lehn N (from English) เลน lane (of a highway)

lehw ADJ เลว bad (of a person)

lêhw ADJ เหลว the opposite of solid, e.g. liquid-like

lék ADJ เล็ก little, small, diminutive

lèk N เหล็ก iron, metal

lèk klâa N เหล็กกล้า steel

lék nói ADJ เล็กน้อย small, not much, a tiny bit

lêm N เล่ม classifier used when counting or referring to numbers of books, candles, knives

len N เลนส์ (from English) lens (of a camera)

lên V เล่น to play

lên pai thûa V เล่นไปทั่ว to play around

lên tôh khlûehn V เล่นโต้คลื่น to surf/to ride a surfboard

lép N เล็บ nail(s) – as in fingernail(s), toenail(s), also – for animals – 'claws'

lia V เลีย to lick

lian V เลียน to imitate, copy, mimic; (also, more fully) **lian**

bàehp v เลียนแบบ to copy (e.g. someone else's style of dressing etc.)

lían ADJ เลียน greasy, oily, fatty (food)

líang v เลี้ยง to bring up, raise (children or animals); to treat (someone/a friend/ acquaintance, e.g. by taking them out for drinks or dinner – food or drinks)

líao v เลี้ยว to turn, make a turn

líao klàp v เลี้ยวกลับ to turn around

lín N ลิ้น tongue

lín-chák N ลิ้นชัก drawer

ling N ลิง monkey

lín-jìi N ลิ้นจี่ lychee (fruit)

lip N (from English) ลิฟต์ lift, elevator

lít N (from English) ลิตร liter

lôehk v เลิก to cease/stop/give up (e.g. smoking cigarettes)

lôehk kan v เลิกกัน to break off a relationship

loei N เลย a word used in a number of senses such as: therefore, so, beyond; also used to intensify adjective, often in conjunction with 'no/not' – in this sense meaning '… at all'. For example: 'no good at all' **mâi dii loei** ไม่ดีเลย, or 'not expensive at all' **mâi phaehng loei** ไม่แพงเลย

lôh N โหล dozen

lôhk N โลก the earth, world

loi v ลอย to float

loi náam v ลอยน้ำ to float in the water

lom N ลม wind, breeze

lôm ADJ ล่ม capsized/ overturned (boat)

lóm v ล้ม to topple, fall over, collapse; to overthrow (a government)

lom bâa mŭu N ลมบ้าหมู epilepsy

lom hăai jai N, v ลมหายใจ breath, breathe

lom jàp v (COLLOQUIAL) ลมจับ about to faint, about to have a fainting spell; (also, more commonly) **pen lom** เป็นลม to faint/pass out

lóm lá-laai v ล้มละลาย to go bankrupt, to be wiped out financially

lom phát ADJ, v ลมพัด windy,

216

the wind is blowing

lŏng v หลง to be infatuated (with), to be crazy about (someone or something)

long v ลง to go downwards; to land (plane), get off (transport)

lŏng (thaang) v หลง (ทาง) to get lost/to lose one's way (literally and metaphorically)

long kha-naehn siang v ลงคะแนนเสียง to vote

long maa v ลงมา come down

long phung v (COLLOQUIAL) ลงพุง to get paunchy, to develop a gut

long tha-bian v ลงทะเบียน to register

long thun v ลงทุน to invest (e.g. in a business)

lóp v ลบ to subtract, deduct, minus (in doing mathematical calculations); to erase (e.g. the writing on a blackboard)

lòp v หลบ to avoid, evade, duck, shy away from

lót v ลด to reduce, decrease, lower

lót long v ลดลง decrease, lessen, reduce

lót náam-nàk v ลดน้ำหนัก to lose weight, to diet (the English word 'diet' has also found its way into Thai and pronounced in a similar way)

lót raa-khaa v ลดราคา to discount or reduce the price

lŭam ADJ หลวม loose (the opposite of 'tight')

lúan ADV ล้วน all/the whole lot, completely

lŭang ADJ หลวง great, (owned by) the) state, royal: **thànŏn lŭang** N ถนนหลวง public road/thoroughfare; **mueang lŭang** N เมืองหลวง capital city; (COLLOQUIAL) **nai lŭang** ในหลวง His Majesty the King

lúang v ล่วง to go beyond/exceed (rules, the law); to trespass (against someone), violate, infringe

lúang krà-păo v ล้วงกระเป๋า to pickpocket

lûat N ลวด wire

lûat năam N ลวดหนาม barbed wire

lŭea v เหลือ to be left over

lûeai N เลื่อย a saw

217

lúeai v เลื้อย to crawl, slither (as a snake)

lûeak v เลือก to pick, choose, select

lûeak dâi v เลือกได้ to be optional, to have the choice

lûean v เลื่อน to put off, delay

lûean àwk pai v เลื่อนออกไป to postpone, delay

lǔeang เหลือง yellow (for a list of the most common colours see the entry under **sǐi** สี which means 'colour')

lûeat N เลือด blood

luehm v ลืม to forget

luehm taa v ลืมตา to open one's eyes

luehm tua v ลืมตัว to forget oneself, lose one's self-control

lûehn v, ADJ ลื่น to slip, to be slippery

lúek ADJ ลึก deep (e.g. water), profound

lúek láp ADJ ลึกลับ to be mysterious

lúk v ลุก to stand, get up, rise

lúk khûen v ลุกขึ้น get up (from bed)

lǔm sòp N หลุมศพ grave

lún v (COLLOQUIAL) ลุ้น to back/support/cheer (e.g. a team); to win (a prize in a competition)

lung N, PRON ลุง uncle – either parent's older brother; also used as a pronoun (i.e. 'you' or 'he') to refer to an older unrelated male in a friendly way

lûuk N ลูก child (offspring); classifier for small round objects, e.g. fruit, and 'ball-like' things

lûuk anthá v ลูกอัณฑะ (medical term) testicle(s)

lûuk chaai N ลูกชาย son

lûuk chín N ลูกชิ้น meat/pork/fish ball(s), one of the main ingredients in noodle soup

lûuk fàet N ลูกแฝด twins

lûuk kháa N ลูกค้า customer, client

lûuk khǒei N ลูกเขย son-in-law

lûuk khrûeng N ลูกครึ่ง person of mixed race (e.g. European+Asian = 'Eurasian')

lûuk lǎan N ลูกหลาน descendant(s)

lûuk măa N ลูกหมา puppy/ puppies

lûuk maeo N ลูกแมว kitten(s)

lûuk náwng N ลูกน้อง employee(s)

lûuk phîi lûuk náwng N ลูกพี่ ลูกน้อง cousin

lûuk phûu chaai N, ADJ ลูก ผู้ชาย man; (to be) manly

lûuk săaw N ลูกสาว daughter

lûuk-sà-phái N ลูกสะใภ้ daughter-in-law

lûuk taa N (commonly pronounced **lûuk-àtaa** ลูกตา) ลูกตา eyeball(s)

lûuk thûng N ลูกทุ่ง country/ hillbilly; **phlehng lûuk thûng** N เพลงลูกทุ่ง (Thai) popular country music; also used for 'country music' more generally

M

máa N ม้า horse (NOTE: **máa laai** ม้าลาย zebra)

măa N หมา dog

maa V มา to come; also indicates time up to the present; direction

maa jàak มาจาก come from, originate

maa jàak năi มาจากไหน common question form: 'Where do you come from/ where does it come from?' etc.

maa láew V (COLLOQUIAL) มาแล้ว to have arrived, to have come already: e.g. **kháo maa láew** เขามาแล้ว 'He's/she's come; he's/she's already here'

maa nîi V (COLLOQUIAL) มานี่ Come here

maa săai V (COLLOQUIAL) มาสาย to be late (e.g. for school, work, etc.)

maa sí V (COLLOQUIAL) มาสิ Come on, come along there

măi lêhk thoh-rásàp N หมายเลขโทรศัพท์ telephone number

mâak ADJ มาก many, much, a lot ADV very

màak N หมาก betel nut (which was widely used/chewed in Thailand in the past, leaving a dark reddish stain on the lips, gums, teeth)

màak fàràng N หมากฝรั่ง chewing gum

mâak khûehn ADJ มากขึ้น more, increasing (e.g. the cost of living, the number of tourists)

mâak koehn pai มากเกินไป too much

mâak kwàa ADJ มากกว่า more than (something else), e.g. to like something more than another thing

màak rúk N หมากรุก chess

mâak thîi sùt ADJ มากที่สุด (the) most

maa-lehsia N มาเลเซีย Malaysia, Malaysian

mâan N (pronounced 'marn' with a falling tone) ม่าน curtains, drapes

maandaa N มารดา (formal term for) mother

maa-rá-yâat N มารยาท conduct, behavior, manners, etiquette

maa-rá-yâat dii ADJ มารยาทดี to have good manners, to be well-mannered

mâat-trà-thăan N มาตรฐาน standard, specification(s) (e.g. of goods/services, etc.)

mâeh N แม่ mother

mâeh bâan N แม่บ้าน housekeeper, housewife, lady of the house

mâeh khrua N แม่ครัว cook (female)

mâeh kunjaeh N แม่กุญแจ a padlock

mâeh mâai N แม่ม่าย a widow

mâeh náam N แม่น้ำ river

mâeh să-mii N แม่สามี mother-in-law; also **mâeh yaai** N แม่ยาย

máeh tàeh แม่แต่ even (though), not even

máeh wâa แม้ว่า though, if, no matter

maeo N แมว a cat

maeo náam N แมวน้ำ a seal

má-hăa-chon N มหาชน the public, the masses

má-hăa sà-mùt N มหาสมุทร ocean

máhăa sèht-thĭi N มหาเศรษฐี millionare, a very wealthy person

má-hăa wítthá-yaa-lai N มหาวิทยาลัย university, (COLLOQUIAL) **máhăălai** มหาลัย

mâi ADV ไม่ no, not (used with verbs and adjectives)

220

mãi ไหม common question particle used at the end of an utterance, e.g. 'is it good/is it any good?' (written with a rising tone but commonly pronounced with a high tone) *dii mãi* ดีไหม

mài ADJ ใหม่ new

mái N ไม้ wood

mǎi N ไหม silk

mai N ไมล์ (from English) mile

mâi V ไหม้ to burn

mâi châwp V ไม่ชอบ not to like (something/somebody), to dislike

mâi jampen ADJ ไม่จำเป็น to be unnecessary, not necessary

mái jîm fan ไม้จิ้มฟัน toothpick(s)

mái khiit fai N ไม้ขีดไฟ matches

mâi khít ngoen (COLLOQUIAL) ไม่คิดเงิน free of charge

mâi khoei ADV ไม่เคย never

mâi khôi mii (COLLOQUIAL) ไม่ค่อยมี there's hardly any, hard to find, scarce

mâi kìi... ไม่กี่... few..., e.g. **mâi kìi khon** ไม่กี่คน few people

mái kwàat N ไม้กวาด broom

mâi mâak kâw nói (COLLO-

QUIAL) ไม่มากก็น้อย more or less

mâi mii ไม่มี no (in response to questions such as 'have you a.../have you got any?'), there's none/there isn't any (NOTE: when translated literally **mâi mii** means 'no have' — an expression you commonly hear in Thailand from those who haven't really studied English)

mâi mii àrai ไม่มีอะไร (COLLOQUIAL) 'no/nothing' in response to such questions as 'what's the matter?', 'what's on your mind?', 'what are you thinking?'

mâi mii khâw phùuk mát (EXPRESSION) ไม่มีข้อผูกมัด to be free of commitments

mâi mii khrai ไม่มีใคร nobody (e.g. there is nobody at home/ I don't have anyone [to help me etc.])

mâi mii khwaam sùk ADJ ไม่มีความสุข to be unhappy

mâi mii prà·yòht ADJ ไม่มีประโยชน์ to be of no use, to be useless

mâi mii thaang (COLLOQUIAL)
ไม่มีทาง no way (I'm doing
that)

mâi nâa chûeah ADJ
(COLLOQUIAL) ไม่น่าเชื่อ
unbelievable, incredible

mái pàa diao kan ไม้ป่า
เดียวกัน **(SLANG EXPRESSION)**
homosexual (male) – i.e.
'wood from the same jungle/
forest'

mâi pen rai (common
idiomatic Thai expression)
ไม่เป็นไร don't mention
it!, never mind!, you're
welcome!, it doesn't matter,
it's nothing

mâi phaehng ADJ ไม่แพง to
be inexpensive

mâi phèt ADJ ไม่เผ็ด mild (not
spicy)

mâi prà-sòp phŏn sămrèt
ADJ (SOMEWHAT FORMAL) ไม่
ประสบผลสำเร็จ to fail, to be
unsuccessful

mâi run raehng ADJ ไม่รุนแรง
mild (not very strong, e.g.
taste), (or, alternatively) not
violent (**run raehng** รุนแรง
means 'violent')

mâi rúu-jàk v ไม่รู้จัก (pronounced something like
'roo-juck') **(COLLOQUIAL)** not to
know someone or something

mâi sàbaai jai ADJ ไม่สบายใจ
(to feel) upset, unhappy

mâi săm-khan ADJ ไม่สำคัญ
not important, unimportant

mâi siap N ไม้เสียบ skewer
(e.g. a satay stick)

mâi sùk ADJ ไม่สุก (to be)
unripe

mâi su-phâap ADJ ไม่สุภาพ
impolite, rude

mái tháo N ไม้เท้า walking
stick, cane

mák jà ADV ... มักจะ... often,
usually, regularly

má-kà-raa-khom N มกราคม
January

má-khǎam N มะขาม tamarind
(fruit)

má-khǔea mûang N มะเขือ
ม่วง eggplant, aubergine

má-khǔea thêht N มะเขือเทศ
tomato

mák-khú-thêht N มัคคุเทศก์
guide (i.e. tour guide)

má-laehng N แมลง insect
(general term)

má-laehng wan N แมลงวัน fly (insect)

má-lá-kaw N (**kaw** pronounced like 'gore') มะละกอ papaya, pawpaw

málí N มะลิ jasmine

má-mûang N มะม่วง mango

má-naaw N มะนาว lemon, lime (citrus fruit)

má-phráo N มะพร้าว coconut

má-reng N มะเร็ง cancer

man มัน (**SLANG**) excellent, most enjoyable, to be fun, that's great

man PRON, N, ADJ มัน it; potato-like vegetables; shiny, brilliant

măn ADJ หมัน to be sterile, barren

mân N หมั้น to engage (promise to marry)

man fá-ràng N มันฝรั่ง potato(es)

màn sâi (**COLLOQUIAL**) หมั่นไส้ to be disgusted (with), to be put off (by)

man thêht N มันเทศ yam(s)

mâng khâng ADJ มั่งคั่ง (to be) wealthy

mang sà-wí-rát N, ADJ

มังสวิรัติ vegetarian

mang-khút N มังคุด mangosteen (fruit)

mân-khong ADJ มั่นคง to be firm, definite, secure

mánút N มนุษย์ human (being)

máo N (from English) เมาส์ mouse (computer)

mao ADJ เมา drunk, intoxicated, stoned, wasted

mao kháang V (**COLLOQUIAL**) เมา ค้าง to have a hangover

máruehn níi ADV มะรืนนี้ (the) day after tomorrow

mâw N (pronounced 'mor' with a falling tone) หม้อ (cooking) pot

măw N (pronounced 'mor' with a rising tone) หมอ doctor

maw-rà-dòk N มรดก inheritance, legacy

maw-rà-kòt N มรกต emerald

maw-rà-sŭm N มรสุม monsoon

màw sŏm ADJ เหมาะสม to be suitable/appropriate

màwk N หมอก mist, fog

măwn N หมอน pillow, cushion

mawng V มอง watch, to stare at

223

mawng mâi hĕn v มองไม่เห็น to be invisible, unable to see

mâwp hâi v มอบให้ to hand over, bestow (e.g. power to incoming government/a university degree to a graduate)

mâwp tua v มอบตัว to give oneself up, to surrender (to the police); to report (for duty, work etc.)

mawtoehsai N (from English) มอเตอร์ไซค์ motorcycle

mêhk mâak ADJ เมฆมาก overcast, cloudy

meh-nuu N (from English) เมนู menu

meh-săa-yon N เมษายน April

méht N เมตร metre

mĕn v, ADJ เหม็น to stink, to be stinky (NOTE: in Thai just this one word can be a whole sentence – the equivalent of 'It stinks/It smells foul' etc.)

mét N (also pronounced **mel-ét**) เมล็ด seed; classifier for small seed-like objects, e.g. pills

mí nâa là มิน่าล่ะ (COLLOQUIAL EXPRESSION) no wonder!

mia N เมีย (COLLOQUIAL) wife, defacto partner, sometimes simply 'girlfriend'

mia nói N เมียน้อย mistress

mii N หมี a bear

mii N หมี่ vermicelli, fine noodles

mii v มี to have, own; there is, there are

mii amnâat ADJ มีอำนาจ to have power, to be powerful

mii chii-wít มีชีวิต live (be alive), living

mii chûeh ADJ มีชื่อ to be famous, to be well known

mii chúu v มีชู้ (for a married person) to have a lover

mii it-thí-phon v มีอิทธิพล to have influence (to get things done), to have connections

mii jèht-tà-naa v มีเจตนา to intend, to have the intention (to)

mii khâa v มีค่า to be valuable, precious, to have worth/be useful

mii khon thoh maa (COLLOQUIAL) มีคนโทรมาsomeone's on the phone (i.e. someone's called me/you)

224

mii khun khâa v มีคุณค่า to have value (e.g. for a medicine to be useful)

mii kwaam mân-jai v มีความมั่นใจ to have confidence, to be confident

mii kwaam sùk v มีความสุข to be happy

mii klìn v มีกลิ่น to have an odour, to smell bad

mii laai ADJ มีลาย patterned (to have a pattern on it), striped; (COLLOQUIAL) **tháwng laai** ท้อง ลาย for a woman to have 'stretch marks'

mii-naa-khom N มีนาคม March

mii phít v มีพิษ to be poisonous

mii phŏn tàw v มีผลต่อ... to affect

mii pràjam duean v มีประจำ เดือน (SOMEWHAT FORMAL) to men- struate, to have one's period

mii prà-sòpkaan v มีประสบ- การณ์ to have experience, to be experienced

mii prà-yòht v มีประโยชน์ to be useful

mii sà-maa-thí v มีสมาธิ to concentrate, to be mindful

mii sà-nèh v (COLLOQUIAL) มีเสน่ห์ to be personable, alluring, appealing, to have charm

mii sên v มีเส้น (COLLOQUIAL) to have influence/connections

mii sùan rûam v มีส่วนร่วม to participate/co-operate

mii tháksà v มีทักษะ skilful, to be skilled, to have skills

mii thúrá v มีธุระ to be busy, to have something to do

mîit N (pronounced like 'mead' with a falling tone) มีด knife

mít N มิตร (SOMEWHAT FORMAL) friend

mít-chǎa-chìip N มิจฉาชีพ wrongful/unlawful occupation; a person who makes their living from some form of criminality

mí-thù-naa-yon N มิถุนายน June

mìti N มิติ dimension (e.g. as in 3D – **sǎam miti** สามมิติ)

moh-hŏh ADJ โมโห to be cross/angry

mohng N โมง o'clock, e.g. **6 mohng** 6 o'clock, hours

môi N หมอย (RUDE) pubic hair

225

mon-lá-phaa-wá N มลภาวะ
pollution, also **mon-lá-phít**
มลพิษ

mòt aàyú หมดอายุ v to expire
(e.g. a license, a passport),
past its use-by date (e.g.
milk, etc.)

mòt láew ADJ (COLLOQUIAL)
หมดแล้ว used up, all gone,
none left

mót lûuk N มดลูก uterus,
womb

mòt raehng (COLLOQUIAL) หมด
แรง to have no energy left,
tired out

mûa ADV/ADJ (COLLOQUIAL) มั่ว
haphazardly, indiscriminately,
chaotic, erratic

muai N มวย boxing (general
term)

muai sǎa-kon N มวยสากล
Western-style boxing

muai thai N มวยไทย Thai
boxing

mùak N หมวก hat, cap

mûang/sǐi mûang N (สี) ม่วง
purple

mûea khuehn níi ADV เมื่อคืน
นี้, (or simply) **mûea khuehn**
เมื่อคืน last night

mûea kìi níi N (COLLOQUIAL) เมื่อ
กี้นี้, (or simply) **mûea kìi** เมื่อ
กี้ just a moment ago

mûea rài เมื่อไหร่ when?

mûea rài kâw dâi เมื่อไหร่ก็ได้
(a common response to the
question 'when?') whenever,
any time

mûea waan níi ADV เมื่อวานนี้,
(or simply) **mûea waan** เมื่อ
วาน yesterday

mûea waan suehn níi ADV
เมื่อวานซืนนี้ the day before
yesterday

mǔean ADJ เหมือน to resemble,
be similar to, like, as

mueang N เมือง town, city;
also country as in the
common name for Thailand
mueang thai เมืองไทย

mǔeang N (COLLOQUIAL) เหมือง,
(more fully) **mǔeang râeh**
เหมืองแร่ a mine

mueang jiin N เมืองจีน China

mueang thai N เมืองไทย
Thailand (NOTE: the most
common way Thai people
refer to their own country)

mǔean-kan เหมือนกัน to
be identical; too, either, (in

conversation if you are of the same view as the person you are talking to you can say) likewise

mueh N มือ hand

múeh N มื้อ mealtime, a meal (also commonly used when referring to the number of meals eaten)

mueh thǔeh N มือถือ cell phone, mobile phone

mùehn N หมื่น ten thousand

mûeht ADJ มืด dark

mûeht khrúem ADJ มืดครึ้ม to be cloudy, overcast

mùek N หมึก ink

múk N มุก pearl

mum N มุม corner, angle

mǔn V หมุน to turn, rotate (e.g. a knob/dial)

múng N มุ้ง mosquito net

múng lûat N มุ้งลวด fly screen

mûng pai V มุ่งไป to head for, towards

mút-sàlim มุสลิม Muslim

mǔu N หมู pig, hog, boar

mùu bâan N หมู่บ้าน a village

mǔu haem N (from English) หมูแฮม ham

N

ná นะ a particle used at the end of a sentence to convey a number of different meanings, e.g. 'right?' **mâi dii ná** ไม่ดีนะ 'That's no good, right?'; 'okay/OK?'; **tòk-long pai dûai kan ná** ตกลงไปด้วยกันนะ 'Agreed, let's go together, OK?'

nâa ADJ หนา thick (of things)

naa N นา (irrigated) rice field, paddy field

náa N น้า aunt, uncle (a younger brother or sister of one's mother)

nâa N หน้า face, page, front (ahead); e.g. season – **nâa ráwn** หน้าร้อน summer (Feb–April); **nâa nǎaw** หน้าหนาว winter/cool season (Nov–Jan); **nâa fǒn** หน้าฝน rainy season (May–Oct)

nâa น่า a prefix used with verbs/adjectives to form words with endings such as -ful, -able, -y, -ing; also used to suggest that something's worth doing, trying, sampling etc., e.g. **nâa kin** น่ากิน – appetizing, tempting, delectable, to look delicious

nâa bùea ADJ น่าเบื่อ boring, dull

nâa fang v น่าฟัง worth listening to

nâa itchǎa ADJ น่าอิจฉา envious

nâa jùup ADJ น่าจูบ kissable

nâa kàak N (pronounced 'gark' with a low tone) หน้ากาก a mask

nâa kàwt ADJ น่ากอด huggable, cuddlesome

nâa khǎai nâa ADJ น่าขายหน้า to be shameful; (COLLOQUIAL) **khǎai nâa** ขายหน้า to lose face

nâa klìat ADJ น่าเกลียด ugly – can refer to both a person or thing as well as unseemly behaviour

nâa klua ADV น่ากลัว scary, frightening

nâa lá-aai น่าละอาย (to be) ashamed, embarrassed; to be embarrassing

nâa òk N หน้าอก chest; also breast(s), chest

nâa phàak N หน้าผาก forehead

nâa plàehk jai ADJ น่าแปลกใจ surprising, weird

nâa prà-làat jai ADJ น่าประหลาดใจ unusual, strange, wonderful

nâa rák ADJ น่ารัก cute, appealing, lovely, pretty (NOTE: this term is used in Thai to refer not only to people or animals, but also behaviour)

nâa rák mâak ADJ น่ารักมาก very cute

nâa rang-kìat ADJ น่ารังเกียจ disgusting

nâa sà-nùk ADJ น่าสนุก to be fun, to look like fun (i.e. it looks like fun)

nâa sàp sŏn ADJ น่าสับสน to be confusing

nâa sǒn-jai ADJ น่าสนใจ to be interesting

nâa sŏng sǎan ADJ น่าสงสาร to feel/express pity/sympathy for someone else: Oh, what a pity!

nâa tàang N หน้าต่าง window (in house)

228

nâa thîi N หน้าที่ duty (responsibility)

naa thîi N นาที a minute

nâa tùehn tên ADJ น่าตื่นเต้น to be exciting

nâa wái jai ADJ น่าไว้ใจ trustworthy, dependable, reliable

naai N นาย Mr, Mister, Sir, owner, employer, chief, boss

naai jâang N นายจ้าง employer

naai phâet N (FORMAL TERM) นายแพทย์ doctor

naai phon N นายพล general (in the armed forces)

naai rueah N นายเรือ captain (of a ship/vessel)

naai tamrùat N นายตำรวจ police officer

naai thá-hǎan N นายทหาร army officer

naai thun N นายทุน capitalist

naalí-kaa N นาฬิกา wristwatch, clock; o'clock in 24 hour system (i.e. **1 naalikaa** = one o'clock in the morning; **13 naalikaa** = one o'clock in the afternoon)

náam N น้ำ water, liquid, fluid (also see entries under **náam...** below)

náam àt lom N น้ำอัดลม soft drink, fizzy drink (Coke, Pepsi, etc.)

náam chaa N น้ำชา tea

náam hǎwm N น้ำหอม perfume

náam jai N น้ำใจ (an important Thai word expressing a very desirable trait – someone with): spirit, heart, goodwill, thoughtfulness, a willingness to help

náam jîm N น้ำจิ้ม sauce (for dipping, e.g. spring rolls, curry puffs, etc.)

náam khǎeng N น้ำแข็ง ice

náam khûen N น้ำขึ้น high tide; **náam long** N น้ำลง low tide

náam man N น้ำมัน gasoline, petrol

náam man khrûeang N น้ำมันเครื่อง engine oil

náam man ngaa N น้ำมันงา sesame oil

náam nàk N น้ำหนัก weight

náam nàk khûen V น้ำหนักขึ้น to gain weight, to put on weight

náam nàk lót v น้ำหนักลด to lose weight

náam phŏn-lá-mái N น้ำผลไม้ fruit juice

náam phú N น้ำพุ a spring/fountain

náam phú ráwn N น้ำพุร้อน hot spring

náam phûeng N น้ำผึ้ง honey

náam plaa N น้ำปลา fish sauce

náam prà-paa N น้ำประปา piped water, tap water, water supply (e.g. in a town/city)

naam sà-kun N นามสกุล surname, last name

náam sôm N น้ำส้ม orange juice; also (Thai) vinegar used as a condiment that can used to flavour such things as noodle soup

náam súp N น้ำซุป soup, broth

náam taa N น้ำตา tear(s)

náam taan N น้ำตาล brown (colour), sugar

náam thûam N, v น้ำท่วม a flood/to flood

náam tòk N น้ำตก a waterfall

naan ADJ, ADV นาน long, lasting, for a long time, ages

naan thâo-rài นานเท่าไหร่ (for) how long?

naa-naa châat ADJ นานาชาติ international

naang N นาง woman, lady; Mrs (title)

naang èhk N นางเอก leading actress, female lead, heroine

naang ngaam N นางงาม a beauty queen; **naang ngaam jàkkrawaan** นางงามจักรวาล Miss Universe

naang săaw N นางสาว unmarried woman, Miss/Ms (title)

năaw ADJ หนาว cold weather, to be cold (body temperature)

năaw sàn v หนาวสั่น to shiver

naa-yók N นายก chairman, president (of a company)

naa-yók rát-thà-montrii N นายกรัฐมนตรี prime minister (colloquially referred to simply as **naa-yók** นายก)

nâeh jai ADJ แน่ใจ certain, sure

nâeh nawn ADV แน่นอน certainly!, of course, exactly

nâen ADJ แน่น to be crowded; solid, tight

náe-nam v แนะนำ to suggest, advise, recommend

náe-nam tua v แนะนำตัว to introduce someone

náe-nam tua ehng v แนะนำตัวเอง to introduce oneself

naew N แนว line, row (e.g. of chairs etc.)

năi ADV ไหน where? which?

nai PREP ใน in, at (space), inside, within

nai à-diit ADV ในอดีต in the past

nai à-naakhót ADV ในอนาคต in the future

nai-lâwn N (from English) ในล่อน nylon

nai lŭang N (COLLOQUIAL) ในหลวง the King (of Thailand)

nai mâi cháa ADV ในไม่ช้า soon, shortly, before long

nai mueang ในเมือง downtown, urban

nai ra-wàng ADV ในระหว่าง during (e.g. the trip to the coast), between

nai thîi sùt ADV ในที่สุด finally, eventually, in the long run

nàk ADJ หนัก to be heavy

nák นัก used as a prefix to form a word meaning – an expert, one skilled (in), or

-er, fancier (see the following entries)

nák bin N นักบิน a pilot, aviator

nák doehn thaang N นักเดินทาง traveler

nák khàaw N นักข่าว journalist

nák khian N นักเขียน writer

nák-lehng N นักเลง tough guy, hoodlum, ruffian

nák ráwng N นักร้อง a singer

nák rian N นักเรียน a student

nák thâwng thîao N นักท่องเที่ยว a tourist

nák thúrákit N นักธุรกิจ businessperson

ná-khawn N นคร city, metropolis, the first part of the name in a number of Thai towns/cities/provinces, e.g. Nakhon Pathom, Nakhon Sawan, Nakhon Phanom, Nakhon Naiyok, Nakhon Sithammarat

nam v นำ to guide, lead; to head, escort

nam khâo v นำเข้า to import

nam pai v นำไป to lead (to guide/take someone somewhere)

nam thîao v นำเที่ยว to guide, to take (a person) around, lead a tour

nán นั้น that

nân lâe! (COLLOQUIAL) นั้นแหละ exactly! just so!

nâng v นั่ง to sit

nǎng N หนัง leather

nǎng N หนัง film, movie (NOTE: the same word as 'leather', this being related to a perceived likeness between the screening of early films and traditional shadow puppets whose images were illuminated on a thin leather/parchment type of screen)

nâng long v นั่งลง to sit down

nâng rót v นั่งรถ to ride (in a car, van, etc.)

nǎngsǔeh N หนังสือ book

nǎngsǔeh doehn thaang N หนังสือเดินทาง passport (the English word 'passport' is commonly used in Thailand, pronounced something like 'pars-port')

nǎngsǔeh nam thîao N หนังสือนำเที่ยว guidebook (such as *Lonely Planet*)

nǎngsǔeh phim N หนังสือพิมพ์ newspaper

nâo ADJ เน่า to be rotten, spoiled, for food, etc. to have gone off, decayed, corrupted

náp v นับ count, reckon

náp thǔeh v นับถือ to respect, to hold in high regard, to believe in (a particular religion/faith)

nárók N นรก hell, purgatory

nát v (pronounced similar to 'nut' with a high tone) นัด to fix/set a time, to make an appointment; also to sniff (a substance) up the nose

nát-mǎai N นัดหมาย an appointment

nàw mái N หน่อไม้ bamboo shoot(s)

ná-wá-níyaai N นวนิยาย novel

nâwk ADJ นอก outside, beyond, outer, external

nâwk jàak PREP นอกจาก apart from, excluding, except, unless

nâwk jàak níi นอกจากนี้ besides, in additon, for another thing

nâwk jai v นอกใจ to be unfaithful, adulterous

nâwk khâwk ADJ นอกคอก to be unconventional, offbeat, eccentric, non-conformist

nǎwn N หนอน worm, maggot

nawn v นอน to lie down, recline, to go to bed

nawn khwâm v นอนคว่ำ to lie face down, to sleep on one's stomach

nawn làp v นอนหลับ to sleep, to be asleep; the opposite – **nawn mâi làp** นอนไม่หลับ – to be unable to sleep

nawn lên v นอนเล่น to take a rest, lay about, repose

nawn ngǎai v นอนหงาย to lie/sleep on one's back

náwng N น่อง calf (lower leg)

náwng N น้อง (COLLOQUIAL) younger brother or sister (also commonly used by Thais when speaking to an 'inferior' such as the staff in a restaurant, etc.)

náwng chaai N น้องชาย younger brother

náwng khǒei N น้องเขย younger brother-in-law

náwng mia N น้องเมีย wife's younger sibling

náwng sǎamii N น้องสามี husband's younger sibling

náwng sǎaw N น้องสาว younger sister

náwng sà-phái N น้องสะไภ้ younger sister-in-law

náwt N น็อต a bolt, nut (for building etc.)

ná-yoh-baai N นโยบาย policy (e.g. government policy)

nékthai N (from English) เน็คไท necktie

nian rîap ADJ เนียนเรียบ to be smooth (of surfaces)

nǐao ADJ เหนียว sticky, tough (e.g. chewy); (COLLOQUIAL) stingy – more fully **khîi nǐao** ขี้เหนียว

níi (PRON) นี่ this; also (COLLOQUIAL; calling attention to something) hey!

nǐi v หนี to flee, run away, escape, get away

níi ADJ นี้ this: e.g. **yàang níi** อย่างนี้ 'like this'; **wan níi** วัน นี้ 'today (i.e. this day)'

nîi sǐn N หนี้สิน debt, obligation

nîng ADJ นิ่ง still, quiet

ní-sǎi N นิสัย habit, disposition, character

nít nòi ADV นิดหน่อย slightly, a little bit

niu N นิ้ว finger; also part of the word for 'toe' **níu tháo** นิ้วเท้า; the names of the different fingers: **níu pôhng** นิ้วโป้ง thumb; **níu chíi** นิ้วชี้ index finger; **níu klaang** นิ้วกลาง middle finger; **níu naang** นิ้วนาง ring finger; **níu kôi** นิ้วก้อย little finger/pinky

niu-sii-laehn N นิวซีแลนด์ New Zealand

ní-yom ADJ นิยม to be interested in (e.g. fast cars); **rótsàni-yom** N รสนิยม taste, preference (e.g. in fashion, music etc.)

noehn khǎo N เนินเขา a hill

noei N เนย butter

noei khǎeng N เนยแข็ง cheese

nôhn ADV โน่น yonder, over there

nóhn ADV โน้น there, way over there (further than **nôhn** โน่น)

nói ADJ น้อย little, small, not much, few

nói kwàa น้อยกว่า less (smaller amount)

nói nàa N น้อยหน่า custard apple (fruit)

nói thîi sùt น้อยที่สุด least (the smallest amount)

nók N นก bird

nom N นม milk; breasts

nonthá-bùrii N นนทบุรี Nonthaburi, provincial capital northwest of central Bangkok on the east bank of the Chaopraya River. Nowadays it is virtually a part of the greater Bangkok metropolitan area

nùat N หนวด moustache

nûat V นวด to massage

nûea ADV, N เหนือ above, beyond; north

núea N เนื้อ beef, meat

núea kàe N เนื้อแกะ lamb, mutton

núea mǔu N เนื้อหมู pork (NOTE: when ordering food – simply **mǔu** หมู)

nùeai ADJ เหนื่อย to be exhausted, weary

núek V นึก to recall, to think of; (COLLOQUIAL) **nùek àwk láew** นึกออกแล้ว 'I've remembered it/I can recall it now'

234

nùeng หนึ่ง one

nûeng v นึ่ง to steam

nùeng khûu หนึ่งคู่ a pair of

nùeng thîi หนึ่งที่ once

nûm ADJ นุ่ม soft

nùm ADJ, N หนุ่ม young, youth-
ful; young man, adolescent

nùm săaw N หนุ่มสาว teen-
agers, young men and
women

nûng v นุ่ง to wear, put on, be
clad in; **nûng phâa thŭng** นุ่ง
ผ้าถุง to be wearing a sarong

nŭu N หนู a mouse or rat
(NOTE: this word is also
used by, generally, younger
women as a first person [i.e.
'I'] pronoun)

NG

NOTE: 'ng' ง is a distinct letter
in Thai quite separate from
'n' น, although here words
beginning with this letter are
grouped together under 'N'.

ngaa N งา sesame seeds

ngaa cháang N งาช้าง an
elephant tusk, ivory

ngâai ADJ ง่าย to be simple,
easy

ngâai tháwng ADJ หงายท้อง
overturned, upside down
(e.g. a vehicle that has rolled
over onto its roof)

ngaam ADJ งาม to be beautiful,
attractive; fine, good

ngaan N งาน job, work; also
party (as in 'a birthday party'),
ceremony; a measure of land
the equivalent of 400 sq. m.

ngaan àdirèhk N งานอดิเรก
a hobby

ngaan bâan N งานบ้าน
housework

ngaan líang N งานเลี้ยง
banquet

ngaan sòp N งานศพ funeral

ngaan tàeng-ngaan N งาน
แต่งงาน wedding

ngâeh N แง่ (an) angle

ngai (COLLOQUIAL) ไง what; how;
(COLLOQUIAL EXPRESSIONS) pen
ngai เป็นไง 'How are things?',
'How are you?', 'And then
what?'; **láew ngai** แล้วไง
'So?', 'So what?'; **wâa ngai**
ว่าไง 'What did you
say?', 'What did he/she say?'

235

ngán-ngán (COLLOQUIAL) งั้นๆ average (so-so, just okay)

ngáo ADJ เหงา lonely

ngao N, ADJ เงา shadow, reflection; glossy, shiny, lustrous

ngá-w ADJ โง่ to be stupid

ngâwk V งอก to sprout, shoot, germinate; **thùa ngâwk** N ถั่วงอก beansprout(s)

ngîan N, ADJ เงี่ยน (a) strong urge (for), craving (for); horny, randy, to have the hots for (someone)

ngîap ADJ, V เงียบ to be quiet, silent; (also used to say – rather brusquely) 'be quiet!'

ngoen N เงิน money, silver

ngoen duean N เงินเดือน salary

ngoen fàak N เงินฝาก deposit (money deposited in a bank)

ngoen mát-jam N (pronounced 'mutt-jum') เงิน มัดจำ a deposit (e.g. on a car, etc)

ngoen sòt N เงินสด cash, money

ngoen traa N (FORMAL TERM) เงิน ตรา currency

ngóh N (**óh** pronounced very short like in 'Oh!oh') เงาะ rambutan (fruit)

ngom-ngaai V งมงาย to be credulous, believe in something blindly

ngong ADJ งง to be puzzled, stunned, befuddled

ngùang ADJ ง่วง to be sleepy, tired

ngùea N เหงื่อ sweat; **ngùea àwk** V เหงื่อออก to perspire, sweat

ngûean khǎi N เงื่อนไข a condition/proviso (e.g. a pre-condition for something to take place)

nguu N งู snake

nguu-nguu plaàplaa (COLLOQUIAL EXPRESSION) งูๆ ปลาๆ a little bit, not much, rudimentary (e.g. to speak a language, be able to do something requiring a degree of skill)

nguu sà-wàt N งูสวัด shingles, *herpes zoster*

O

ôh hoh (exclamation expressing surprise) โอ้โฮ Wow! Gosh! Oh!

oh-kàat N โอกาส chance, opportunity

oh-liang N โอเลี้ยง iced black coffee (Thai-style)

oh-thii ADJ (from English) โอที overtime (work)

oh-yúa N โอยั๊วะ hot black coffee (Thai-style)

ohn V โอน to transfer (e.g. money to another bank account/overseas, etc.)

òhng N โอ่ง earthen jar, (large) water jar

ôi N อ้อย sugarcane

om V อม to keep in the mouth, to suck (e.g. a lolly/lozenge)

ong-kaan/ong-kawn องค์การ/องค์กร (an) organization

ongsǎa N องศา degree(s) (of temperature)

òp V, ADJ อบ to bake, to roast; baked

òp choei N อบเชย cinnamon

òp ùn ADJ อบอุ่น warm

òp-phá-yóp V อพยพ to migrate, evacuate

òt V อด to give up, abstain from

òt aa-hǎan V อดอาหาร to fast, to go without food, to abstain from food

òt taai V อดตาย to starve to death

òt thon V อดทน to be patient, to have tenacity, stamina

P

NOTE: this letter should not be confused with the English 'p'. This Thai 'p' ป is not a sound commonly found in English although it is similar to the 'p' sound in the word 'spa'.

pá V ปะ to patch (a tyre/inner tube of bicycle/a piece of clothing)

pâa N ป้า aunt, the older sister of either parent

pàa ป่า N forest, jungle; ADJ wild (of animals)

pâai N ป้าย sign, signboard; **pâai rót** N ป้ายรถ bus stop

pàak N ปาก mouth, entrance

pàak sĭa ADJ (COLLOQUIAL) ปาก
เสีย to say unpleasant things,
(to have) a big mouth

pàak soi N ปากซอย the
entrance of a Soi (laneway,
side road)

pàak-kaa N ปากกา pen

pâehng N แป้ง flour, (talcum)
powder

pàeht แปด eight

pàeht sip แปดสิบ eighty

páep diao (COLLOQUIAL
EXPRESSION) แป๊ปเดียว in a
jiffy, in a sec (second), (wait)
just a second/moment

pai V ไป to go, depart, move;
(COLLOQUIAL) to tell someone to
'Go, get out/go away' simply
say **pai** ไป with emphasis.
One other sense the word is
commonly used is to express
the idea of 'too/too much',
e.g. **phaehng pai** แพงไป too
expensive; **dang pai** ดังไป
too loud

pai ao maa V (COLLOQUIAL) ไป
เอามา to fetch, to go and
(literally, 'go'-'take'-'come')

pai doehn lên V (COLLOQUIAL)

ไปเดินเล่น to go for a walk

pai dûai V (COLLOQUIAL) ไปด้วย
to go along, to go as well

pai kan V ไปกัน to go together,
let's go; (COLLOQUIAL) also **pai
dûai kan** ไปด้วยกัน 'let's go'
together'

pai khâang nâa V ไปข้างหน้า
to go forward

pai năi maa (COLLOQUIAL) ไป
ไหนมา Where have you been?

pai nawn V ไปนอน to go
to bed

pai pen phûean V (COLLOQUIAL)
ไปเป็นเพื่อน to accompany,
to go along with someone to
keep them company

pai sòng V ไปส่ง to give
(someone) a lift (home), to
see (someone) off (e.g. at the
airport, etc.)

pai súeh khăwng V ไปซื้อของ
to shop, to go shopping

pai thát-sà-naa-jawn V (**thát**
pronounced 'tat' with a high
tone) ไปทัศนาจร (SOMEWHAT
FORMAL) to go sightseeing

pai thîi năi (QUESTION) ไป
ที่ไหน where are you going?
(COLLOQUIAL – also used as a

238

common greeting) **pai nǎi**
ไปไหน

pai yîam v ไปเยี่ยม to go visit
(e.g. a friend/relative etc.)

pàk v ปัก to embroider, to
implant

pàkàti ADJ ปกติ normal, regular,
usual, ordinary

pám náam man N ปั๊มน้ำมัน
gas/petrol station

pân v ปั้น to model (clay),
mold, sculpt

panhǎa N ปัญหา problem;
(COLLOQUIAL) **mâi mii panhǎa**
ไม่มีปัญหา 'No problems'

pào v เป่า to blow (e.g. the
candles out on a birthday
cake)

pào hǔu v (COLLOQUIAL) เป่าหู
to insinuate, to whisper
something in someone's ear
(to get them on your side/
believe you rather than
someone else)

pào mǎai N เป้าหมาย goal,
objective

pàrin-yaa N ปริญญา a degree
(i.e a university/college
degree)

pàtibàt v ปฏิบัติ (FORMAL) to

operate, perform

pàtibàt tàw v ปฏิบัติต่อ
(FORMAL) to behave towards

pàti-kiri-yaa N ปฏิกิริยา
reaction

pàtisèht v ปฏิเสธ to decline,
refuse, deny

pà-ti-thin N ปฏิทิน calendar

pàt-jù-ban nii ปัจจุบันนี้
(FORMAL) nowadays, these
days, currently

pàwk v ปอก to peel (e.g. an
orange)

pâwm N ป้อม fortress, citadel

pawn N ปอนด์ pound (money);
also used to refer to a loaf
of bread

pâwn v ป้อน to feed someone,
to spoonfeed

pâwng kan v ป้องกัน to
prevent, to protect; to defend
(in war)

pàwt N ปอด lung(s)

pêh N เป้ a backpack

pen v เป็น (the Thai equivalent
to the verb 'to be') to be
someone or something; to
know how to do something

pen hèht hâi เป็นเหตุให้ to be
the cause or reason

239

pen ìtsàra **ADJ** เป็นอิสสระ to be free, independent

pen jai **V** (COLLOQUIAL) เป็นใจ to favour, sympathize (with), side (with); to be an accomplice (of)

pen jâo khǎwng **V, N** เป็น เจ้าของ to own; the owner

pen kan ehng **ADJ** (COLLOQUIAL) เป็นกันเอง to be friendly, outgoing; (COMMON EXPRESSION) 'make yourself at home/take it easy, just be yourself'

pen khǎwng... **v** เป็นของ... to belong to..., e.g. **pen khǎwng khǎo** เป็นของเขา 'It's his/ hers'

pen man **ADJ** เป็นมัน oily (skin); shiny, glossy

pen mǎn **ADJ** เป็นหมัน to be sterile, infertile

pen nîi (PHRASE) เป็นหนี้ to owe, be in debt to someone

pen pai dâi **ADJ** (EXPRESSION) เป็นไปได้ to be possible

pen pai mâi dâi **ADJ** (EXPRESSION) เป็นไปไม่ได้ to be impossible

pen rá-bìap **ADJ** เป็นระเบียบ to be orderly, organized

pen tham **ADJ** เป็นธรรม to be fair, just, equitable

pen thammá-châat **ADJ** เป็น ธรรมชาติ natural

pen thammá-daa **ADJ** เป็น ธรรมดา to be typical, normal

pen thîi niyom **ADJ** เป็นที่นิยม to be popular

pen thîi phaw jai **ADJ** เป็นที่พอใจ to be satisfying

pen wàt เป็นหวัด to have a cold

pèt **N** เป็ด duck

pìak **ADJ** เปียก to be wet, soaking

pii **N** ปี year, years old

pii nâa ปีหน้า next year

pii thîi láew **ADV** ปีที่แล้ว last year

pìik **N** ปีก wing (of a bird or aeroplane)

piin **v** ปีน climb (e.g. a mountain)

pîng **v, ADJ** ปิ้ง to grill/toast; to be grilled, toasted

pìt **v** ปิด to close, cover, shut; off, to turn something off

pìt láew **ADJ** ปิดแล้ว turned off, closed

pìt prà-tuu **v** ปิดประตู to close the door

pit ráan v ปิดร้าน to close the shop/store

pit thà-nŏn v ปิดถนน to close the road

plaa N ปลา fish

plaa chà-lăam N ปลาฉลาม shark

plaa mùek N ปลาหมึก squid (literally, 'fish'-'ink')

plaai N ปลาย end (e.g. of the road), tip (e.g. of the tongue)

pláatsàtik N (from English) พลาสติก plastic

plaeh v แปล to translate

plaeh wâa... แปลว่า... it means...; a question to elicit the above response 'it means…': **plaeh wâa arai** แปลว่าอะไร 'what does it/ this mean?'

plàehk ADJ แปลก strange, unusual, odd; **khon plàehk nâa** คนแปลกหน้า a stranger

plàehk jai ADJ แปลกใจ surprised, puzzled

plák N (from English) ปลั๊ก plug (bath)

plák fai N ปลั๊กไฟ plug/socket (electric)

plào ADJ เปล่า empty, void; one

of the ways of saying 'no' in Thai, for example when someone asks a question assuming a positive reponse but instead gets a reply of 'no' (A: 'Do you want to go and see [name of film]? Everyone says it is great.' B: **plào** 'No')

plawm v ปลอม to forge, counterfeit, fake

plawm tua v ปลอมตัว to disguise oneself

plàwt phai ADJ ปลอดภัย to be safe (from harm)

plàwt prôhng ADJ ปลอดโปร่ง to be clear (the weather)

plian v เปลี่ยน to change (e.g. clothes, plans, etc.)

plian jai v เปลี่ยนใจ to change one's mind

pling N ปลิง a leech

plòi v ปล่อย to free, release, drop/let go

plôn v ปล้น to rob (e.g. a bank), plunder

plòt kàsian ADJ ปลดเกษียณ to be retired

plùak N ปลวก termite, white ant

241

plueai ADJ เปลือย to be naked, nude

plùeak N เปลือก the peel (of an orange), the shell (of a nut)

plùk v ปลุก to awaken/to wake up (someone); to arouse, excite

plùuk v ปลูก to plant, grow, build, construct

poehsen N (from English) เปอร์เซ็นต์ percent, percentage

pòeht v เปิด open, to open; turn or switch something on

pòeht banchii v เปิดบัญชี to open an account (e.g. bank account)

pòeht phòei v เปิดเผย to reveal, to make known

póh ADJ โป๊ indecent, revealing (clothing), scantily dressed; **năng póh** หนังโป๊ N an X-rated/pornographic film/DVD etc.

pòk khrong v ปกครอง to take care of, to govern, rule, administer

praa-kòt v ปรากฏ to appear, become visible

pràap v ปราบ to control,

suppress (e.g. the drug trade), exterminate

praà-sàat N ปราสาท castle

pràat-sajàak ADV (FORMAL) ปราศจาก without

pràat-thànăa v ปรารถนา (somewhat more formal than the colloquial **wăng** หวัง) to wish (for something), to desire, to be desirous

prà-chaa-chon N ประชาชน the public, the people, populace

prà-chaa-kawn N ประชากร population

prà-chaakhom N (FORMAL) ประชาคม community (e.g. used for the EEC, or ASEAN Community)

prachaa-sămphan N ประชาสัมพันธ์ public relations

prà-chót v ประชด to mock, ridicule, deride; to spite (someone)

prà-chum v ประชุม to meet, hold a meeting, have a conference

prà-dàp v ประดับ to decorate, adorn

242

prà-dìt v ประดิษฐ์ to invent, make up, create

praehng N แปรง a brush

praehng sǐi fan N แปรงสีฟัน toothbrush

prai-sànii N ไปรษณีย์ post office; **prai-sànii klaang** N ไปรษณีย์กลาง GPO, central post office

prà-jaan v ประจาน (a traditional Thai practice) to humiliate publicly, disgrace, to shame (the modern version of this is for criminals to re-enact their crimes – usually in handcuffs – with the police and general public looking on. Photographs are taken and published in the popular press together with details about the particular crime/offence)

pràjam ADV ประจำ regular(ly); **prajam thaang** N ประจำทาง the regular/scheduled (e.g. bus) route

pràjam duean N (formal medical term) ประจำเดือน (menstrual) period

pràjam pii ADJ, ADV ประจำปี annual

pràjam wan ADJ, ADV ประจำวัน daily

pràjòp v ประจบ to flatter, fawn (on, over); to please or humour someone (i.e. to kiss ass/arse)

prà-kàat v ประกาศ to announce, proclaim, declare, give notice

prà-kàat-sànii-yá-bàt N ประกาศนียบัตร a certificate (for completing a course of study)

prà-kan v ประกัน to guarantee, to insure; to put up bail/security

prà-kan chii-wít N ประกันชีวิต life insurance

prà-kàwp v ประกอบ to assemble, put together

prà-kàwp dûai v ประกอบด้วย be made up of, comprising, consist of

prà-kùat v ประกวด to show (in competition), to enter a competion, contest

prà-làat ADJ ประหลาด strange, odd, unusual, extraordinary

prà-làat jai ADJ ประหลาดใจ to be surprised

prà-maan v, ADV ประมาณ

to estimate; about, approximately, roughly

prà-màat ADJ ประมาท to be negligent, careless (e.g. doing something with a high risk of causing an accident)

prà-muun v ประมูล to bid/tender/auction

prà-muun khǎi v ประมูลขาย (to be) auctioned off

pràp v ปรับ to adjust (e.g. airconditioning)

pràp aa-kaat ADJ ปรับอากาศ air conditioned

pràp tua v ปรับตัว to adjust, adapt (e.g. oneself to a new situation)

prà-phêht N ประเภท class, category, type

prà-phrúet v (FORMAL) ประพฤติ behave

prà-sàat N ประสาท nerve; **sên prà-sàat** N เส้นประสาท a nerve; (COLLOQUIAL) **prà-sàat** ประสาท to be nuts/crazy

prà-sòpkaan N ประสบการณ์ experience

prà-thaa-na thíp-bawdii N ประธานาธิบดี president

prà-tháp jai ADJ ประทับใจ to

be impressed; impressive

prà-thát N ประทัด fireworks, firecrackers

prà-thêht N ประเทศ country (nation)

prà-thúang v ประท้วง to protest, go on strike

prà-tuu N ประตู door, gate; goal in football/soccer

prà-tuu náam N ประตูน้ำ a water gate; a very busy, lively area in the central part of Bangkok commonly written 'Pratunam'

prà-wàt N ประวัติ history (i.e. a personal history), record, resume

pràwàtti-sàat N ประวัติศาสตร์ history (the formal discipline of the study of the past)

prà-yàt v, ADJ ประหยัด to economize; economical, to be thrifty, frugal

prà-yòhk N ประโยค a sentence (i.e. a sentence of text)

prà-yòht N ประโยชน์ useful-ness, utility, (for the) benefit (of), advantage

priao ADJ เปรี้ยว sour (to the taste); spirited, vivacious,

244

wild, untamed (of people – generally women still in their prime)

prîao wăan ADJ เปรี้ยวหวาน sweet and sour (e.g. fish, pork, etc.)

prìap kàp เปรียบกับ compared with

prìap thîap V เปรียบเทียบ to compare

prùeksăa V ปรึกษา to consult, talk over with

pùai ADJ ป่วย to be ill, sick

pùat V ปวด to ache (e.g. toothache), be sore (e.g. sore back)

pûean ADJ เปื้อน to be soiled, dirty

puehn N ปืน gun (general term)

pŭi N ปุ๋ย fertilizer

pûm pûi ADJ (COLLOQUIAL – playful) ปุ้มปุ้ย pudgy, a bit of a fatty

pùu N ปู่ grandfather (paternal)

puu N, V ปู a crab: to lay, spread, put (sheets/mat) on (bed/floor)

pùu yâa taa yaai N ปู่ย่าตายาย grandparents, forebears, ancestors

puun N ปูน cement

PH

NOTE: 'ph' is very similar to the 'p' sound in English

phâa N ผ้า cloth, material, fabric, textile

phàa V ผ่า to split (e.g. a piece of wood with an axe)

phaa V พา to take or lead someone somewhere

phâa chét tua N ผ้าเช็ดตัว towel

phâa hòm N ผ้าห่ม blanket

phâa khîi ríu N ผ้าขี้ริ้ว a rag; tripe/offal

phâa mâan N ผ้าม่าน curtain(s), drapes

phâa puu N ผ้าปู sheet (for bed) (NOTE: the most common way of referring to bedsheets: **phâa puu thîi nawn** ผ้าปูที่นอน)

phâa puu tó N ผ้าปูโต๊ะ tablecloth

phâa sîn N ผ้าซิ่น Thai long one-piece sarong-like skirt

phàa tàt V ผ่าตัด to operate, to perform an operation or surgery

phaai N พาย a paddle; **phaai rueah** V พายเรือ to paddle/row a boat

phaai nai PREP ภายใน in (time, years), within

phaai nai pràthêht ภายในประเทศ internal, domestic, within the country

phàan V ผ่าน to pass, go past; (to go) via, through

phâap N ภาพ picture

phâap kwâang N ภาพกว้าง panorama

phâap wâat N ภาพวาด painting

phâap-phayon N ภาพยนตร์ motion picture, film

phaa-rá N ภาระ obligation, responsibility, burden

phaa-sǎa N ภาษา language

phaa-sǎa angkrit N ภาษาอังกฤษ English (language)

phaa-sǎa jiin N ภาษาจีน Chinese (language)

phaa-sǎa kha-mêhn N ภาษาเขมร Khmer/Cambodian (language)

phaa-sǎa thai N ภาษาไทย Thai (language)

phaa-sǎa thin N (pronounced 'tin', not 'thin') ภาษาถิ่น local language, dialect

phaa-sǐi N ภาษี tax(es)

phaa-wá N ภาวะ state, condition, status

phaa-yú N พายุ storm

phà-choehn V เผชิญ to meet, confront

phà-choehn nâa V เผชิญหน้า to meet, to face up to (someone or something), confront

pháe N แพะ goat

phaeh N แพ a raft, houseboat

pháeh V แพ้ to lose, be defeated; to be allergic (e.g. to some types of food, medication)

phǎehn N แผน a plan, scheme

phǎehn bohraan ADJ แผนโบราณ traditional, old style, e.g. **nûat phǎehn bohraan** นวดแผนโบราณ traditional Thai massage

phǎehn thîi N แผนที่ map

phaehng ADJ แพง expensive, dear, costly

phàen N แผ่น classifier used when counting flat objects, e.g. CDs/DVDs, sheets of paper etc.

246

phàen-din wăi N แผ่นดินไหว an earthquake

phâet N **(FORMAL TERM)** แพทย์ doctor, physician

phâi ไพ่ card(s) (game); **(COLLOQUIAL) lên phâi** เล่นไพ่ to play cards

phai N ภัย danger, peril

phài N ไผ่, (more fully) **mái phài** ไม้ไผ่ bamboo

phai phíbàt N ภัยพิบัติ disaster

phai-lin N ไพลิน sapphire

phàk N ผัก vegetable(s)

phák N พรรค party (political), group

phák V พัก to stay (at, over), to rest, stop for a while

phàk bûng N ผักบุ้ง Thai morning glory

phàk chii N ผักชี coriander, cilantro

phàk kàat khăaw N ผักกาดขาว Chinese cabbage

phàk phàwn V พักผ่อน to relax, rest

phàk sòt N ผักสด fresh vegetables

phá-lang N พลัง energy, power (e.g. physical energy, solar

energy, wind power, etc.)

phá-lang ngaan N พลังงาน energy

phà-lìt V ผลิต to manufacture, produce

phá-mâa N พม่า Burma, Burmese

phan พัน thousand

phan láan พันล้าน billion

phà-nàehk N แผนก division, section (e.g. of a government department)

phá-naehng/kaehng phanaehng N พะแนง/แกง พะแนง name of mildish curry (often written in English as 'panang' – apparently originating in Penang, Malaysia)

phánák-ngaan N พนักงาน employee in a department store/large enterprise

phánák-ngaan khăay N พนักงานขาย sales assistant

phá-nan V พนัน gamble; **lên kaan phá-nan** เล่นการพนัน to gamble; **(COLLOQUIAL) phá-nan kan măi** พนันกันไหม do you want to bet?

phà-năng N ผนัง wall,

(internal) partition in a building

phang ADJ พัง (pronounced like 'hung' with a 'p' in front – 'phung') broken down, destroyed, in ruins, ruined

phanràyaa/phanyaa N (POLITE FORMAL TERM) ภรรยา/ภริยา wife

phansǎa N พรรษา rainy season retreat/Buddhist Lent: **khâo phansǎa** เข้าพรรษา to enter/begin the rainy season retreat/Buddhist Lent

phào N เผ่า tribe, ethnic group

phǎo V เผา to burn, cremate, to set fire (to)

pháp V พับ to fold, to double over

phà-sǒm V ผสม to mix, combine

phàt V, ADJ ผัด to stir fry; stir fried

phátlom N พัดลม fan (for cooling)

phátsàdù N พัสดุ supplies, things, stores

phát-thá-naa V พัฒนา to develop (e.g. a project); for a child to 'develop/progress'

in their ability/knowledge or understanding

phaw ADV พอ (pronounced 'pour' with a mid tone) enough; as soon as, when

phâw N (pronounced 'pour' with a falling tone) พ่อ father

phaw dii ADV พอดี just right (i.e. just the right amount), just then (i.e. 'just then someone came to the door')

phaw jai ADJ พอใจ to be satisfied, contented, to be pleased

phaw khuan ADV พอควร enough, moderately, reasonably

phâw mâai N พ่อม่าย widower

phâw mâeh N พ่อแม่ parents

phaw phiang พอเพียง a notion closely associated with King Phumiphon Adunyadet which refers to what is generally called in English 'the sufficiency economy' (i.e. something along the lines of self sufficiency)

phaw sǎw N (pronounced 'por saw') พ.ศ. Buddhist era, B.E.

248

A year in the Buddhist era (which begins from the year of the Buddha's 'passing') is calculated by adding 543 to a given year in the Christian Era

phaw sŏmkhuan ADJ พอ สมควร reasonable (price), appropriate/sufficient

phaw thîi (COLLOQUIAL) พอที Enough (already), stop (doing what you're doing)

phăwm ADJ ผอม thin, lean, slim

phawn V, N พร (commonly written in English 'porn' or 'phorn') blessing, benediction, good wishes

phá-yaa-baan N พยาบาล nurse

phá-yaan N พยาน witness

phá-yâat N พยาธิ worm, parasite (in the body)

phá-yaa-yaam V พยายาม to try, attempt, make an effort

pheh-daan N เพดาน ceiling

phêht N เพศ gender, sex

phèt ADJ เผ็ด to be hot (spicy), sharp, peppery

phét N เพชร diamond

phiang ADV เพียง just, only

phiang phaw ADV เพียงพอ enough, sufficient, adequate

phiang tàeh ADV เพียงแต่ only

phîi PRON พี่ older brother or sister; commonly used as a polite, somewhat deferential, second person pronoun (you) when talking with a friend, or a stranger, who is older (but often not much older), or in a position of greater power or authority

phĭi N ผี ghost, spirit, ghoul, apparition

phîi chaai N พี่ชาย older brother

phîi khŏei N พี่เขย older brother-in-law

phîi săaw N พี่สาว older sister

phîi sà-phái N พี่สะใภ้ older sister-in-law

phĭi sûea N ผีเสื้อ butterfly (literally, 'ghost'-'shirt')

phí-jaàrànaa V พิจารณา to consider, have a considered opinion

phí-kaan ADJ พิการ to be disabled, handicapped

249

phim v พิมพ์ to print, publish; to write on a computer

phim diit v พิมพ์ดีด to type (with a typewriter)

phi-nai-kam n พินัยกรรม a will, testament

phí-phít thá-phan n พิพิธภัณฑ์ museum

phísèht ADJ พิเศษ special, exceptional, particular

phí-sùut v พิสูจน์ to prove, show, demonstrate

phit ADJ ผิด to be false (not true); guilty (of a crime); wrong (false)

phí-thii n พิธี ceremony, ritual

phit kòtmăai ADJ ผิดกฎหมาย to be illegal

phit phlâat ADJ ผิดพลาด to be mistaken, to be wrong

phit wăng ADJ ผิดหวัง to be disappointed

phĭu n ผิว skin, complexion; surface, covering

phlâat v พลาด to be mistaken, make an error/a mistake; to miss (i.e. the bus, a target)

phlǎeh n แผล scar, cut, wound

phlàk v ผลัก to push

phlehng n เพลง song, tune

phóeh ADJ เพ้อ to ramble on, to be delirious; (COLLOQUIAL) **phóeh jôeh** เพ้อเจ้อ to refer to utterances that are nonsensical, way over the top, inane

phôehm v เพิ่ม to add, increase, extra

phôehm khûen v เพิ่มขึ้น to increase

phôehm toehm ADV เพิ่มเติม further, in addition

phôeng ADV เพิ่ง just now, e.g. **kháo phôeng klàp bâan** เขาเพิ่งกลับบ้าน he's just gone home

phŏm n ผม hair (on the head only)

phŏm PRON ผม I, me (male speaking)

phŏn n ผล effect, result

phŏn prá-yòht n ผลประโยชน์ benefit (which accrues to someone)

phŏn-lá-mái n ผลไม้ fruit

phŏn-sùt-tháai (EXPRESSION) ผลสุดท้าย finally, in the end

phŏng sák fâwk n ผงซักฟอก detergent

phóp v พบ to find, meet

phóp kan mài (COLLOQUIAL EXPRESSION) พบกันใหม่ see you later!

phót-jà naa-ànú-krom N (FORMAL TERM) พจนานุกรม dictionary

phrá พระ (a Buddhist) monk; (also colloquially used to refer to) Buddhist amulets, images

phrá aa-thít N พระอาทิตย์ the sun

phrá aa-thit khûen พระอาทิตย์ขึ้น sunrise

phrá aa-thit tòk din พระอาทิตย์ตกดิน sunset

phrá jâo N พระเจ้า, also phrá phûu pen jâo N พระเป็นเจ้า God

phrá má-hăa kà-sàt N พระ มหากษัตริย์ king, monarch

phrá raa-chí-nii N พระราชินี, (COLLOQUIAL) raa-chí-nii N queen

phrá râat-chá-wang N พระราชวัง royal palace

phrá-w CONJ เพราะ because; ADJ mellifluous, to sound pleasing to the ear

phráwm ADJ, ADV พร้อม to be ready

phrík N พริก chilli, chilli pepper

phrík thai N พริกไทย pepper/ black pepper

phrom N พรม carpet

phrúet-sà-ji-kaa-yon N พฤศจิกายน November

phrúet-sà-phaa-khom N พฤษภาคม May

phrûng níi N, ADV พรุ่งนี้ tomorrow

phŭa N ผัว husband (colloquial but somewhat rude, better left unsaid in polite company)

phûak N พวก group

phûak khăo PRON พวกเขา they, them

phûang v พ่วง to trail, trailing; to be attached to (e.g. a trailer)

phuang N พวง bunch, cluster; phuang kunjaeh N พวงกุญแจ key ring/bunch of keys; phuang maa-lai N พวงมาลัย garland; also steering wheel

phûea àrai N เพื่ออะไร what for?

phûea thîi เพื่อที่ in order that, so that

phùeak N เผือก taro; also

251

cháang phùeak ช้างเผือก
albino – white elephant

phûean N เพื่อน friend

phûean bâan N เพื่อนบ้าน
neighbour(s)

phûean rûam ngaan N เพื่อน
ร่วมงาน co-worker, colleague

phúehn N พื้น floor

phúehn din N พื้นดิน ground,
earth

phúehn thîi N พื้นที่ area

phûeng N ผึ้ง bee(s); **náam
phùeng** น้ำผึ้ง honey

phút-thá sàat-sà-nǎa N พุทธ
ศาสนา Buddhism/Buddhist
religion

phûu N ผู้ a prefix meaning
'one who (is or does something in particular)'; also
male, e.g. to refer to male
animals **tua phûu** ตัวผู้; a
male cat is a **maeo tua phûu**
แมวตัวผู้

phûu aa-sǎi N ผู้อาศัย
resident, inhabitant

phûu am-nuai-kaan N
ผู้อำนวยการ director (of
company)

phûu chaai N ผู้ชาย male,
man

phûu chá-ná N ผู้ชนะ winner

phûu chûai N ผู้ช่วย assistant,
helper

phûu dohy-sǎan N ผู้โดยสาร
passenger

phûu fang N ผู้ฟัง (pronounced 'fung') listener (e.g.
to a radio program)

phûu jàtkaan N (pronounced
'jut garn') ผู้จัดการ manager

phuu-khǎo N ภูเขา mountain

phuu-khǎo fai N ภูเขาไฟ
volcano

phûu nam N ผู้นำ leader

phûu phí-phâak-sǎa N
ผู้พิพากษา judge (in a court
of law)

phûu thaen N ผู้แทน
representative (e.g. of a
company), delegate

phûu yài N ผู้ใหญ่ adult;
(COLLOQUIAL) a person of
consequence

phûu yài bâan N ผู้ใหญ่บ้าน
village headman

phûu ying N ผู้หญิง woman

phùuk V ผูก to tie, fasten,
secure

phuu-mí-phâak N ภูมิภาค
region

phuum-jai ADJ ภูมิใจ to be proud (of accomplishing something)

phûut v พูด to speak, talk, say

phûut lên v พูดเล่น to be joking/kidding

phûut rûeang... พูดเรื่อง... (to) talk about...

phûut wâa... พูดว่า... say/said that, used as follows: **kháo phûut wâa kháo mâi sabaai** เขาพูดว่าเขาไม่สบาย 'he said he (was) sick'

R

raa-chaa N ราชา king, monarch, rajah

ráai ADJ ร้าย wicked, evil, malicious, ferocious; **khon ráai** คนร้าย a bad person

raai chûeh N รายชื่อ list (of names)

raai jàai N รายจ่าย expense(s), expenditure

raai-kaan N รายการ list (of names), item, particulars

raai-kaan aa-hăan N รายการ อาหาร menu

raai-kaan krà-jaai sĭang N

รายการกระจายเสียง a (radio) broadcast, program

raai-kaan sòt N รายการสด (a live) show, performance

raai ngaan N, v รายงาน a report; to report

ráai raehng ADJ ร้ายแรง serious (severe), violent

râak v ราก root (of plant or a tooth); foundation; also to throw up, retch

raa-khaa N ราคา price, value, worth; (COLLOQUIAL) **raa-khaa khàat tua** ราคาขาดตัว bottom price, lowest price, best price

ráan N ร้าน shop, store, vendor's stall

ráan aa-hăan N ร้านอาหาร restaurant

ráan khăi yaa N ร้านขายยา pharmacy, drugstore, chemist

ráan sŏehm sŭai N ร้านเสริม สวย beauty parlour/salon

râang kaai N ร่างกาย body

raangwan N รางวัล a prize, reward (for the arrest of...)

râap ADJ ราบ flat, level, even, smooth

râap rûehn ADJ ราบรื่น harmonious (relations)

râat V ราด to pour (something) on (something else) (e.g. curry over rice **khâaw râat kaehng** ข้าวราดแกง)

râat-chá-kaan N ราชการ government service, the bureaucracy

râat-chá-wong N ราชวงศ์ dynasty, royal house

raaw-raaw ADV ราวๆ around (approximately)

rábaai sǐi V ระบายสี to paint (in the artistic sense)

rá-biang N ระเบียง verandah, porch

rá-biap N ระเบียบ order, regulations, rules

rá-bòp N ระบบ a system (e.g. of organizing/processing things)

rá-dàp N ระดับ level (standard), degree

râeh N แร่ mineral, ore; **náam râeh** น้ำแร่ mineral water

râehk ADJ แรก beginning, start, original, first, initial

raehng N แรง strength, force, power

râi N ไร่ a Thai measurement of land (1 **râi** = 1,600 sq m)

rái sǎa-rá ADJ ไร้สาระ nonsense

rák V รัก to love, to be fond of

rák châat V รักชาติ to love one's country, to be patriotic

rák ráeh N รักแร้ armpit(s)

ráksǎa V รักษา to care for (someone who is ill); to maintain, preserve (the peace etc.)

ráksǎa khwaam láp V รักษาความลับ to keep a secret

ráksǎa láew ADJ รักษาแล้ว recovered, cured

ram V รำ (pronounced 'rum') to dance (also commonly say **tên ram** เต้นรำ), to perform a Thai traditional dance

ramkhaan V รำคาญ to be annoyed, irritated; to be annoying

rán ADJ รั้น to be stubborn, headstrong

rang N (pronounced like 'rung') รัง nest (e.g. a bird's nest)

rang-kaeh V รังแก to bother, annoy, bully, mistreat

rang khaeh N รังแค dandruff

rangkiat V รังเกียจ to mind

254

(e.g. someone's (bad) behaviour); dislike, have an
aversion (to/for)

ráp รับ to receive; to take, get,
to pick someone up (e.g.
from the airport)

ráp chái รับใช้ to serve

ráp jâang v รับจ้าง to take
employment, for hire; to
be employed/hired (to do
something)

ráp ngoen duean v รับเงิน
เดือน to get/receive (one's)
salary/wages

ráp phit châwp v รับผิดชอบ
to be responsible

ráp rawng v รับรอง to
guarantee

ráp thoh-rá-sàp v (**sàp**
pronounced 'sup' with a low
tone) รับโทรศัพท์ to answer
the phone

rát N รัฐ (pronounced 'rut'
with a high tone) state (of a
country), government (in the
sense of 'the state')

rát-thà-baan N (the **rát** sound
is pronounced like 'rut'
with a high tone) รัฐบาล
government

raw v รอ (pronounced 'raw')
to wait (for, at, in, on)

rá-wàang ADV ระหว่าง during,
between, among, while

rá-waehng ADJ ระแวง to be
wary, suspicious, mistrustful

rá-wang ADJ, v ระวัง to be
careful; beware (of), watch
out (for)

ràwk หรอก a particle of
speech used at the end of a
statement meaning: on the
contrary (to what the other
party has said or expressed)

ráwn ADJ ร้อน hot
(temperature)

ráwng hâi v ร้องไห้ to cry, weep

ráwng phlehng v ร้องเพลง
to sing

rawng tháo N รองเท้า shoe(s)

rawng tháo tàe N รองเท้าแตะ
thongs, flip flops, sandals,
slippers

râwp N รอบ (a) round (like
a lap of the park), circuit,
trip; also used to refer to the
12-year cycle (the Chinese
zodiac)

râwp-râwp ADV รอบๆ around
(surrounding)

râwt chii-wit v รอดชีวิต to survive (e.g. a car crash)

ráyá N ระยะ interval, distance, bar (in music)

ráyá thaang N ระยะทาง distance (e.g. of a journey)

ráyá wehlaa N ระยะเวลา period (of time)

rêng v เร่ง to hurry, accelerate; (COLLOQUIAL) step on it

rêng dùan ADJ เร่งด่วน to be urgent

rew ADJ เร็ว fast, rapid, quick

rew kwàa pàkàti ADV เร็วกว่าปกติ earlier/faster than usual

rew pai ADV เร็วไป too soon, too fast, premature

rew-rew ADV เร็วๆ hurry up!

rîak v เรียก to call, demand, summon

rîak chûeh v เรียกชื่อ to call (someone) by name

rîak ráwng เรียกร้อง to urge, push for, demand

rian N เหรียญ a coin, dollar (initial consonant actually written with an 'r' but commonly pronounced with an 'l')

rian v เรียน to learn, study, take lessons

rian nǎngsǔeh v เรียนหนังสือ to go to school/college etc.

riang khwaam N เรียงความ (university/college/school) essay

rîap ADJ เรียบ even (smooth), flat, level; plain (not fancy)

rîap rói ADJ เรียบร้อย neat, orderly, tidy

rîip v รีบ to hurry, to rush

rîit v รีด to squeeze, wring, to put through a wringer; to iron, press

rîit sûea v รีดเสื้อ to iron (clothing)

rim N ริม edge, rim

rim fàng mâeh náam N ริมฝั่งแม่น้ำ bank (of river)

rim fǐi pàak N ริมฝีปาก lip(s)

rin v ริน to pour (a drink)

rǒeh (NOTE: this word is actually written **rǒeh** but commonly pronounced with an 'l' rather than 'r') เหรอ really?, is that so?; a question word at the end of a sentence (often expressed with some doubt or surprise) that seeks confirmation

rôehm v เริ่ม to begin, start, commence, initiate; also **rôehm tôn** เริ่มต้น to begin, start; **rôehm tôn mài** เริ่มต้น ใหม่ to make a fresh start, begin again

rôhk n โรค disease

rôhk káo n โรคเกาต์ gout

rohng n โรง building, house, hall, shed, factory, godown (general term)

rohng lá-khawn n โรงละคร theatre, playhouse (drama)

rohng náng n โรงหนัง cinema, movie house

rohng ngaan n โรงงาน factory

rohng phá-yaa-baan n โรง พยาบาล hospital

rohng raehm n โรงแรม hotel

rohng rian n โรงเรียน school

rohng rót n โรงรถ garage (for parking)

rói n ร้อย hundred

roi n รอย trace, mark, track (e.g. fingerprints, footprints)

roi pûean n รอยเปื้อน stain

rók ADJ รก (for a room to be) in a mess, untidy, cluttered; (for a garden to be) overgrown

rôm n ร่ม shade, umbrella

róp kuan v รบกวน to bother, disturb

rót n รถ car, automobile (wheeled vehicles in general)

rót n รส flavour, taste

rót v รด to water (plants); **rót náam tôn-mái** รดน้ำต้นไม้ to water the plants/garden

rót banthúk n รถบรรทุก truck

rót fai n รถไฟ train; **rót fai tâi din** รถไฟใต้ดิน under-ground railway, subway

rót jàk-kràyaan n รถจักรยาน bicycle, pushbike

rót khěn n รถเข็น (super-market) trolley, pram, cart (of the type used by street hawkers)

rót meh n รถเมล์ bus

rót phá-yaa-baan n รถพยาบาล ambulance

rót phûang n รถพ่วง trailer; (COLLOQUIAL) to refer to a motobike with some sort of attached trailer/sidecar

rót tháeksíi n รถแท็กซี่ taxi (or simply **tháeksíi** แท็กซี่)

rót thua n รถทัวร์ an air-conditioned tour bus/coach

257

rót tit N รถติด (a) traffic jam

rót túk-túk N รถตุ๊กตุ๊ก tuk-tuk/motorized trishaw (or simply **túk-túk** ตุ๊กตุ๊ก)

rót tûu N (COLLOQUIAL) รถตู้ minibus/minivan

rót yon N รถยนต์ automobile, car

rúa N รั้ว a fence

rûa V รั่ว to leak

ruai ADJ รวย to be rich, well off, wealthy

ruam V รวม to total, to add together, to join, altogether

rûam V ร่วม to live together, associate (with), participate (in)

rûam kan V ร่วมกัน (to do/put) together

rûam phêht V (FORMAL/POLITE) ร่วมเพศ to have sex, or sexual intercourse

ruam tháng V รวมทั้ง include, including (e.g. service charges, etc.); CONJ as well as

rûap ruam V รวบรวม to assemble, gather

ruea N เรือ boat, ship

ruea khâam fâak N เรือข้าม ฟาก ferry

ruean N เรือน house, home, dwelling building; the classifier used when counting (i.e. referring to the number of) watches or clocks

rûeang N เรื่อง story, record, account, issue (as in 'there are many issues he has to face')

rûeang lék N เรื่องเล็ก a small matter, an insignificant thing

rûeang mâak ADJ เรื่องมาก (COLLOQUIAL) to be fussy; someone who is hard to please (i.e. a pain in the arse/ass); to be picky

rúe-duu N (FORMAL TERM) ฤดู season; (COLLOQUIAL) see **nâa** หน้า

rúe-duu bai mái phlì ฤดู ใบไม้ผลิ spring (temperate climates)

rúe-duu bai mái rûang ฤดูใบไม้ร่วง autumn/fall (temperate climates)

rúe-duu fŏn N (FORMAL) ฤดูฝน rainy season

rúe-duu nǎaw N (FORMAL) ฤดู หนาว cool season, winter

rúe-duu ráwn N (FORMAL) ฤดู

ร้อน hot season, summer

rǔeh หรือ or **rǒer (COLLOQUIAL)** question particle that comes at the end of an utterance asking for confirmation (perhaps with some doubt or surprise); e.g. **jing rǔeh** 'is that so?/really?'. Sometimes it also serves as a sort of jaded response to a comment/statement made by someone else along the lines of 'oh?', or 'oh, yeah?'

rǔeh CONJ หรือ

rûn N รุ่น model (type), vintage; 'class' of people, e.g. the class of 2001 – those graduating from high school in 2001

run raehng ADJ รุนแรง severe, violent

rúng N รุ้ง a rainbow

ruu N รู a hole

rúu V รู้ to know, realize, be aware of

rúu-jàk V รู้จัก to know a person/a place, be acquainted with

ruu jà-mùuk N รูจมูก nostril(s)

rúu răa ADJ หรูหรา luxurious

rúu-sùek V รู้สึก to feel/sense, have a feeling (of, that)

rúu-sùek phìt รู้สึกผิด to feel guilty

rûup N รูป shape, picture

rûup khài N รูปไข่ oval (shape – 'egg-shaped')

rûup pân N รูปปั้น sculpture, statue

rûup phâap N รูปภาพ picture

rûup râang N รูปร่าง form (shape), appearance

rûup thài N รูปถ่าย photograph

rûup wâat N รูปวาด drawing

S

sà-àat ADJ สะอาด to be clean

sà-dueh N สะดือ navel, belly button

sà phŏm V สระผม to shampoo the hair

sà wâai náam N สระว่ายน้ำ swimming pool

săa-hàt ADJ (**hàt** pronounced like 'hut' with a low tone) สาหัส severe, serious, grave (condition)

săa-hèht N สาเหตุ cause, reason (for)

sáai ADJ, N (long vowel) ซ้าย left (direction)

saai N (long vowel) ทราย sand

săai (long vowel) สาย ADJ (to be) late; N classifier for connecting things, e.g. roads, routes and telephone lines

săai mâi wâang (long vowel) สายไม่ว่าง (for the phone) line is engaged/busy

sáai mueh ADV (long vowel) ซ้ายมือ on the left-hand side

săa-khăa N สาขา a branch (e.g. the branch of a bank/a particular junk food chain)

săa-lii N สาลี่ wheat

săam สาม three

săam liam N สามเหลี่ยม triangle

săam sip สามสิบ thirty

săa-mâat v สามารถ to be able to, to be capable of, can

săa-man ADJ สามัญ regular, common, ordinary

săa-mii N (POLITE TERM) สามี husband

săan N ศาล court (of law)

săan jâo N ศาลเจ้า a (Chinese) temple, joss house

sâang v สร้าง to build, construct, create

sâang khwaam pràtháp jai สร้างความประทับใจ to create/ make an impression

sâap v (pronounced 'sarp' with a falling tone) ทราบ to know (more polite/formal term than **rúu** รู้)

sâap súeng v, ADJ ซาบซึ้ง to appreciate, to be grateful (for); heartfelt

sàt-sà-năa N ศาสนา religion

sàat-sa-năa khrít N ศาสนา คริสต์ Christianity

sàat-sà-năa phút N ศาสนา พุทธ Buddhism

săaw N (long vowel) สาว young woman; (COLLOQUIAL) **săaw kàeh** สาวแก่ an old maid

sàbaai ADJ สบาย to feel comfortable/relaxed/good; **sàbaai-sàbaai** สบายๆ laid back

sàbaai dii rŭeh/mǎi (COLLOQUIAL EXPRESSION) สบายดี หรือ/ไหม how are you?

sàbaai jai ADJ สบายใจ to be happy, satisfied

sà-bùu N สบู่ soap

260

sà-daehng v แสดง to display, show; to express (an opinion)

sàdùak ADJ สะดวก to be convenient

săehn แสน hundred thousand

săehng aa-thít N แสงอาทิตย์ sunlight

sàehp v, N แสบ to sting, smart; a stinging sensation

saeng v แซง to overtake/pass (e.g. another car/vehicle)

saeo v (COLLOQUIAL) แซว to tease (someone)

sàhà-râatchá-aa-naàjàk N สหราชอาณาจักร (formal name of the) United Kingdom, (COLLOQUIAL) yuu kheh ยูเค, (or more commonly) ang-grìt – i.e. England

sàhà-rát àmehrikaa N สหรัฐอเมริกา (formal name of the) United States

sài v (shortish vowel) ใส่ to wear, put on; to load; to put in, insert

săi ADJ ใส (shortish vowel) clear, bright, unclouded

sài phaw dii (shortish vowel) ใส่พอดี (e.g. for clothing) to fit

săiyá-sàat N ไสยศาสตร์ sorcery, magic (of the non-stage variety), supernatural arts

sàk ADV สัก about, at least, approxiamately

sàk N, v สัก (a) tattoo, to tattoo (someone); teak (wood) – more fully mái sàk ไม้สัก

sàk khráng สักครั้ง just this once

sàk khrûu สักครู่ (in) just a moment

sàk phâa v ซักผ้า to do the washing/laundry

sàk phák N สักพัก for a while

sàk rîit v ซักรีด to wash and iron (clothing)

să-kon ADJ สากล international, universal, western

sà-kòt v สะกด to spell (a word)

sàk-sĭi N ศักดิ์ศรี dignity, honour, prestige

sàksit ADJ ศักดิ์สิทธิ์ sacred, holy, revered, hallowed

sàlàk v สลัก to carve, chisel out, engrave

sàlàp v สลับ to alternate

sàlàt N สลัด salad; **phàk sàlàt** ผักสลัด lettuce

sàlòp v สลบ to pass out, lose consciousness

sà-maa-chík N สมาชิก member

sà-maak-hom N สมาคม society/association

sà-măi N สมัย time, period, age, era

sà-măi kàwn สมัยก่อน in the past

sà-măi mài ADJ สมัยใหม่ modern, contemporary

sà-măi níi สมัยนี้ nowadays, these days

sà-măwng N สมอง brain, mind

sà-mǐan N เสมียน clerk

sămkhan ADJ สำคัญ important, significant

sămlii N สำลี cotton wool

sămnao N สำเนา photocopy, (a) copy

sămnuan N สำนวน an idiom, idiomatic expression; style of writing

sà-mǒeh ADV เสมอ always

sămphâat v, N สัมภาษณ์ (to) interview (someone); (an) interview

sămràp PREP สำหรับ for, to, intended for

sămrawng v สำรอง to reserve (for), to have in reserve, a spare (e.g. tyre); put on a waiting list

sămrèt ADJ สำเร็จ to be finished, completed, accomplished, successful; v to succeed

sà-mùt N สมุด notebook, exercise book

sà-mùt dai aà-rìi N (from English) สมุดไดอารี่ a diary

sân ADJ สั้น brief, short (concise)

sàn v สั่น to shake, vibrate, tremble

sà-năam N สนาม a yard, field, empty space

sà-năam bin N สนามบิน airport

sà-năam yâa N สนามหญ้า lawn

sănchâat N สัญชาติ nationality

sà-nèh ADJ เสน่ห์ charm, attraction, appeal

sàng v (pronounced similar to 'sung' with a low tone) สั่ง to order, command; to order something

săngkèht v สังเกต to notice

săngkhom n สังคม society

sà-ngòp ADJ สงบ peaceful, calm

sà-nöeh v เสนอ to bring up (topic), propose (a matter) present; to offer, suggest

sănti-phâap n สันติภาพ peace

sà-nùk ADJ สนุก fun, enjoyable, entertaining, to have a good time

sănyaa v, n สัญญา to promise; a contract

sănyálák n สัญลักษณ์ symbol, sign, token

săo ADJ เศร้า sad, sorrowful

săo n เสา post, pole, column

săo aa-thít n เสาอาทิตย์ the weekend

sà-òht sà-ong ADJ สะโอด สะอง slender

sàp v สับ to chop, mince, e.g. **mŭu sàp** หมูสับ minced pork

sáp sáwn ADJ ซับซ้อน complicated, complex

sàp sŏn ADJ สับสน to be

confused; disorderly

sàpdaa n (FORMAL) สัปดาห์ week

sàpdaa nâa n (FORMAL) สัปดาห์ หน้า next week

sà-phaan n สะพาน bridge

sà-phaan loi n สะพานลอย a foot bridge (over a road), overpass

sà-phâap n สภาพ condition (of a house, car)

sà-phái n สะใภ้ female in-law

sàppàrót n สับปะรด pineapple

sà-pring n (from English) สปริง (a) spring

sà-rúp v สรุป to summarize, sum up, recapitulate

sà-sŏm v สะสม to accumulate, amass, save, to collect (e.g. stamps), to build up

sàt n สัตว์ animal (general term)

sàt liang n สัตว์เลี้ยง pet (animal)

sà-taang n สตางค์ old unit of Thai currency, money; (COLLOQUIAL) **tang** ตังค์ money

sà-tăa pàttà-yá-kam n สถาปัตยกรรม architecture

sà-tàat v (from English) (pronounced 'sar-tart')

263

สตาร์ท to start (e.g. a car; also used in the broader English sense – 'the sale starts tomorrow')

sà-taehm N (from English) แสตมป์ stamp (postage)

sà-thǎa-nii N สถานี station (general term – used in conjunction with other words to form such terms as – radio station, television station, police station, space station, etc.)

sà-thǎa-nii rót fai N สถานีรถไฟ train station

sà-thǎa-nii rót fai hǔa lam-phohng N สถานีรถไฟ หัวลำโพง Hualampong, Bangkok's main railway station

sà-thǎa-nii rót meh N สถานี รถเมล์ bus station

sà-thǎan-nákaan N สถานการณ์ situation

sà-thǎan thîi N สถานที่ place

sà-thǎan thûut N สถานทูต embassy

sà-tháwn V สะท้อน to reflect (off the glass, the water, the window, etc.), to rebound, bounce (up, back)

sàttà-wát N ศตวรรษ (a) century

sàt-truu N ศัตรู enemy

sà-wàang ADJ สว่าง bright, brilliant (light)

sà-wǎn N สวรรค์ heaven, paradise

sàwàt dii สวัสดี (common polite form of greeting at any time of day) hello (good morning/good afternoon, etc.); also (CASUAL/COLLOQUIAL) **wàt dii** หวัดดี 'Hi'

sà-wít N (from English) สวิทช์ switch

sâwm N ส้อม (a) fork (utensil for eating)

sâwm V ซ่อม to repair, mend, fix

sǎwn V สอน to teach, instruct

sâwn V ซ่อน to hide, conceal

sâwn yùu ซ่อนอยู่ (to be) hidden

sawng N ซอง envelope

sǎwng N สอง two

sâwng N ซ่อง brothel, hiding place, den (of iniquity)

sâwng kà-rii N ซ่องกะหรี่ (SLANG – rude, better left

unsaid in polite company)
whorehouse

săwng săam ADJ สองสาม
(COLLOQUIAL) a few

săwng thăew N **(COLLOQUIAL)**
สองแถว common term for
a pick-up truck with bench
seats (the name **săwng thăew**
means 'two rows [of seats]
facing one another') in the
back that is used to take
paying passengers on shortish journeys – primarily
found in provincial towns/
cities

săwng thâo ADJ สองเท่า
double (e.g. double the
price), twice as much

sàwp V สอบ to examine, test,
take an examination; to
verify, inquire

sàwp phàan V สอบผ่าน to
pass a test/an exam

săwt N (from English) ซอส
sauce

sàwt phrík N ซอสพริก chili
sauce

sĕh-rii ADJ เสรี free, independent

sèht N เศษ remainder, what is
left over, scrap(s), fraction

sèht nùeng sùan sìi N เศษ
หนึ่งส่วนสี่ (¼) one quarter
(part of something)

sèht sà-taang N เศษสตางค์
small change

sèht-thà-kìt N (pronounced
'set-àgìt') เศรษฐกิจ economy

sèht-thĭi N เศรษฐี a wealthy/
rich/affluent man

sèht-thĭi-nii N เศรษฐินี a
wealthy/rich/affluent woman

sen N เซ็นต์ centimetre

sên N เส้น thread, line (mark),
blood vessel; classifier for
counting string-like things,
e.g. noodles, hair

sen V เซ็น to sign

seng ADJ (COLLOQUIAL) เซ็ง to be
bored, fed up (with)

séng V เซ้ง to sell, for sale;
sublet

sèohp V (from English) เสิร์ฟ
serve

sèt V เสร็จ to finish; (SLANG) to
climax, have an orgasm

sèt láew เสร็จแล้ว (for
something to be) done,
finished, completed, ready

sèt sĭn เสร็จสิ้น over, done,
completed

265

sí ซิ a particle that is used at the end of an utterance to request/urge (with some force) or persuade the other party do something, e.g. **pòeht thii wii sí** เปิดทีวีซิ 'come on, turn on that TV will you'; **duu sí** ดูซิ 'Look at that!/do look, will you'

sìa เสีย ADJ to be spoiled, broken, out of order, spoiled; to have gone off (food); v to spend, pay; to be dead; to die

sìa chii-wít v เสียชีวิต to die, pass away

sìa chûeh v เสียชื่อ to get a bad name, spoil one's reputation, be discredited, look bad

sìa daai เสียดาย to regret, be sorry; (EXPRESSION) 'what a shame', 'too bad'

sìa jai เสียใจ to feel sorry, regretful, be disappointed

sìa ngoen v เสียเงิน to waste money; to pay/spend

sìa phaa-sǐi v เสียภาษี to pay tax(es)

sìa sà-là v เสียสละ to sacrifice, give up (something)

sìa tua v (COLLOQUIAL) เสียตัว (for a woman) to lose her virginity, to have sex the first time, to sleep with (a man)

sìa wehlaa v เสียเวลา to waste time

sǐang N เสียง a sound, noise, tone; voice

sìang v เสี่ยง to risk, take a risk, take a chance

sìang chii-wít v เสี่ยงชีวิต to risk one's life

sǐang dang ADJ เสียงดัง to be loud, noisy

sǐao เสียว to have hair raising, chilling; to feel a thrill of pleasure/pain; (sexually) exciting

sìi สี่ four

sǐi N สี colour, also the word for paint (Here is a list of common colours: white **sǐi khǎaw** สีขาว; black **sǐi dam** สีดำ (pronounced 'dum'); green **sǐi khǐao** สีเขียว; red **sǐi daehng** สีแดง; orange **sǐi sôm** สีส้ม; yellow **sǐi lǔeang** สีเหลือง; brown **sǐi náam-taan** สีน้ำตาล; (sky) blue **sǐi fáa** สีฟ้า; (navy/royal) blue **sǐi**

náam ngoen สีน้ำเงิน; pink **sĭi chomphuu** สีชมพู; gray/grey **sĭi thao** สีเทา

sĭi dii N (from English) ซีดี CD

sĭi ĕiu N ซีอิ๊ว soy sauce (salty)

sĭi ĕiu wǎan N ซีอิ๊วหวาน soy sauce (sweet)

sĭi lìam สีเหลี่ยม square (shape)

sĭi sìp สีสิบ forty

sĭi tòk V สีตก (for the colour of clothing, for example) to run

sĭi yâehk N สีแยก (four way) intersection

sí-kâa N (from English) ซิการ์ cigar

sìng N สิ่ง item, individual thing

sĭng N สิงห์ a lion (NOTE: this is the name of the well-known Thai beer – written in English as Singha but which is actually pronounced **sĭng** or, more fully **bia sĭng** เบียร์ สิงห์ = Singha beer)

sìng khǎwng N สิ่งของ thing(s), object(s)

sìng kìit khwǎang สิ่ง กีดขวาง (a) hindrance, (an) obstruction

sìng wâeht láwm N สิ่ง

แวดล้อม the environment, surroundings

sĭng-hǎa-khom N สิงหาคม August

sĭngkhá-poh N สิงคโปร์ Singapore

sĭnlá-pà N ศิลปะ art

sĭnlá-pin N (commonly pronounced **sĭlapin**) ศิลปิน artist

sìp สิบ ten; the numbers 11–19 are as follows: **sìp èt** สิบเอ็ด eleven; **sìp sǎwng** สิบสอง twelve; **sìp sǎam** สิบสาม thirteen; **sìp sìi** สิบสี่ fourteen; **sìp hâa** สิบห้า fifteen; **sìp hòk** สิบหก sixteen; **sìp jèt** สิบเจ็ด seventeen; **sìp pàeht** สิบแปด eighteen; **sìp kâo** สิบเก้า nineteen

sĭri mongkhon ADJ สิริมงคล (to be) auspicious, lucky, favourable

sìtthi N (commonly pronounced 'sìt' with a low tone) สิทธิ rights (e.g. legal rights)

sôh N โซ่ chain

sohfaa N (from English) โซฟา couch, sofa

sŏhm N โสม ginseng

sohm V, ADJ โทรม to

deteriorate, decline (of a person); (to look) run down/ worn out

sŏh-pheh-nii N (POLITE) โสเภณี prostitute

sòht ADJ โสด single, unmarried

soi N ซอย lane, side street (sometimes virtually a main road)

sôi N สร้อย bracelet

sôi khaw N สร้อยคอ necklace

sòkkàpròk ADJ สกปรก dirty, filthy

sôm N ส้ม orange (citrus fruit)

sŏm hèht phŏn สมเหตุผล reasonable, sensible, logical

sŏm khuan ADJ สมควร should, worthy (of), proper, appropriate

sôm oh N ส้มโอ pomelo (a type of tropical grapefruit)

sŏmbàt N (pronounced 'sombut') สมบัติ property, wealth

sŏmbuun ADJ สมบูรณ์ to be whole, entire, complete, plentiful; healthy; to have put on weight

sŏmmút V สมมติ to suppose, assume, hypothetical; e.g. **sŏmmút wâa** สมมติว่า

'suppose (that)…'

son ADJ ซน naughty, mischievous, playful

sòng V ส่ง to send, deliver

sòng àwk V ส่งออก to export

sòng fáek V ส่งแฟกซ์ to send a fax

sòng ii-mehl V ส่งอีเมล to (send an) email

sŏng kraan N สงกรานต์ traditional Thai New Year (mid April – 13–15 April)

sŏngkhraam N สงคราม war

sŏngsăan V สงสาร to pity, feel sorry (for)

sŏngsăi V สงสัย to doubt, suspect

sŏn-jai ADJ สนใจ (to be) interested in

sòp N ศพ corpse, cadaver

sòt ADJ สด fresh

suai ADJ ซวย to be unlucky, accursed, (to have) bad luck; (mild expletive) Damn it!

sŭai ADJ สวย beautiful, attractive, pretty (of places, things), beautiful

sûam N ส้วม toilet, lavatory

sùan N ส่วน a portion, share, section, piece, part (not the

whole)

sŭan N สวน garden, orchard, plantation, park

sùan koen N ส่วนเกิน (pronounced 'gurn') surplus, excess

sùan nùeng ส่วนหนึ่ง partly, one part

sŭan săa-thaa-rá-ná N สวน สาธารณะ public garden/park

sŭan sàt N สวนสัตว์ zoo

sùan tua ADJ ส่วนตัว private, personal (e.g. matters)

sùan yài ADV ส่วนใหญ่ mostly, for the most part

sùat mon V สวดมนต์ to chant/ pray (Buddhist style)

sûea N เสื่อ mat

sûea N เสือ tiger; (SLANG) bandit, gangster

sûea N เสื้อ (general term for items of clothing/upper garments) shirt, blouse, coat

sûea bai N (COLLOQUIAL) เสื้อไบ bisexual

sûea chán nai N เสื้อชั้นใน underwear/undercolthing (general term)

sûea chóeht N (from English) เสื้อเชิ้ต shirt

sûea dam N เสือดำ (dam pronounced similar to 'dum') leopard (literally, 'tiger'+'black')

sûea kák N เสื้อกั๊ก a vest, waistcoat

sûea kan năaw N เสื้อ กันหนาว coat, jacket, windcheater

sûea khlum N เสื้อคลุม robe, cloak, cape; bathrobe

sûea klâam N เสื้อกล้าม undershirt, muscle shirt

sûea nâwk N เสื้อนอก jacket, coat

sûea nawn N เสื้อนอน pyjamas

sûea phâa N เสื้อผ้า clothes, clothing, garments

sûea yûeht N เสื้อยืด T-shirt, undershirt

súeh V ซื้อ to buy, purchase

sùeh V สื่อ to communicate

sùeh muanchon N สื่อมวลชน mass media

sùeh-sàt ADJ ซื่อสัตย์ to be honest

sùek-săa N, V ศึกษา education; to educate, to study

sùk ADJ สุก to be ripe, to be

269

ready (e.g. to be eaten), to be cooked

sùk láew ADJ สุกแล้ว to be done (cooked)

sùksăn wan kòeht (FORMULAIC EXPRESSION – not commonly used) สุขสันต์วันเกิด happy birthday!

sùksăn wan pii mài (FORMULAIC EXPRESSION) สุขสันต์ วันปีใหม่ happy new year!

su-nák N (FORMAL/POLITE) สุนัข dog/canine

sù-phâap ADJ สุภาพ to be polite, courteous, well-mannered

sù-phâap sàtrii N สุภาพ สตรี lady

sù-rào N สุเหร่า mosque

sùt ADJ สุด end, utmost, most, -est, e.g. the tallest person – **khon** คน (person) **sŭung** สูง (tall) **thîi sùt** ที่สุด (-est)

sùt sàpdaa N (FORMAL) สุด สัปดาห์ weekend

sùt thâai ADJ สุดท้าย final, last

sùt yâwt (COLLOQUIAL) สุดยอด That's cool/Great!/Tops! The best!

sùu PREP สู่ to, towards

sûu V สู้ to fight (physically), fight back, oppose, resist

sùu khăw V สู่ขอ to ask for the hand (of someone) in marriage

sûu khwaam V สู้ความ to contest a legal action

suu-poehmaa-ket N (from English) ซูเปอร์มาร์เก็ต supermarket

sûu róp V สู้รบ battle, engage in combat

sûu taai V (COLLOQUIAL) สู้ตาย to fight to the bitter end

sŭun N ศูนย์ zero, naught

sŭun klaang ADJ ศูนย์กลาง centre

sŭung ADJ สูง high, tall

sùup V สูบ to smoke (cigarettes); to pump (in, out, up, away)

sùut N (from English) สูท suit (clothes)

sùut N สูตร formula, method, recipe

sùut aa-hăan N สูตรอาหาร recipe (for food)

270

T

NOTE: This letter should not be confused with the normal English 't' sound. It is pronounced somewhere between a 'd' and a 't', similar to the sound of the 't' in the word 'star'

taa N ตา eye; (maternal) grandfather

taa bàwt ADJ ตาบอด to be blind, sightless

taa châng N ตาชั่ง scales

taa daehng N, ADJ ตาแดง conjunctivitis; bleary eyed, red-eyed

taai V ตาย to die, pass away; EXCLAM 'Oh!', 'Damn!'

taai tua ADJ ตายตัว to be fixed (e.g. a fixed or set price of something)

tàak V ตาก to dry, to expose to the air

tàak hâehng V ตากแห้ง (to) dry out (in the sun)

tàak phâa V ตากผ้า to dry the clothing out (in the sun)

taam V ตาม to follow, accompany; in accordance with; along

taam jai V ตามใจ to go along with (whatever you think/ want to do); to give in to; to please, indulge (someone)

taam khoei ADV ตามเคย as usual (as expected/as he/she does habitually)

taam kòtmǎai ADV ตาม กฎหมาย legally, according to the law

taam lamdàp ADV ตามลำดับ in order, respectively

taam lǎng V ตามหลัง to follow behind

taam pàkati ADV ตามปกติ ordinarily, usually, normally

taam thîi ADJ ตามที่.... according to... (e.g. what he said)

tàang ADJ, V ต่าง each; other; different; differ

tàang châat ADJ ต่างชาติ alien, foreign (e.g. people)

tàang hàak ADV ต่างหาก extra, separately (i.e. additional/ extra fees apply, etc.)

tàang hŭu N ต่างหู earring(s)

tàang prà-thêet N ต่าง
ประเทศ overseas, abroad

tàang-tàang ADJ ต่างๆ
different, diverse, various

taaraang wehlaa N ตาราง
เวลา timetable, schedule

taa-rang N ตาราง square (also
used to refer to square metres
taa-raang mét ตารางเมตร)

tàe V (pronounced with a very
short vowel sound) แตะ to
touch

tàeh CONJ แต่ but, however,
only; (COLLOQUIAL) **tàeh wâa** แต่
ว่า 'but (she said…)'

tàeh lá ADJ แต่ละ each, every:
e.g. **tàeh lá pii** แต่ละปี each/
every year; **tàeh lá khon**
แต่ละคน each/every person

tàehk V, ADJ แตก to be broken,
shattered, cracked

tàehk là-ìat V แตกละเอียด
break, shatter into tiny
pieces

tàehk ngoen V (COLLOQUIAL)
แตกเงิน to get change, to
break (a bill)

tàehk yâehk ADJ แตกแยก
divided, disunited, broken
apart

taehng N แตง melon (general
term)

tàehng V แต่ง to write,
arrange, compose (letters,
books, music)

taehng kwaa N แตงกวา
cucumber

taehng moh N แตงโม
watermelon

tàehng ngaan V แต่งงาน to
marry, get married

tàehng ngaan láew ADJ
แต่งงานแล้ว to be married

tàehng tua V แต่งตัว to get
dressed

tâi PREP ใต้ under, below; south

tai N ไต kidney(s)

tai V ไต่ to go up, climb (hills,
mountains)

tâifùn N ไต้ฝุ่น typhoon

tàk N ตัก lap (i.e. 'the baby is
sitting on her lap')

tàk N ตัก (pronounced similar
to 'tuck' with the 'star' sound
and a low tone) to draw,
scoop up – **tàk khâaw** ตักข้าว
to help oneself/others to rice;
to dish out the rice

tà-khǎw N ตะขอ hook

tà-khrái N ตะไคร้ lemon grass

272

tà-kìap N ตะเกียบ chopstick(s)

tà-kiang N ตะเกียง lamp, lantern

tà-kohn V ตะโกน to cry out, shout, yell

tà-krâa N ตะกร้า basket

tà-làat N ตลาด market, bazaar

tà-làat náam N ตลาดน้ำ floating market (the most notable being in Ratburi/Ratchaburi province)

tà-làat nát N ตลาดนัด occasional market (common in Thailand) – perhaps once or twice a week/month, etc. in different spots in a given locality

tà-làp N ตลับ (very) small box, compact (for make-up), case

tà-làwt PREP, ADV ตลอด through, throughout, all the time, from beginning to end

tà-làwt chii-wìt ตลอดชีวิต for life, throughout one's life

tà-làwt pai ตลอดไป forever, always, all the time

tà-lòk ADJ ตลก funny, comical, ridiculous

tàm ADJ ต่ำ low, inferior, base

tam V ตำ to pound, beat

(part of the word for the Northeastern Thai dish 'green papaya salad' **sôm tam** ส้มตำ)

tambon N ตำบล sub-district: an administrative unit in Thailand, often spelled in English as 'tambol'. In the Thai spelling the final letter is the letter 'l' but it is pronounced as an 'n'

tam-naan N ตำนาน legend, chronicle

tam-nàeng N ตำแหน่ง position (in an organization)

tam-rùat N ตำรวจ police

tâng jai V ตั้งใจ to intend, pay attention

tâng-tàeh ADV ตั้งแต่ since

tâng tôn N ตั้งต้น start, beginning

tâng yùu V ตั้งอยู่ to be situated, located

tao N เตา a stove (gas/electric), a traditional style charcoal cooker/brazier

tào N เต่า turtle

tào hûu N เต้าหู้ beancurd, tofu

tao òp N เตาอบ oven

tào tà-nù N เต่าตนุ (sea) turtle

273

tàp N (pronounced similar to 'tup' with a low tone) ตับ liver (vital organ)

tà-puu N ตะปู a nail (spike)

tàt V ตัด to cut, cut off, sever

tàt phŏm V ตัดผม to have a haircut

tàt sĭn jai V ตัดสินใจ to decide, make a decision

tàw V ต่อ to extend (e.g. a visa); to lengthen; to join, reconnect (e.g. a severed limb)

tàw pai ต่อไป next (in line, sequence)

tàw ráwng V ต่อรอง to bargain, negotiate

tàw tâan V ต่อต้าน to oppose

tà-wan àwk N ตะวันออก east

tà-wan àwk chĭang nŭea N ตะวันออกเฉียงเหนือ north-east

tà-wan àwk chĭang tâi N ตะวันออกเฉียงใต้ south-east

tà-wan tòk N ตะวันตก west

tà-wan tòk chĭang nŭea N ตะวันตกเฉียงเหนือ north-west

tà-wan tòk chĭang tâi N ตะวันตกเฉียงใต้ south-west

tawn N ตอน part, period; episode

tâwn V ต้อน to castrate, geld, neuter, spay

tawn bàai N ตอนบ่าย in the afternoon

tawn klaang khuehn N ตอนกลางคืน at night, during the night

tawn lăng ADV ตอนหลัง later on, subsequently

tâwn ráp V ต้อนรับ to welcome, greet, receive (someone)

tawn rôehm tôn N ตอนเริ่มต้น (at the) beginning

tawn thîang N ตอนเที่ยง at noon, noontime

tawn yen N ตอนเย็น evening

tâwng AUX V ต้อง have to, must

tâwng hâam ADJ ต้องห้าม to be forbidden, prohibited; taboo

tâwng kaan AUX V ต้องการ to want, desire, must have

tàwp V ตอบ to answer, respond; reply

tàwp sà-năwng V ตอบสนอง to respond, react

tèh V เตะ to kick, boot (e.g. a football)

tem ADJ เต็ม to be full, complete, filled up

tên ram v เต้นรำ to dance

tîa ADJ เตี้ย to be short, low

tiang N เตียง bed, bedstead

tii v ตี hit, strike, beat

tii raa-khaa v ตีราคา to estimate the value/price, give an estimate; set the price (of something)

tii sà-nìt v (COLLOQUIAL) ตีสนิท to get on familiar terms, to get close (to), to become 'mates'/'buddies'; to befriend (for ulterior motives)

tìt v (not pronounced like the English word 'tit') ติด to stick, to get stuck; to be addicted to; to be close to; to owe, be owed

tìt kan ADJ ติดกัน next, adjoining; stuck together

tìt kàp v ติดกับ to be trapped; next to

tìt khúk v ติดคุก to be gaoled/jailed, go to gaol/jail; to be imprisoned

tìt tâng v ติดตั้ง to install, put in (e.g. air conditioning)

tìt tàw v ติดต่อ to communi-cate with, contact, get in touch with; contagious/infectious (e.g. disease)

tìt thúrá v ติดธุระ to be busy, tied up (with some other matter)

toehm v เติม to add, put in (e.g. petrol)

toh ADJ (pronounced with a long vowel sound) โต to be big, large, mature

tó! N (pronounced very short!) โต๊ะ desk, table

toh khûen v โตขึ้น to grow larger (e.g. a tree); growing up (e.g. children)

tôh tàwp v โต้ตอบ to reply to, retort, to argue

tòi v ต่อย to punch, box, strike; (for a bee to) sting

tòk v ตก to fall, to drop, diminish, decrease

tòk jai ADJ ตกใจ alarmed, startled

tòk ngaan v ตกงาน to be out of work, to lose one's job

tòk plaa v ตกปลา to fish

tòk rót v (COLLOQUIAL) ตกรถ to miss (a bus, train)

tòk yâak v ตกยาก to fall on

hard times; to be impoverished; to suffer misfortune

tòk-long v ตกลง to agree; OK, agreed!

tòk-long tham v ตกลงทำ to agree to do something

tôm v ต้ม to boil (water); (COLLOQUIAL/SLANG) take (someone) for a ride, swindle; to be taken in, cheated (out of something)

tôm khàa N ต้มข่า mildish coconut/cream soup flavoured with galangal, kaffir lime, etc.

tôm yam N (pronounced similar to 'tom yum') ต้มยำ a Thai (generally clear) soup with a spicy, lemony taste

tôn mai N ต้นไม้ plant, tree

tòp tàeng v ตบแต่ง to beautify, to improve the appearance; to marry off one's daughter

tòt N, v ตด a fart; to fart/pass wind

traa N ตรา seal, stamp, chop, brand

trài trawng v ไตร่ตรอง to consider, think (something over), ponder

trà-kuun N ตระกูล lineage, family

tràwk N ตรอก alley, narrow passage

triam v เตรียม prepare, make ready

triam phráwm v เตรียมพร้อม to be prepared, ready for action

triam tua v เตรียมตัว to get ready

trong ADJ ตรง straight; accurate; direct, non-stop (e.g. flight)

trong khâam ADJ, PREP ตรง ข้าม opposite (facing): **trong kan khâam** ตรงกันข้าม on the contrary; conversely

trong klaang ADJ ตรงกลาง in the middle/centre

trong pai khâng nâa ADJ, ADV ตรงไปข้างหน้า (go/it's) straight ahead

trong wehlaa ADV ตรงเวลา (to be) on time, punctual

trùat v ตรวจ to inspect, examine, check

trùat sàwp v ตรวจสอบ to check, verify, test

tua ɴ ตัว body; thing classifier for counting animals, tables, chairs and clothes

tŭa ɴ ตั๋ว ticket (for transport, entertainment)

tua àksăwn ɴ ตัวอักษร letter, character (written), alphabet

tua jing ɴ ตัวจริง original, (the) genuine (article), (the) real (thing)

tua lêhk ɴ ตัวเลข number, numeral, figure

tua mia ɴ ตัวเมีย female (used to refer to animals/plants)

tŭa pai klàp ɴ ตั๋วไปกลับ return ticket

tua phûu ɴ ตัวผู้ male (used to refer to animals/plants)

tŭa thîao diao ɴ ตั๋วเที่ยวเดียว one-way ticket

tua yàang ɴ ตัวอย่าง example, sample

tua yàang chên ตัวอย่างเช่น such as, for example

tuean v เตือน to remind, warn

tûehn v ตื้น to be shallow, not deep, superficial

tùehn v ตื่น to wake up, be awake

tùehn tên v, ᴀᴅᴊ ตื่นเต้น to be excited; exciting

tù-laa-khom ɴ ตุลาคม October

tûm hŭu ɴ ตุ้มหู earring(s)

tûu ɴ ตู้ cupboard, cabinet, closet

tûu nǎngsŭeh ɴ ตู้หนังสือ bookshelf

tûu yen ɴ ตู้เย็น refrigerator

TH

NOTE: This 'th' sound is the same as the English 't'. For example, in the words 'tie–Thai' – spelled differently, but pronounced exactly the same way

thâa ᴄᴏɴᴊ ถ้า if, although; suppose

thaa v ทา to coat, paint, apply (e.g. sunscreen)

thâa ruea ɴ ท่าเรือ harbour, port; wharf, pier

thaa sĭi v ทาสี to paint (e.g. a house, a wall)

tháa thaai v ท้าทาย to challenge, defy; to provoke

thâa thaang ɴ ท่าทาง appearance, manner, bearing

277

thàai v ถ่าย to decant, pour out, discharge, throw away; **(FORMAL/POLITE)** to defecate

thàai rûup v ถ่ายรูป to take a picture, to photograph

thàai sămnao v ถ่ายสำเนา to make a photocopy

thăam v ถาม to ask, enquire

thăam kìao kàp v ถามเกี่ยว กับ to ask about

thăn N ฐาน base (e.g. military), foundation, basis

thân PRON ท่าน (polite form of address directly to, or when talking about, a higher status individual) he, she; him, her, you; sir

thaan v **(COLLOQUIAL/POLITE)** ทาน to eat (also 'drink'; the colloquial equivalent is **kin**); donation, charity

thaan aa-hăan yen v **(COLLOQUIAL/POLITE)** ทานอาหาร เย็น to eat dinner

thaan khâaw thîang v **(COLLOQUIAL/POLITE)** ทานข้าว เที่ยง to eat lunch

thăa-ná N ฐานะ position, status, standing

thaang N ทาง way, path, direction

thaang àwk N ทางออก exit, way out

thaang kaan ADJ ทางการ official, formal; **phaa-săa thaang kaan** N ภาษาทางการ official/formal language

thaang khâo N ทางเข้า entrance, way in

thaang lûeak v, ADJ ทางเลือก choice, alternative

thaang rótfai N ทางรถไฟ railroad, railway

thaa-rók N **(FORMAL)** ทารก baby, infant

thàat N ถาด a tray

thăa-wawn ADJ ถาวร permanent, fixed, enduring

thaa-yâat N ทายาท heir, descendant

thaehn v, ADJ แทน to represent; to substitute (for), in place of, instead (of); **tua thaehn** ตัวแทน an agent, a representative (e.g. of a company)

thaehn thîi แทนที่ instead of

thaehn thîi jà... แทนที่จะ... rather than...

tháeksĭi N (from English) แท็กซี่ taxi

thǎem v แถม to give something extra, give in addition (e.g department store giveaways that often go with purchases above a certain amount; when a vendor gives you something 'extra' when buying fruit/fish etc. in a market)

thaeng v แทง to stab, pierce, prick

tháeng v แท้ง to abort; **tham tháeng** ทำแท้ง to have an abortion; **tháeng lûuk** แท้งลูก to have a miscarriage

thǎew N แถว a row, line; area

thǎew níi ADJ แถวนี้ around here (e.g. 'where's the bike shop?' 'around here/in this area')

thá-hǎan ทหาร soldier; **(COLLOQUIAL)** general term for someone in the armed services

thá-hǎan aa-kàat N ทหารอากาศ airman, airwoman; (the) air force (in general)

thá-hǎan bòk N ทหารบก soldier in the army; (the) army (in general)

thá-hǎan ruea N ทหารเรือ sailor; (the) navy (in general)

thai ไทย Thai, Thailand; **khon thai** คนไทย a Thai person/Thai people; **châat thai** ชาติไทย the Thai nation; **prà-thêht thai** ประเทศไทย (the country) Thailand; **phaa-sǎa thai** ภาษาไทย (the) Thai language

thák thaai v ทักทาย to greet; to say hello

thá lá-w v, N ทะเลาะ to argue; an argument

thá-leh N ทะเล sea

thá-leh saai N ทะเลทราย a desert

thá-leh sàap N ทะเลสาบ a lake

thâm N ถ้ำ a cave

tham N ธรรม Dharma, the Buddha's teaching, the Doctrine

tham v ทำ do, perform an action, make, act, undergo; see **tham hâi** ทำให้ below – a very important aspect of the Thai language – commonly these two words go together to express the idea of 'to do

279

(something) to/for (someone else)'

tham aa-hǎan v ทำอาหาร to cook

tham bun v ทำบุญ to make merit, perform good deeds, give to charity

tham dii thîi sùt v ทำดีที่สุด do one's best

tham dûai ADJ ทำด้วย made of/made from; **tham dûai mueh** ทำด้วยมือ made by hand, handmade

tham dûai mái/tham jàak mái ทำด้วยไม้/ทำจากไม้ to be made from wood/timber; wooden

tham fan v ทำฟัน go to the dentist

tham hǎai v ทำหาย to lose, mislay

tham hâi v ทำให้ to make/do something to/for someone; to cause: e.g. **tham hâi khǎo jep** ทำให้เขาเจ็บ to hurt him (to cause him pain/grief)

tham hâi chamrút v ทำให้ ชำรุด to cause damage

tham hâi hâehng v ทำให้แห้ง to (make something) dry

tham hâi jom náam v ทำให้ จมน้ำ (to cause someone – the cause, for example, being the rough sea) to drown

tham hâi lâa cháa v ทำให้ ล่าช้า to delay

tham hâi mâi phaw jai v ทำให้ไม่พอใจ offend; to offend (someone else)

tham hâi pen rûup v ทำให้ เป็นรูป to form/make into (the) shape (of)

tham hâi pháeh v ทำให้แพ้ to defeat, (or, more precisely) to make (someone) lose

tham hâi phráwm v ทำให้ พร้อม to make ready

tham hâi pùat v ทำให้ปวด to (make) ache/to cause (some bodily part) to ache

tham hâi ráwn v ทำให้ร้อน to heat/to make hot

tham hâi sèt v ทำให้เสร็จ to complete, finish off

tham hâi yen v ทำให้เย็น to (make) cool

tham jai v ทำใจ to accept (e.g. unpleasant news), manage one's emotions/ feelings; come to terms with (it); make the best of (it, a situation, etc.)

tham jing-jing v ทำจริงๆ to do seriously, do (something) in earnest

tham khwaam sà-àat v ทำความสะอาด to clean

tham ngaan v ทำงาน to work, function

tham phìt v ทำผิด (to do something morally) wrong

tham ráai v ทำร้าย to harm, injure, hurt; do violence to

tham sám v (**sám** pronounced similar to 'sum' with a high tone) ทำซ้ำ to repeat

tham sĭa v ทำเสีย to spoil something, ruin, to break

tham sŏngkhraam v ทำ สงคราม to wage war, make war

tham tàw pai ทำต่อไป v to continue on (doing something), to keep doing something

tham tua v ทำตัว to act, behave

tham tua dii ADJ ทำตัวดี to be well-behaved

tham tua hâi sà-nùk v ทำตัว ให้สนุก to enjoy oneself

tham wí-jai v ทำวิจัย to research, to do research

thamlaai v ทำลาย to destroy, demolish, ruin

thamleh N ทำเล location (e.g. a good location for a business), district

thammá-châat N, ADJ ธรรมชาติ nature; natural

thammá-daa ADJ ธรรมดา ordinary, common, simple, normal, undistinguished

thammai (question word) ทำไม why?, what for?, what?

thamnaai v ทำนาย to predict, foretell, prophesy

tham-niam N ธรรมเนียม custom, tradition, practice; **khâa tham-niam** N ค่า ธรรมเนียม a fee (e.g. for a government/offical service)

than ทัน in time (e.g. to get the bus), to have time (to do something); to catch, catch up with

than sà-mǎi ADJ ทันสมัย to be modern, contemporary

than thii ADV ทันที at once, immediately

thá-naai khwaam N ทนายความ, (COLLOQUIAL)

thanai ทนาย lawyer

thá-naa-khaan N ธนาคาร bank (financial institution)

thá-ná-bàt N ธนบัตร (bank) note

thà-nǎwm V ถนอม to take care of, treat with care, cherish, nurture, conserve (e.g. one's complexion, a vintage car, etc.)

thà-nǎwm aa-hǎan ถนอม อาหาร to preserve food; food preservation

thà-nǒn N ถนน road, street, avenue

tháng ADJ ทั้ง all, entire, the whole of

tháng khuehn N ทั้งคืน all night (long)

tháng khûu PRON ทั้งคู่ both, both of them

tháng mòt ADV ทั้งหมด altogether, all, the whole lot

tháng prà-thêht N ทั้งประเทศ the whole country

thanwaa-khom N ธันวาคม December

thâo ADJ เท่า as much as, the same as, equal (to), equivalent (to)

tháo N เท้า foot/feet (used for humans only)

thâo kan ADJ เท่ากัน equal (e.g. amounts of something)

thâo nán ADV, ADJ เท่านั้น just, only (used at the end of a sentence)

thâo rài (question word) เท่าไหร่ how much? (used at the end of a sentence)

thâo thiam ADJ เท่าเทียม to be equal

tháp-phii N ทัพพี a ladle, dipper

thàt pai ADJ ถัดไป (the) next, succeeding (e.g. client, government)

thátsà-ná-khá-ti N ทัศนคติ opinion, view, outlook (on particular matters), attitude

thaw V ทอ to weave

thá-waan nàk N (medical term) ทวารหนัก anus

thá-wíip N ทวีป continent

thǎwn V ถอน to withdraw (e.g. money from the bank), to retract; to uproot, extract, pull out, e.g. **thǎwn fan** ถอน ฟัน to pull out a tooth

thawng N ทอง gold

tháwng N, ADJ ท้อง stomach, belly; to be pregnant

thawng daehng N ทองแดง copper

thawng samrit N ทองสัมฤทธิ์ bronze

thawrá-maan V ทรมาน to torture, punish, torment; to suffer agonizing pain

thàwt V ถอด to take off, remove (clothes, shoes)

thâwt V ทอด to (deep) fry; fried

theh V เท to pour (e.g. water out of a container)

thehp N (from English) เทป adhesive tape

thêht-sà-kaan N เทศกาล festival

thennit N (from English) เทนนิส tennis

thiam ADJ เทียม artificial (e.g. leg), synthetic

thian N เทียน candle

thîang V เถียง to argue, dispute, bicker

thîang khuehn N เที่ยงคืน midnight

thîang wan N เที่ยงวัน midday

thîao N เที่ยว trip, journey

thîao V เที่ยว to go out for fun/pleasure; to go around; to visit

thîao bin N เที่ยวบิน a flight (a trip on an airplane)

thîao diao N เที่ยวเดียว a single trip; one way ticket

thîao phûu-yǐng V (COLLOQUIAL) เที่ยวผู้หญิง to go whoring, for a man to go out and have sex with a prostitute/ prostitutes

thii N ที time, occasion; chance, opportunity; classifier for counting the number of times

thîi N ที่ PREP in, at (space); N site, place, space; that, which, the one who; portion, serve (food)

thîi bâan ADV ที่บ้าน at home

thîi din N ที่ดิน land (a piece of land)

thîi jàwt rót N ที่จอดรถ (a) carpark, parking lot

thîi jing ADV ที่จริง in fact, actually

thîi kiao khâwng ที่เกี่ยวข้อง (that which is) involved; concerning

thîi kwâang ADJ ที่กว้าง spacious

thii lá khon (COLLOQUIAL) ที่ละคน one by one (e.g. were given a vaccination shot one by one)

thii lá lék thii lá nói (COLLOQUIAL) ที่ละเล็กที่ละน้อย little by little, bit by bit; also **(COLLOQUIAL) thii la nit** ที่ละนิด gradually, bit by bit

thii láew ที่แล้ว ago: e.g. **sǎwng pii thii láew** สองปีที่แล้ว two years ago

thii lǎng ADV ที่หลัง later (on), afterwards

thii lǔea ที่เหลือ left, leftover, remaining, the rest

thii nǎi (question tag) ที่ไหน where?

thii nǎi kâw dâi (COLLOQUIAL) ที่ไหนก็ได้ anywhere (at all)

thii nân ADV ที่นั่น there

thii nâng N ที่นั่ง a seat, a place to sit

thii nawn N ที่นอน a mattress

thii nîi ADV ที่นี่ here

thii nôhn ADV ที่โน่น over there

thii phák N ที่พัก accommodation

thii râap N ที่ราบ (a) plain, flatland, flat area

thii rawng jaan N ที่รองจาน tablemat

thii sǎam ที่สาม third (e.g. the third person to go, third place in a race, etc.). In Thai ordinal numbers (1st, 2nd, 3rd, etc.) are created by placing **thii** ที่ in front of a given number: 1st **thii nèung** ที่หนึ่ง; 2nd **thii sǎwng** ที่ สอง, etc.

thii sǎa-thaa-rá-ná N ที่ สาธารณะ public place

thii siap plúk N ที่เสียบปลั๊ก socket (electric)

thii sùt ADV ที่สุด the end, finally; -est (superlative), most, extremely; e.g. **dii thii sùt** ดีที่สุด the best; **rew thii sùt** เร็วที่สุด the fastest; **sǔai thii sùt** สวยที่สุด the most beautiful

thii tham ngaan N ที่ทำงาน place of work, office, etc.

thii thǔeh N ที่ถือ (a) handle

thii wâang N ที่ว่าง (to have) room, space

thii wii N (from English) ทีวี TV, television

thii yùu N ที่อยู่ address

thîi yùu ii-mehl ที่อยู่อีเมล email address

thiim N (from English) (pronounced similar to the English word) ทีม team

thíng V (pronounced like 'ting' with a high tone) ทิ้ง to throw away; desert, abandon

thíng wái V ทิ้งไว้ (to) leave something somewhere (with intent) (The form of use is as follows – **thíng** (object) **wái**, e.g. **kháo thíng rót wái thîi bâan phûean** เขาทิ้งรถไว้ที่บ้านเพื่อน) she left her car at her friend's place

thíp N, V (from English) ทิป (to) tip (gratuity)

thoeh PRON (pronounced similar to 'ter') เธอ you (intimate)

thoehm N (from English) เทอม school term; **pit thoehm** ปิด เทอม the end of (the school) term

thohrá-sàp N โทรศัพท์ telephone

thohrá-sàp mueh thŭeh N โทรศัพท์มือถือ, (COLLOQUIAL) **mueh thŭeh** มือถือ mobile phone

thohrá-thát N โทรทัศน์ (somewhat formal) television

thôht V, N โทษ to blame; punishment, penalty, sentence

thŏi V ถอย to retreat, draw back; to back up

thŏi lăng V ถอยหลัง to go in reverse, back up, backwards

thòk panhăa V ถกปัญหา to discuss

thon V ทน to put up with, tolerate, bear, stand, endure

thon fai ทนไฟ fireproof

thon náam ADJ ทนน้ำ waterproof

thon thaan ADJ ทนทาน lasting, durable, sturdy

thon thúk V ทนทุกข์ to suffer

thonbùrii N ธนบุรี Thonburi, area opposite Bangkok on the west bank of the Chaophraya River. The capital of the Thai kingdom before Bangkok (Krungthep) assumed this role in 1782

thong N ธง flag

thong châat N ธงชาติ national flag

thót lawng V ทดลอง to try,

285

to experiment, test, give (something) a trial

thŭa ADJ ทั่ว all over, throughout

thùa N ถั่ว bean(s), pea(s) (general term)

thùa daehng N ถั่วแดง kidney bean(s)

thùa dam N ถั่วดำ black bean(s)

thùa fàk yaaw N ถั่วฝักยาว (long) green bean(s), stringbean(s)

thùa lantao N ถั่วลันเตา snowpea(s)

thùa lí-sŏng N ถั่วลิสง peanut(s)

thùa ngâwk N ถั่วงอก (mung) bean sprout(s)

thŭa pai ADV ทั่วไป in general, generally

thŭa prà-thêht ADV ทั่ว ประเทศ all over the country; throughout the country

thûai N (pronounced 'two-ay' with a falling tone) ถ้วย cup

thŭeh V ถือ to hold something (in the hands); to believe in (e.g. a religion, faith, set of ideas); to mind (i.e. to be offended by some form of

behaviour, way of dress, etc.)

thŭeh sĭin V ถือศีล to keep/ observe the rules/precepts (of religion)

thŭeh tua ADJ ถือตัว to be aloof, reserved; to have a high opinion of oneself

thŭeng V ถึง to reach, arrive (at), get to

thŭeng láew ถึงแล้ว to have arrived; (COLLOQUIAL) we're here (at the destination)

thŭeng máeh wâa... ถึง แม้ว่า... although, even though

thúk ADJ ทุก each, every, all

thúk chá-nít N ทุกชนิด every type, every kind of

thúk khon PRON ทุกคน everybody, everyone

thúk khuehn ADV, ADJ ทุกคืน every night, nightly

thúk sìng PRON ทุกสิ่ง everything

thúk sìng thúk yàng PRON (COLLOQUIAL) ทุกสิ่งทุกอย่าง everything

thúk thîi ADV ทุกที่ everywhere

thúk thii ADV ทุกที every time, also (more commonly) **thúk khráng** ทุกครั้ง

thun N ทุน funds, funding, capital

thǔng N ถุง bag (i.e. plastic or paper bag)

thǔng mueh N ถุงมือ glove(s)

thǔng tháo N ถุงเท้า sock(s)

thǔng yaang (à-naa-mai) N ถุงยาง (อนามัย), (commonly) **thǔng yaang** ถุงยาง condom

thú-rá N ธุระ business, affairs, work, something to do; **tìt thúrá** ติดธุระ to be busy, tied up, engaged, occupied

thú-rákit N ธุรกิจ business; **nák thu-rakit** นักธุรกิจ business man/woman

thú-rian N ทุเรียน durian (tropical fruit)

thút-jàrìt ADJ ทุจริต dishonest, corrupt, crooked (e.g. officials, etc.)

thǔu V ถู to rub, scrub, polish, wipe, clean (e.g. the floor)

thùuk ADJ ถูก to be cheap, inexpensive; to be right, correct; to touch; also used to create the passive form: e.g. he was hit by a car **khǎo thùuk rót chon** เขาถูกรถชน **thùuk jai** ADJ (COLLOQUIAL) ถูกใจ

to be pleased, satisfied, content (with the outcome of something)

thùuk jàp V ถูกจับ (**jàp** pronounced similar to 'jup' with a low tone) (COLLOQUIAL) to be arrested, apprehended, caught

thùuk láew ADJ (COLLOQUIAL) ถูก แล้ว yes, that's right

thùuk làwk V (COLLOQUIAL) ถูก หลอก to be duped, conned

thùuk luehm V ถูกลืม (to be) forgotten

thùuk tâwng ADJ ถูกต้อง to be correct

thùuk tham laai V ถูก ทำลาย (for something to be) destroyed, ruined

thûup N ธูป incense, joss stick

thûut N ทูต diplomat

U

ùak V อ้วก (COLLOQUIAL) to be sick; vomit, spew, puke

ûan ADJ อ้วน to be fat, stout

ùap ADJ อวบ to be chubby

ùat V อวด to show off, strut, flaunt

287

ùat dii v อวดดี to be vain-
glorious, put on airs

ùat kèng v อวดเก่ง to show off

ùat rúu v อวดรู้ to be a know-
it-all; pretentious

ù-bàat ADJ อุบาทว์ evil, sinister

ù-battihèht N อุบัติเหตุ
accident

ù-bohsòt N อุโบสถ temple,
consecrated assembly hall

ùdom ADJ อุดม rich in (i.e.
fertile); great, excellent

ùe (pronounced very short)
อื้ (COLLOQUIAL) v to defecate;
N poop

ùehn ADJ อื่น other; **khon ùehn**
คนอื่น other people/another
person

ùehn-ùehn PRON, N อื่นๆ
others

ù-jàat ADJ อุจาด obscene,
filthy, shameful

ûm v อุ้ม to carry (e.g. a
baby), hold in one's arms;
(COLLOQUIAL/SLANG) **dohn ûm**
โดนอุ้ม to be illegally taken
and (usually) secretly killed

ùn v, ADJ อุ่น to heat, warm

ùn-hà-phuum N อุณหภูมิ
temperature

ùn kaehng v อุ่นแกง to warm
up the curry

ù-pà-kaa-rá v อุปการะ to
support, look after, take
care (of)

ù-pà-kawn N อุปกรณ์ equip-
ment, instrument, implement

ù-pà-sàk N อุปสรรค obstacle,
difficulty, impediment

ù-pà-thăm v อุปถัมภ์
patronage; support; to give
patronage

ùt-jaà-rá N (FORMAL MEDICAL
TERM) อุจาระ faeces, stool,
excrement

ùt nŭn v อุดหนุน to support,
aid, back (someone or
something)

ùtsàa v อุตส่าห์ to take the
trouble (to do something), to
make an effort (to)

ùt-săa-hà-kam N, ADJ
อุตสาหกรรม industry;
industrial

ùu N อู่ cradle; drydock,
boathouse

ùu rót N อู่รถ garage (for
mechanical repairs)

ùut N อูฐ a camel

W

waa N วา a linear Thai measure equal to 2 metres; **taa-rang waa** ตารางวา 1 square *waa* (or 4 sq.m.)

wâa... ว่า... to speak, say, state, tell; that (introducing a spoken comment, remark, or quotation) – **kháo phûut wâa kháo mâi sàbaai** เขาพูดว่า เขาไม่สบาย he said that he was sick; to scold, rebuke, criticize (someone)

waai N (from English) ไวน์ wine

wáai EXCLAM (COLLOQUIAL) ว้าย Eek!, Oh! Oh my God, etc.

wâai náam V ว่ายน้ำ to swim

wǎan ADJ หวาน sweet (taste); (COLLOQUIAL) **pàak wǎan** ปาก หวาน a smooth talker who uses sweet words and flattery with another person

waang V วาง to lay (something) down, to place (something somewhere)

wâang ADJ ว่าง to be unoccupied, vacant, free; (COLLOQUIAL) **wehlaa wâang**

เวลาว่าง to have spare/free time

wâang ngaan ADJ ว่างงาน to be unemployed, jobless

waang phǎehn V วางแผน to lay plans; to plot, scheme

wâang plào ADJ ว่างเปล่า to be vacant, unoccupied (e.g. piece of land), empty

waa-rá-sǎan N วารสาร magazine, periodical, journal

wâat V วาด to draw, paint, sketch

wâat phâap V วาดภาพ to draw/paint a picture; to portray, depict

wâatsà-nǎa N วาสนา fortune, good luck

wâaw N ว่าว (a) kite; **chák wâaw** V ชักว่าว to fly a kite; (COLLOQUIAL/SLANG) to masturbate (males only)

wáe V (pronounced very short) แวะ to stop by, pay a (quick) visit; (COLLOQUIAL) **wáe pai hǎa** แวะไปหา to pop in/drop by and visit (someone)

wǎehn N แหวน a ring (jewellery)

wǎehn phét N แหวนเพชร (a) diamond ring

wâen taa N แว่นตา, (COLLOQUIAL) **wâen** แว่น (eye) glasses, spectacles; **wâen kan** (pronounced like 'gun') **dàet** N แว่นกันแดด sunglasses

wái v ไว้ an important 'function' word in Thai – meaning 'to place, put; to keep, preserve, reserve'. Some examples of usage: to keep (name of object) [for the foreseeable future] **kèp** (name of object) **wái** เก็บ ไว้; to do something (for some ongoing/continuing purpose) **tham wái** ทำไว้; to leave (something somewhere for a period of time – either for a short period or for an unspecified length of time) **thíng** (pronounced 'ting' with a high tone) **wái** ทิ้งไว้: e.g. leave the bag at home (and come back and get it later) **thíng kràpǎo wái thîi bâan** ทิ้ง กระเป๋าไว้ที่บ้าน

wǎi v ไหว to be able to (to do something), capable (of doing), up to it (a job, task, doing something, etc.);

(COLLOQUIAL) **wǎi mǎi** ไหวไหม Can you do it? Are you up to it? Can you manage it?: (to respond in the negative) **mâi wǎi** ไม่ไหว It's too much, I give up, I don't think I can manage (it)

wai N วัย age (general term used with other words to refer to a particular age demographic or grouping); e.g. **wai rûn** วัยรุ่น youth, adolescent(s), teenager(s); **wai dèk** วัยเด็ก childhood; **wai chá-raa** วัยชรา old age, geriatric

wâi v ไหว้ the traditional Thai form of greeting and fundamental aspect of Thai social relations – to raise the hands pressed together up to the head as a sign of respect (an indicator of the relative status/position of those interacting – a 'junior/inferior' will always 'wâi' a 'superior' – the height of the 'wâi' is a clear indicator of the social standing of the parties involved); pay homage to. The **wâi** is a practice that is best avoided until one has developed a good deal of familiarity with Thai society.

wái jai v ไว้ใจ to trust

wâi jâo v ไหว้เจ้า to make a spirit offering; **wâi phrá** ไหว้ พระ to salute/pay homage to a monk; to do one's chanting (in homage of Buddhism's Triple Gems)

wan N (pronounced similar to 'one') วัน day of the week

wan aa-thít N วันอาทิตย์ Sunday

wan angkhaan N วันอังคาร Tuesday

wan duean pii kòeht N วัน เดือนปีเกิด date of birth (literally, 'day'-'month'-'year'-'birth')

wan jan N วันจันทร์ Monday

wan kàwn (COLLOQUIAL) ADV วัน ก่อน the day before; some days before

wan kòeht N วันเกิด birthday

wan níi ADV วันนี้ today

wan phà-rúe-hàt N วันพฤหัส Thursday (the full word for Thursday is **wan phà-rúe-hàt**

sà-baw-dii วันพฤหัสบดี)

wan phút N วันพุธ Wednesday

wan săo N วันเสาร์ Saturday

wan sùk N วันศุกร์ Friday

wan thíi... วันที่... (the) date (of the month), on the (date)

wan wén wan ADV (COLLOQUIAL) วันเว้นวัน every other day

wan yùt N วันหยุด day off

wan yùt phák phàwn วันหยุดพักผ่อน holiday, vacation

wan yùt râat-chá-kaan N วัน หยุดราชการ public holiday

wan yùt thêht-sà-kaan N วัน หยุดเทศกาล festival holiday

wang N วัง palace

wăng v หวัง to hope

wanná-khádii N วรรณคดี literature

wát N วัด temple, monastery (e.g.Thai, Hindu-Balinese); v to measure (e.g. the length of something); **wát tua** วัดตัว to take someone's measurements

wàt N หวัด (a) cold (i.e. to catch a cold)

wát bohraan N วัดโบราณ (an ancient) temple

291

wát phrá kâew N วัดพระ
แก้ว Temple of the Emerald
Buddha in the precincts of the
old Grand Palace in Bangkok

wát-sàdù N วัสดุ material (e.g.
building material), ingredient

wát-táná-tham N วัฒนธรรม
culture

wátthù N วัตถุ (general term
similar to **wát-sàdù** วัสดุ
above) thing, object, material
(e.g. building material), substance; **wát-thù dìp** N วัตถุดิบ
raw material(s); **wát-thù
níyom** N วัตถุนิยม materialism

wehlaa N เวลา time, at the
time; when; **tà-làwt wehlaa**
ตลอดเวลา all of the time,
continuously, always; **than**
(pronounced similar to 'ton')
wehlaa ทันเวลา (to be) in
time (e.g. to catch a flight)

wehlaa wâang N เวลาว่าง spare
time, free time, leisure time

wehn-kam N เวรกรรม misfortune, ill fated; (COLLOQUIAL)
EXCLAM How awful! God
almighty! etc.

weh-thii N เวที a stage, ring
(e.g. boxing ring)

wén PREP เว้น to skip;
excepting; **yók wén** ยกเว้น
except, excluding, with the
exception of

wép sái N (from English)
เว็บไซต์ website

wîat-naam N เวียดนาม
Vietnam

wí-chaa N วิชา knowledge;
subject/branch of study

wí-chaa chîip N วิชาชีพ
profession, occupation

wí-hăan N วิหาร Buddhist
assembly hall (often written
in English as 'Vihear' or
'Viharn' – despite the fact that
there is no 'v' sound in Thai)

wii N หวี comb

wii-sâa N (from English)
วีซ่า visa

wí-jaan V วิจารณ์ to criticize,
comment (on), review (e.g. a
book, film, etc.); **nák wi-jaan**
นักวิจารณ์ a (professional)
critic, commentator

wí-naa-thii N วินาที a second
(of time)

winai N วินัย discipline,
orderly conduct; Buddhist
disciplinary rules; **mii winai**

ADJ มีวินัย (to be) orderly, disciplined

wîng v วิ่ง to run

wîng nǐi v วิ่งหนี to run away, to flee

win-yaan N วิญญาณ (pronounced 'win yarn') spirit, soul (of the dead)

wít-tha-yaa N วิทยา knowledge, science; **wít-tha-yàakawn** วิทยากร speaker, lecturer; expert

wít-thá-yaa-lai N วิทยาลัย college; **wít-thá-yaa-lai khruu** วิทยาลัยครู teachers' college

wít-thá-yaa-sàat N วิทยาศาสตร์ science; **nák wít-thá-yaa-sàat** N นัก วิทยาศาสตร์ (a) scientist

wí-thii N วิธี way, method, means; **wí-thii chái** วิธีใช้ directions (for use, e.g. medication)

wí-thii N วิถี path, way; **wí-thii chii-wít** วิถีชีวิต way of life, lifestyle (NOTE: the English term 'lifestyle' has made its way into Thai, pronounced something like **lai sàtai**)

wít-thá-yú N วิทยุ radio

wiu N (from English 'view') วิว scenery, view, panorama

wòht N (from English and pronounced something like 'whoat') โหวต to vote; there are also a number of Thai words for 'to vote' such as **àwk sǐang** ออกเสียง and **long khà-naehn** ลงคะแนน

wohy waai v โวยวาย to make a fuss/make a big to do (about/over something), complain (in an animated fashion)

wói mehl N (from English) วอยซ์เมล voicemail

wong N วง a ring, circle

wong dontrii N วงดนตรี (a musical) band/group, orchestra

wong jawn N วงจร (a) circuit (e.g. an electrical circuit)

wong klom N วงกลม (a round) circle

wong phâi N (COLLOQUIAL) วงไพ่ a circle of card players

wong wian N วงเวียน circle (e.g. a traffic circle), roundabout

wua N วัว cow

wún N วุ้น jelly, gelatin, agar; **wún sên** N วุ้นเส้น glass noodles

wûn waai ADJ วุ่นวาย to be busy (crowded); chaotic, turbulent

yàa INJUNCTION อย่า don't (do that)!

yâa N หญ้า grass (of the lawn variety)

yaa N ยา drug, medicine, pills; **yaa bâa** N (literally, 'drug'-'crazy/mad') ยาบ้า methamphetamine (type of smokable speed); **yaa thàai** N ยาถ่าย (a) laxative

yâa N ย่า (paternal) grandmother

yàa V หย่า to divorce

yàa láew ADJ หย่าแล้ว to be divorced

yaa mét N ยาเม็ด tablet(s)

yaa phít N ยาพิษ poison

yaa raksǎa rôhk N ยารักษาโรค pharmaceutical(s)

yaa sà phǒm N ยาสระผม (hair) shampoo

yaa sàmǔn phrai N ยาสมุนไพร herbal medicine(s)

yaa sèp tìt N ยาเสพติด narcotic(s), addictive drug (in Thailand this term is used to refer to all illicit drugs from heroin and ice to marijuana)

yaa sǐi fan ยาสีฟัน toothpaste

yaa sùup N ยาสูบ tobacco

yaai N ยาย (maternal) grandmother

yáai V ย้าย to move (from one place to another), transfer, shift; **yáai bâan** V ย้ายบ้าน to move house

yâak ADJ ยาก (to be) difficult, hard (to do, say, make, etc.), not so easy

yàak V อยาก to want, desire, need, require; to be thirsty/hungry (adventure, sex, etc.)

yàak dâi V อยากได้ would like to get (something), e.g. on seeing a flashy new car a young man/woman says 'I want one/to get one of those' **yàak dâi** อยากได้

yâak jon ADJ ยากจน poor, needy, impoverished, hard up

294

yaam N ยาม watch (i.e. as in the military 'be on watch/guard duty'); time, era (in a general sense); watchman, sentry

yâam N ย่าม (a) shoulder bag (e.g. the type of cloth shoulder bag used by monks and, once upon a time – hippies, aka freaks)

yaam dùek N ยามดึก at night; late at night

yaam kháp khǎn N ยาม คับขัน time of emergency

yâan N ย่าน district; area, quarter (of a city/town)

yaan yon N (formal term, rarely spoken) ยานยนต์ motor vehicle

yaang N ยาง rubber (substance); resin, sap, latex, tar

yàang N อย่าง kind, type, sort, variety; classifier for things

yâang V ย่าง to roast, grill, barbecue

yaang baehn N ยางแบน a flat tyre; also yaang tàehk ยางแตก to have a flat tyre, have a blowout

yàang dii ADJ อย่างดี good quality (e.g. material); well (e.g. makes furniture)

yàang nán ADV อย่างนั้น (COLLOQUIAL; nán pronounced like 'nun' with a high tone) (do it) like that; that's right, correct

yàang nii ADV (COLLOQUIAL) อย่าง นี้ (do it) like this

yàang nói ADV อย่างน้อย at least (e.g. they should try it)

yàang prà-yàt ADJ อย่าง ประหยัด economical

yàang rai (question marker) อย่างไร how? (used at the end of an utterance); (COLLOQUIAL) yang-ngai (pronounced something like 'yang-ngai') ยังไง how?; (COLLOQUIAL – GREETING) pen yang-ngai เป็นยังไง how are you/how are you doing?

yàang rai kâw taam อย่างไร ก็ตาม however

yaang rót N ยางรถ (a rubber) tyre (on a vehicle)

yàang rûat rew ADV อย่าง รวดเร็ว quickly, speedily

yàap khaai ADJ หยาบคาย to be rude, crude

295

yâat N (pronounced like 'yart' with a falling tone) ญาติ relatives (family)

yaaw ADJ ยาว long (in length); **khwaam yaaw** N ความยาว length

yâeh ADJ (pronounced like 'yair' or 'yeah' with a falling tone) แย่ terrible

yâeh long ADJ แย่ลง (to get) worse

yâeh thîi sùt ADJ แย่ที่สุด (the) worst

yâehk V แยก to separate, divide, split; spread apart

yâehk kan V แยกกัน to separate, split up, divide

yaehm N (from English) แยม jam

yâehng V แย่ง to grab, snatch; scramble for; to vie/compete (for)

yài ADJ ใหญ่ large, big, great; major (important); in charge, in command; **yài toh** ADJ ใหญ่โต very big, huge; formidable; powerful

yai N ใย filament, fiber; thread

yai maeng mum N ใยแมงมุม spider web, cobweb

yai săngkhrá-w N ใยสังเคราะห์ synthetic (thread)

yák N ยักษ์ a giant, ogre (frequently appearing in traditional Thai poetic literature and folk tales)

yam N (pronounced like 'yum') ยำ Thai-style spicy salad

yang ADV ยัง still, even now; not yet (as a reply)

yang dèk ADJ (COLLOQUIAL) ยังเด็ก (he/she is) still a child/ still young

yang dii ADJ ยังดี (it's) still good

yang mii... (COLLOQUIAL) ยังมี there is still some left, remaining

yang mii chii-wít yùu ADJ ยังมีชีวิตอยู่ (or, more colloquially) **yang yùu** ยังอยู่ (to still be) alive

yao-wáchon N เยาวชน youth (general term – plural)

yáp ADJ ยับ (pronounced similar to 'yup') wrinkled (clothing), crushed

yát V ยัด to stuff (in, with), cram (in, with), stuffed (with)

yâw v ย่อ to abbreviate, to make shorter; summarize

yaw v ยอ to flatter (somebody)

yâw tua v ย่อตัว to bow down

yáwm v ย้อม to dye, tint (cloth, hair, etc.)

yawm v ยอม to yield, give in, submit; to allow, consent

yawm hâi v ยอมให้ to permit, allow (someone to do something)

yawm pháeh v ยอมแพ้ to surrender, give up, give in (to)

yawm ráp v ยอมรับ to acknowledge, accept, agree; to admit, confess

yawm taai v (COLLOQUIAL) ยอม ตาย I'll never give in

yâwt N ยอด summit, peak, top

yâwt yiam ADJ ยอดเยี่ยม to be excellent

yeh suu N เยซู (although this may seem somewhat odd, this name is pronounced 'yeah sue') Jesus; also **phrá yeh-suu** พระเยซู

yen ADJ เย็น to be cool, cold

yép v เย็บ to sew, to stitch, to pin; to staple

yét v เย็ด (COLLOQUIAL – EXTREMELY RUDE) to fuck

yiam ADJ เยี่ยม first rate, great, tops; **yâwt yiam** ADJ ยอดเยี่ยม top, superb

yiam v เยี่ยม to visit, call on, go to see (someone)

yiao N, v (COLLOQUIAL) เยี่ยว urine; to urinate, piss, pee

yiap v เหยียบ to step on, put one's foot on; **yiap brèhk** v (**brèhk** from English) เหยียบ เบรค to brake, to put one's foot on the brakes (of a car)

yiat v เหยียด to look down on, hold in contempt, despise, be contemptuous (of); **yiat phiu** N เหยียดผิว (to be a) racist (literally, 'despise'+'skin')

yii-pùn N ญี่ปุ่น Japan

yii sip ยี่สิบ twenty; **yii sip èt** ยี่สิบเอ็ด twenty one; (COLLOQUIAL) ยี่สิบเอ็ด

yik v, ADJ หยิก to pinch; **phǒm yik** ผมหยิก wrinkled/kinky/curly/fuzzy hair

yím v ยิ้ม to smile

yím yáehm ADJ ยิ้มแย้ม (to be) cheerful

yin dii ADJ ยินดี to be glad,

pleased, be happy (for, to); **yin dii thîi dâi rúu–jàk (EXPRESSION)** ยินดีที่ได้รู้จัก 'glad to meet you'; 'it's a pleasure to meet you'

yin dii tâwn ráp (formal public type of greeting) ยินดี ต้อนรับ welcome!

yìng ADJ หยิ่ง (to be) haughty, stuck up, conceited, vain, proud, aloof

yìng ADV ยิ่ง exceedingly

yǐng N หญิง female (humans only)

yíng v ยิง to shoot, to fire (a gun/cannon)

yìng khûen ADV ยิ่งขึ้น more and more, increasingly

yìng yài ADJ ยิ่งใหญ่ grand, great, momentous

yóeh yáe (COLLOQUIAL) (both words pronounced with very short vowels) เยอะแยะ lots of, many, **(SLANG)** heaps of/ tons of (e.g. great music)

yohn v โยน to throw, toss

yòk N หยก jade (semi precious stone)

yók v ยก raise, lift; also a round in boxing

yók lôehk v ยกเลิก cancel (e.g. a contract)

yók rá–dàp v ยกระดับ to elevate, upgrade, raise the level/ standard (e.g. of teaching)

yók song v ยกทรง bra, brassiere (literally, 'lift'+'shape')

yók thôht v ยกโทษ to forgive, pardon (someone/a prisoner)

yók tua yàang ยกตัวอย่าง for example, for instance; to give an example

yók wén v ยกเว้น to except, excluding, not including; exempt from

yók yaw v ยกยอ to flatter, praise

yók yâwng v ยกย่อง to praise

yót N ยศ rank (military, police); insignia of rank

yú v ยุ to incite, provoke

yûa ADJ, v ยั่ว provocative; to provoke, arouse, entice; **yûa yuan ADJ** ยั่วยวน provocative, sexy, seductive

yùeak N เหยือก a jug, pitcher

yuehm v ยืม to borrow

yuehn v ยืน to stand, get on one's feet

yûehn ADJ ยื่น to project, stick out; to hand, to offer, to present

yûehn àwk maa ADJ ยื่นออกมา to protrude

yuehn khûen v ยืนขึ้น to stand (up)

yûet ADJ ยืด to expand, stretch; yûet wehlaa ADV ยืดเวลา to prolong; to extend the time (for doing something)

yúet thùeh v ยึดถือ to grasp hold of; seize

yúk N ยุค time; period, age: e.g. yúk hĭn ยุคหิน the Stone Age

yung N ยุง mosquito

yûng ADJ, V ยุ่ง to be busy/ hectic (work, etc.); to inter-fere/meddle (in someone else's affairs); to fool around (with); troublesome, bothersome; (COLLOQUIAL) yàa yûng อย่ายุ่ง 'leave it/me/ alone', 'don't interfere', 'don't mess/fool around with

(someone or something)'

yûng yŏehng ADJ ยุ่งเหยิง tangled up; to be in a muddle, in a state of

yú-rôhp N ยุโรป Europe

yùt v หยุด to stop, halt

yùt ná (COLLOQUIAL) หยุดนะ stop it!

yút-ti-tham ADJ ยุติธรรม to be just, fair, equitable

yùu v อยู่ to stay, remain; to live, dwell; to be alive

yùu bâan v (COLLOQUIAL) อยู่บ้าน to be at home, stay home

yùu kàp thîi v อยู่กับที่ stay, remain

yùu kin ADJ (COLLOQUIAL) อยู่กิน, (or, more fully) yùu kin dûai/ dûai kan อยู่กินด้วย/ด้วยกัน to live (together, with)

yùu pen phûean v (COLLOQUIAL) อยู่เป็นเพื่อน to keep another company

yùu trong khâam ADV อยู่ตรง ข้าม to be opposite (facing) (e.g. the cinema)

The Tuttle Story:
"Books to Span the East and West"

Many people are surprised to learn that the world's largest publisher of books on Asia had its humble beginnings in the tiny American state of Vermont. The company's founder, Charles E. Tuttle, belonged to a New England family steeped in publishing.

Immediately after WW II, Tuttle served in Tokyo under General Douglas MacArthur and was tasked with reviving the Japanese publishing industry. He later founded the Charles E. Tuttle Publishing Company, which thrives today as one of the world's leading independent publishers.

Though a westerner, Tuttle was hugely instrumental in bringing a knowledge of Japan and Asia to a world hungry for information about the East. By the time of his death in 1993, Tuttle had published over 6,000 books on Asian culture, history and art—a legacy honored by the Japanese emperor with the "Order of the Sacred Treasure," the highest tribute Japan can bestow upon a non-Japanese.

With a backlist of 1,500 titles, Tuttle Publishing is more active today than at any time in its past—inspired by Charles Tuttle's core mission to publish fine books to span the East and West and provide a greater understanding of each.